Mikhail Gorbachev was in charge of the portfolio and running up against exceptionally bad weather conditions.

Economic prospects faded after the initial years. So did Brezhnev's hopes in foreign policy. Détente with the United States collapsed in 1979, the Afghanistan disaster began, butter was sacrificed for war machines. Brezhnev bequeathed his successors a monster military and an economy near Third World levels. In the Soviet Union there were fewer miles of paved highways than in the State of Texas; the highway network actually shrank by five percent during Brezhnev's tenure. There were as few cars in the U.S.S.R. as the United States or Japan produced in one year alone – about seven million.

"These and other infrastructure problems," wrote Seweryn Bialer, a leading Sovietologist, "are more characteristic of a third world nation than of an advanced industrial power. . . . One cannot understand the Soviet Union without regarding it as both a developed and an underdeveloped country, one that combines a successful space program with an inability to produce durable shoes or sharp razor blades."[3]

The extent of the corruption and embezzlement under Brezhnev was described by prominent Soviet jurist Arkady Vaksberg. There existed "a huge clan of bribetakers and embezzlers who turned their high offices into festering ulcers, into marketplaces where everything, absolutely everything, was for sale – duties, titles and awards, diplomas and country houses."[4]

By his last years, said Daniel Granin, a Soviet writer, Brezhnev had become such a medal lover and glory seeker that battle heroics had to be invented for his biography so he could have more. "He accepted this shower of medals totally convinced of his merits, having long overstepped the bounds of reality. . . . Zealous work by expert toadies at all levels kept him cut off from the life of the people and brought benefits only to the bootlickers themselves."[5]

In the 1980s the ultraconvenient rationalization for the Soviet Union's backwardness – that materialism is bad for the people – was still around. "Materialism is dangerous," insisted a professor at Moscow State University. "It invisibly emasculates a man's soul, making him a slave to cars, dachas, expensive furniture and trendy clothes." His spartanism was countered by a colleague of the other sex, Natalia Rimashevskaya: "It seems to me we should seriously ask ourselves why we write about labour with such breathless respect, yet about consumer demand with such shameless scorn."

As 1986 began, Andrei Gromyko, the 77-year-old president, ventured out among the proletariat to ask them about their quality of life. Never the populist, it was a safe bet that it wasn't his own idea. The people he spoke to complained about the lack of vegetables and fruit and meat and milk and fish, of thin winter boots, of dim fabric colours and so on and so on. At the same time, the Soviet Academy of Sciences had the gall to release a so-called poll of 10,000 Soviets. It showed that nine out of ten had no worries about their future, that only two percent considered their lives unsatisfactory, that 95 percent believed they were fairly well off.

Brezhnev had been sheltered enough from reality to perhaps believe such nonsense. But Gorbachev knew better. He could see through the windows of his car.

3/An Open-Minded Soviet Man

IN STAVROPOL, the pretty, tulip-filled town 1,000 miles south of Moscow, I was staring from across the street at the modest house where Gorbachev lived for so many years, listening to a local journalist retrace the route his leader used to take to work every morning. Sergei Morozov was recalling how Gorbachev, as the de facto mayor of Stavropol, used to wear a funny hat and bound along the streets bantering with the townsfolk about their problems. "It's hard to say what it was about him," Sergei told me. He paused, then added quietly, "He was always different from the rest of us."

It was a thought – the idea that Gorbachev was an atypical Soviet man well before he became leader – that I would hear often in Stavropol.

Morozov, head bent and low-key, took me past the circus. Stavropol was not even in the top hundred in population among Soviet cities. It didn't, by this yardstick, merit its own circus. But Gorbachev, who lived in Stavropol from 1955 to 1978, decided as mayor that he would bring the city's youth a circus. In Moscow his bid for financing was rejected out of hand: the Kremlin had a thousand other financial priorities. So Gorbachev, taking a "to hell with Moscow" attitude, began raising money locally. He launched a private cooperative venture. It worked. Soon little Stavropol had its own Big Top.

We went to the Stavropol Agricultural Institute. Gorbachev took evening classes there for several years and graduated in the mid-1960s, supplementing his law degree from Moscow State University. In the meantime he became the city's foremost political figure. The sight of a top Communist Party boss taking exams with students half his age was not a common one anywhere in the Soviet Union, but Gorbachev saw it through. I looked for some observance in the school of its most famous graduate but found nothing. "It's the way Gorbachev wants it," Morozov said.

Morozov introduced me to Professor Yuri Duder, a big, soft-spoken, balding man. He had once lived on Dzerzhinski Street, as had the Gorbachevs, just a stone's throw from the large building that serves as the city's KGB headquarters. When Gorbachev returned from Moscow with his law degree, he would have been a prime young candidate for recruitment by the KGB. But he didn't choose that route.

Duder and I stopped at a tea house that was cozy and warm – a rare find in the Russian Republic. Over hot cakes he explained how he first met Gorbachev in 1961 when the future Soviet leader, 30 years old at the time, was head of the local chapter of the Komsomol, or young Communist league. It was not so long after Castro's revolution in Cuba; Gorbachev was looking for comrades to send there to help the Cubans with their agriculture. Duder travelled to Cuba and reported back to Gorbachev on his strange reception. "American propaganda had painted us in crazy ways at that time," he recalled. "People over there thought we were bears who ate our children. They came up and touched us to find out if we were real." The Soviets were sending meat to Cuba but at first the Cubans wouldn't accept it. "They were afraid to eat it," said Duder. "They thought it was made from humans."[1]

Gorbachev listened keenly. His wife Raisa, who taught at the institute, invited Duder to her class, where he told her students about Cuba's revolution. "She stayed in the background that day," Duder recounts, "and let me be the teacher."

Stavropol had been occupied during the Second World War but not destroyed. The prewar buildings were still standing when Gorbachev became mayor, and he fended off any pressure from the central authorities to replace the quaint Russian look with industrial architecture. As a result the city maintains a Russian flavour that not many others have.

Early on, Gorbachev developed an antipathy to centralization policies. In 1967 he complained to a visiting friend from his student years, a Czechoslovakian named Zdenek Mlynar, that the Moscow bureaucrats were far too meddlesome. Gorbachev told Mlynar that his major criticism of Khrushchev, who had been overthrown three years earlier, was that he had preserved the old policy of arbitrary intervention from the centre in the life of the whole country. From Brezhnev, Gorbachev added, he expected greater autonomy. Mlynar, then a Central Committee member in the reformist government of Alexander Dubcek, told an envious Gorbachev about the exhilarating liberal movement taking place in Czechoslovakia.

The two old friends spent the entire day together trading notes and enjoying some drinks. Gorbachev wasn't known as a reveller of any kind. When he returned home very late that day, uncharacteristically tipsy under his panama hat, Raisa was waiting at the door. She gave him a blast.[2]

Gorbachev had visited France the previous year and was now making plans to return there with Raisa and tour the entire country by automobile – 5,000 kilometres in a Renault. They carried out that plan and toured Italy as well. Gorbachev also visited Belgium and West Germany as a member of Soviet delegations.

Never burdened by Stalin-era xenophobia to the extent other Russians were, Gorbachev was developing a broad mental framework. By the time he came to power in 1985, he had something that earlier Soviet leaders – with the exception of the peripatetic Lenin – never had. He had perspective.

The unusual degree of foreign influence in the making of Gorbachev, a marking that would some day result in the "new thinking" of the Soviet Union, began early in his home town with the occupation by the Nazis. It continued with the uncommon degree of international material in his university curriculum and a college friendship with a foreigner. And it was heightened by his many direct experiences abroad before taking power, among them trips to Canada and Britain.

When Gorbachev was ten, a schoolboy in the village of Privolnoye, which means "free," he got his first pictures of how brutal the world can be. The Germans occupied the Stavropol area for five months and, according to Soviet estimates, left 10,000 dead. Yuri Duder, who was there, said anyone who lived through it could not be anything but a fierce peace advocate. "I remember the horrors. I have never been so hungry as I was then. All the stores were closed. I don't understand how mother ever got the food for us. I was only seven at the time but remember it well. Mikhail Sergeyevich was a few years older."

It is not known whether young Gorbachev was evacuated from his one-storey brick home in what today has become a more modern village with a shopping concourse and a war memorial on which the names of seven relatives of the Soviet leader are inscribed. Mikhail's childhood was so poor, the official story goes, that he missed three months of schooling while in the fifth form because he had no shoes. His father, Sergei, a combine/harvester driver, on the front at the time, wrote home ordering his wife to sell household items in order to get shoes, "Misha must go to school," he said.

By top grades and labour honours, including the Order of the Red Banner of Labour for toiling hard in the fields during Stavropol's good harvest year of 1949, Gorbachev was able to gain admittance to the country's best school – Moscow State University. He boarded the train to Moscow in 1950. "I travelled through Stalingrad which had been destroyed, through Voronezh which had been destroyed, through Rostov which was destroyed. Kharkov was destroyed. Nothing but ruins everywhere. I travelled as a student and saw it all, the whole country in ruins."[3]

Gorbachev had grown up during the war years, when the Soviets saw the Americans as strong allies in arms. That attitude changed in the early postwar years. When he visited Canada in 1983, his host Eugene Whelan, the agriculture minister, was surprised at how often he brought up the war and how bitter he was about the experience and its aftermath. "He told me about his growing up as a boy – the hardship, the lack of food, the friends and relatives killed and wounded in the war."[4]

Gorbachev told Whelan that "we fought beside you and we lost 20 million people during the war to destroy a monster." And when it was over, Gorbachev added, the Soviets were told to change their ideology or else. "They never told us that when we fought the war together and died together."

In Moscow, Gorbachev, who except for Lenin is the only Soviet leader to hold a university degree, would have preferred to study physics rather than law. But he could not gain admittance to the former and, like Lenin, he took law. The law curriculum was not limited to turgid Marxist-Leninist texts, but included general humanities, most notably a two-year course on the history of political ideas. Gorbachev studied the works of Hegel, Hobbes, Rousseau, Aquinas. He studied Roman law, Latin, the American Constitution, Machiavelli's history of Florence. The law side of the studies included training on courtroom speech and rhetoric – a grounding that a politician can well afford to have.

Gorbachev is remembered at the university as having an officious, dogmatic, disciplinarian side to him when his ambitions warranted such behaviour. When the so-called Doctors' Plot – Stalin's anti-Semitic campaign – was in full force, Gorbachev, being the good Komsomol school leader that he was, joined the anti-Jewish rhetoric on cue.

But the more dominant memory of Gorbachev is as a nonconformist. Behind the scenes he was an opponent of much of what Stalin stood for. After the leader's death in 1953 he was not afraid to discuss these views openly, including – and this would be a harbinger of Gorbachev in power – his opposition to Stalin's having isolated the Soviet Union from the rest of the world.

Gorbachev as a student was not without courage. Classmate Vladimir Lieberman remembered him becoming very annoyed when a professor simply read out a Stalin text to his class. Gorbachev wanted analysis, discussion. With Lieberman's complicity he passed an anonymous note up to the teacher informing him that everyone in the class was capable of reading on their own. According to David Aikman, a biographer of Gorbachev's young years, the instructor grew livid, accusing the note's authors of anti-socialist behaviour. Gorbachev rose to acknowledge himself as the source and explained his opposition to the teaching method in more detail. No serious disciplinary action was taken against him.

Another time, Gorbachev laughed at a Soviet film he was watching glorifying Stalin's collectivization of Soviet farms. Part of the film showed how happy everyone was in the Stavropol region. The student from Stavropol told the others it wasn't that way at all.

Perhaps more significant than his curriculum at Moscow State was a friendship he made there. Zdenek Mlynar, whose room was next to Gorbachev's for five years, was tantamount to a Western influence. Czechoslovakia had only been brought into the Soviet camp a few years earlier. That the Soviet leader became such a close friend of a foreigner was notable in itself. "Gorbachev was completely open to me," Mlynar recalled. "It made no difference to him that I was a foreigner. And that was unusual at the time because many Soviet students were afraid of us." The Soviets in fact were so suspicious of their neighbours to the west that incoming mail from Czechoslovakia and other countries was intercepted. Once when they were still students, Mlynar sent a postcard to his friend in Stavropol and the authorities there made Gorbachev explain what was going on.

Mlynar noted that as well as being open-minded, Gorbachev had "an intelligence which never led him to arrogance. He knew how to listen and was willing to do so to others. He was honest and goodwilled. He had acquired a natural rather than a formal authority. . . . He was reformist by nature." But perhaps the most prominent feature of Gorbachev's personality, according to Mlynar, was self-assurance. "This could also be a danger," his old friend added, "because he is such a self made man and could overestimate his qualities."

Another strong trait of Gorbachev the student was his reluctance to accept a rigid reading of Soviet ideology. For him the ideas of Soviet leaders were to be debated and explored, not saluted by a population in straitjackets. He agreed with a paper written by Mlynar asserting that the State should be the watchdog of economic life rather than the organizer of its every aspect. Mlynar recalled Gorbachev saying in college something that he would repeat often as Soviet leader – that the distribution of rewards under socialism should follow the merit principle, that is, should be based on the quality and quantity of work. On crime and punishment Gorbachev referred on more than one occasion to Lenin's humane treatment of his political opponent, Julius Martov. By Stalin's time public deviation from the party line had come to be considered a severe crime. But Gorbachev applauded Lenin for allowing Martov to go abroad rather than incarcerating him.

Gorbachev won top marks as a student. But his biggest victory at Moscow State may have been over the horde of would-be suitors for the bright, cultured, and attractive Raisa Maximovna Titorenko. What won over "Riya," Mlynar suggested, was Gorbachev's "lack of vulgarity" toward women – a characteristic that set him apart from other Russian men. Gorbachev had gone to a ballroom-dancing class with the intention of having a few fraternal laughs at the footwork of his friend, Vladimir Lieberman. He met Raisa there and the courtship began.

At home in Stavropol, Gorbachev had learned how to mix with peasants and provincials. At the university he quickly took to the milieu of intellectuals and foreigners. And now, with the well-read and fashionable Raisa, he would add a cultural dimension. She took him in hand to the theatre and ballet, she built a home library containing many of the Western literary classics, she gave him style. Before he met her he had once spent an entire year wearing one pair of pants. With her influence he would soon be wearing panama hats.

They courted each other in the student dorm. In those days they packed several male students into each small, cold room. There was running water but no bath; for want of real tea, they drank "student tea" – a mix of hot water and sugar. Privacy was impossible, so students in Gorbachev's wing arranged a schedule whereby each would periodically get the room alone for an hour with a female friend. Mikhail and Raisa were married in 1954 while they were still students. They had a little reception in the corner of the dorm. In honour of the occasion, according to Aikman, the students gave the newlyweds a room for not just one hour but the whole night.

Gorbachev returned to Stavropol in 1955 and began a remarkably swift rise through the ranks. He gained the leadership of the area Komsomol, then moved to the senior party in 1962. In 1966 he became first secretary for the city of Stavropol and in 1970 he made the big leap to first secretary of the entire Stavropol *krai*, or region.

In 1978 he was called to Moscow and in 1980 appointed a full Politburo member. By the age of 40 he was a member of the Central Committee, the Soviet policy-making body of 300-plus members that is second in importance only to the Politburo. He was the youngest of anyone on the body. With his two degrees, he was also among the better educated, many of the others having only one diploma from an engineering or pedagogical institute.[5]

Gorbachev had political smarts and other good qualities. But as well – and this was vital to his swift rise – he had the luck of geography. Stavropol was a vacation area for Politburo members, and so one of the best places in the Soviet Union for making contacts: when the country's leaders flew to Stavropol, Gorbachev was there to greet them. It was also the real home of Mikhail Suslov, the party's ideology chief; and Fyodor Kulakov, who was a Politburo star until his mysterious death in 1978.

In Stavropol the most frequent adjectives I heard people use to describe Gorbachev were "tough," "open," "innovative," and "pragmatic." Pierre Trudeau had emphasized this last one to me in a chat before I left for Moscow.

Gorbachev, while accessible and outgoing during his Stavropol days, was not one to brook any violation of the socialist order. He would visit state farms unannounced, catching the slackers by surprise. He preferred to mix and learn rather than run things from the desk. Despite his high position, he was never too proud to hop on one of the tractors and do some of the work himself – just as he was not too proud as mayor to be a student.

The *glasnost* side of his personality was apparent long before his Kremlin days. In Stavropol, which had a population of about 150,000 in the 1960s, the custom as elsewhere was for the newspapermen to take their cue from the local party bosses, who would frequently brief them. But Gorbachev encouraged them not to be bound by the party line. He told editors to show some imagination, to write about real problems. He would often ask, "Is anyone reading what you write?"

One of *glasnost*'s future architects was Alexander Yakovlev, who was Ambassador to Canada when Gorbachev, as the Kremlin's agriculture secretary, made his visit there. Yakovlev, who would win the confidence of Gorbachev during the visit, had a very open relationship with the rotund Whelan. "We were just a couple of old peasants," Whelan said of their rapport. "Neither of us could stand a lot of b.s."

Yakovlev had an artificial leg, the result of the Siege of Leningrad. "I used to tease him about his metal leg," Whelan said. "I'd tell him, 'That's where you keep your electronic listening device.'"

During the visit, Yakovlev told Whelan to talk to Gorbachev in that very blunt style. So, "I would get going, telling Gorbachev why Canada's methods were superior and Alex would sneak in behind him and start waving his arms, urging me to give Gorbachev the real goods. I think Yakovlev realized our food production system was the best and he wanted Gorbachev to realize it too."

Gorbachev "looked at us and said, 'You rehearsed all this.' But we hadn't. Sometimes we gave 24 hours' notice if we were visiting a farm but that's it. We went to a supermarket once on an hour's notice. Gorbachev couldn't believe the products on the shelves." Gorbachev mocked Whelan about the Canadian senate, asking how the population could tolerate an unelected body. He quizzed Alberta farmers about bull semen and livestock embryos. He showed an immense appetite for information.

Visiting Politburo members usually wouldn't have put themselves in situations where they had to answer tough questions. When they did, it didn't help the image much. For decades, off and on, Gromyko had been appearing on Western TV screens looking as if all the blood had been sucked from him. But Gorbachev had no hesitation in appearing before the Senate's Standing Committee on External Affairs and National Defence. In Canada and in Britain he demonstrated another trait he would later manifest as general secretary – an ability to reverse the anti-Soviet spin, to put the shoe on the other foot. Never one to cover up his own country's past problems, Gorbachev grew annoyed when foreigners looked at those in isolation from their own.

When a Canadian senator asked him why the Soviets had to maintain nuclear missiles in Asia, Gorbachev flipped the question over. "What do you expect from us? There are [American] missiles in South Korea and in ships in the Pacific. The Nakasone government has agreed to turn Japan into an unsinkable missile carrier and militaristic plans are being hatched. What position are we to adopt?"[6]

When the Canadians fired Cold War spy talk at him, Gorbachev played with them, saying that it was typical Soviet negative stuff and nothing would come of it. "I will tell you bluntly. As they say in our country, in Central Asia, the wind blows, the dogs bark and the caravan moves on."

In Britain, when he was attacked on human rights, he testily fought back, using Northern Ireland as an example. "I can quote you a few facts about human rights in the United Kingdom. For example you persecute entire communities, entire nationalities. You have 2.3 million unemployed. You govern your society, you leave us to govern ours."

In London, Gorbachev recalled from his international studies a line from Lord Palmerston: "England does not have eternal friends or eternal enemies, but eternal interests." As Jerry Hough, Duke University's Soviet specialist, noted, "It was scarcely the simplistic Marxist view of economic determinism."

The Canadian media didn't follow Gorbachev closely in 1983; but by the time of the 1984 British visit many outsiders considered him the Kremlin's heir apparent. The attention focussed on him was enormous, the reviews he was given, flattering. Thatcher was admiring, and the veteran pol, Dennis Healy, was driven to poetry. "He is a man of exceptional charm with a relaxed, self-deprecating sense of humour. Emotions flicker over a face of unusual sensitivity like breezes on a pond. In discussion he was frank and flexible with a composure full of inner strength." Healy had hit on a key descriptive – inner strength. But in the final analysis the Brit was puzzled: "How could someone so nice and human run the Soviet system?"

Mikhail Gorbachev, though a product of the Soviet system, the Communist Party establishment, was not really part of that system, that establishment. Too many things set him apart – his exposure to the West, his education, his youth, his openness, his perspective. He was, as Mlynar put it, "a reformist by nature." He was, as a Moscow intellectual told me, "a humanist by nature." He was, in contrast to Brezhnev, the new atypical Soviet man.

4/Out of the Blocks

THE POLITBURO'S election of Gorbachev was the equivalent, in a sense, of the election of the liberal opposition party in a democracy such as Canada or the United States. Within the Soviet Union's one Communist party were conservative and reformist wings not unlike political divisions in the West. In the U.S.S.R. the wings represented change within the confines of socialism. In the case of America the two parties represent change within the confines, more or less, of capitalism. There, of course, changes are decided in democratic elections, whereas in the U.S.S.R. they have been made by party-hierarchy decree.

Once in power, the Gorbachev wing, the reform wing, moved quickly in some respects but slowly on the economy, a decision it would live to regret. In a country thick with conservative tradition, Gorbachev felt he lacked the mandate for immediate and sweeping economic change. As well, as he would acknowledge later, he failed at first to appreciate the urgency of his economic crisis.

In foreign affairs, Gorbachev was more convinced of the required direction, faced less entrenched opposition, and could score more quickly. He put Washington on the defensive with a unilateral moratorium on nuclear-test explosions. Only eight months into office, he attended a summit where, with Ronald Reagan in Geneva, he demonstrated the new, open style of a Kremlin leader. He impressed the world as being genuinely in search of a new era of détente.

But all this, along with some predictable economic measures –
an anti-alcohol campaign, bureaucratic streamlining, an anticorruption drive – still did not represent permanent change. As 1986
opened there was still only Gorbachev's promise of such. "There
should be revolutionary changes," Gorbachev had declared at the
first meeting of his Central Committee in April 1985, "a transfer to
fundamentally new technological systems, to technologies of the
latest generations."

Many signposts were planted in that first, relatively unnoticed
address. On bureaucracy: "It is time to start streamlining the
organizational structures of management, to do away with the
unnecessary management bodies."

On decentralization: "The number of instructions and
regulations which arbitrarily interpret party and government
decisions and thus shackle the independence of enterprises should be
dramatically reduced."

On foreign policy: "Mankind faces a choice: either to increase
further tensions and confrontations or to search constructively for
mutually acceptable agreements which could stop the preparations
for nuclear conflict."

Affixed to his enlightened passages were the Communist cant
and the contradictions. "Today the U.S.S.R. has a powerful, highly
developed economy and skilled work force, specialists and research
personnel," Gorbachev declared. That and another assertion
seemingly pirated from the bible of Brezhnev: "For the first time in
history, the working man has become the master of his country, the
maker of his own destiny."

No sooner had he called for decentralization than, in the late
summer of 1985, he spoke at variance with the message, issuing a
defence of centralized economic controls and attacking reforms
aimed at market socialism. "Some of you look at the market as a
life-saver for your economies," he warned an East European
delegation. "But comrades, you should not think about lifesavers,
but about the ship and the ship is socialism."

About the same time he spoke to the East Europeans, his chief
economic adviser, a wide-waisted, composed, and lucid Armenian
by the name of Aban Aganbegyan, was telling him there was only
one way out of the economic quicksand and that it was the market

solution. End the free ride, he advised, reward the hard workers, punish the slackers, decentralize, give power to the people. Tens of millions had savings that would allow them to improve their housing, Aganbegyan noted, but the system didn't allow them to build. "If there is money and there is a great need for apartments, what is going wrong?"

Much of Gorbachev's 1985 was taken up with consolidating power, moving enemies out, moving allies in, finding some solid ground on which to move. If we are to believe some Soviet experts such as Zhores Medvedev, Konstantin Chernenko's choice as successor was not Gorbachev but the Moscow party boss, Viktor Grishin. As fate would have it, Chernenko died before being able to orchestrate events toward such a scenario. Moreover, Chernenko's March 10 passing came at a time of critical coincidence: two staunch Politburo opponents of Gorbachev – Vladimir Shcherbitsky and Dinmukhamed Kunayev – were far away from the capital, unable to get back in time for the Politburo vote on the successor.[1]

Moved into a position of prominence in the Politburo by Andropov, Gorbachev did not have an exceptional accomplishment with which to campaign for the top spot. His series of mediocre or bad crop years in the agriculture job could be held against him, even though the weather was to blame. In his speech nominating Gorbachev, Andrei Gromyko steered clear of any discussion of agriculture and instead dwelt on Gorbachev's "brilliant" ability to dissect and analyze problems.

The specifics of what the final vote count showed remain unknown. What is known is that Gorbachev did not begin his stewardship in a full command position. Instead it was with a Politburo divided between Brezhnev men and Andropov men.

Andropov's brief term in 1982-83 witnessed the beginnings of the campaign against corruption, of more government candour, of an effort to limit the massive controls the party exerted over all phases of Soviet life. These were all initiatives Gorbachev ascribed to. But neither Andropov nor his followers could be termed radical reformers. Gorbachev was probably alone among the Politburo members of the day in meriting such a description – though he was not showing these full colours quite yet. First he had to build a consensus, to move the blocks into place. His immediate leadership changes brought to the fore Andropov men at the expense of Brezhnevites. They included the posting of Yegor Ligachev, a Siberian with the demeanour of a bulldog, to the number-two Kremlin ranking as ideology chief. Ligachev had a reputation as a strong opponent of corruption but sounded thoroughly Communist in areas of dogma and would come to be identified as a *glasnost* opponent. Nikolai Ryzhkov became prime minister. Ryzhkov was a technocrat, an industry expert from the Urals with an air of competence but no flair. KGB chief Viktor Chebrikov, who, along with the other two, supported Gorbachev in the succession battle, took full Politburo status. Gromyko, the foreign minister, was moved up to perform the titular duties of Soviet president, while a long-time Gorbachev associate, Eduard Shevardnadze of the Georgian Republic, was placed in Gromyko's post, leading many to assume that Gorbachev wanted to run his own foreign policy.

Following the appointments, Gorbachev was soon able to rid himself of major Politburo rivals – Leningrad party boss Grigori Romanov, a heavy-drinking Brezhnev man, and the Moscow mafia's Grishin, a Communist don.

A Moscow woman who worked as a secretary told me she was at a local market one day when Grishin, on an inspection tour of some kind, made an appearance. While red lights whirled atop police escort cars, he arrived in a phalanx of limousines. A flank of KGB toughs bullied their way in, opening a path for him, the woman said, while another cohort of attendants toadied at his every twitch. With an expression of imperial derision, Grishin surveyed the market for a few minutes before screaming away in his limousine regiment.

"How many other 'men of the people' do you have like that?" I asked the woman jokingly. "He isn't the only one," she said, adding with a look of horror, "Can you imagine if he had been elected over Gorbachev?"

In Gorbachev's Politburo, the Kazakh Republic's Kunayev, who rivalled Grishin in immoral turpitude, remained on, as did two other strong conservative voices – the Ukraine's Shcherbitsky, and Mikhail Solomentsev. Gorbachev was not equipped with a majority for radical reform, but he made certain with his early moves that the number of Andropov men outweighed those of the Brezhnev mould.

This was tantamount to being half out of the grave, and the half-measures aimed at economic reform in Gorbachev's first year perhaps reflected the Politburo mix. *Perestroika*, meaning "rebuilding," was not the catchword in 1985 and into 1986. Instead it was *ooskarenya*, meaning "acceleration." The policy included a clampdown on the black market, an anti-alcohol campaign, bureaucratic reorganization, and exhortations to work hard.

"At first," Georgi Arbatov, the astute Kremlin advisor, would later observe, "the situation looked to us somewhat less complicated. For several years, virtually a whole decade, the country, the society, the policies had been in a state of immobility, a kind of hibernation when the leadership was not solving the accumulating problems but was even afraid of acknowledging their existence and facing them." The initial plan, said Arbatov, involved overcoming the stagnation of the Brezhnev era. But "as we started tackling the problems we realized pretty soon that we had to do much more than simply make up for a lost decade."[2]

To go further, the bureaucracy, the leadership, the people themselves needed a brutally frank assessment of the desperate state the country was in. This meant no more cover-ups by the state media. It meant a revolutionary turn away from self-serving propaganda to *glasnost*. If the media were allowed to tell the people what was really going on, Gorbachev reasoned, the demand for radical change would necessarily follow.

Gorbachev hit upon this thought early. In his initial months in power he was quietly mapping out a strategy for a revolution in the Soviet media. Late in the evenings in his residence he held long discussions with Russian liberals, one of whom was Vitaly Korotich.

Korotich was a Ukrainian poet of radical leanings who had once met Gorbachev in Stavropol. I wasn't aware of the tie until one night in 1986 when a woman from Tallin in the Estonian Republic came to my office looking for help. She had a husband who lived in Canada and now she had permission to leave the Soviet Union to join him. But for her son there was no such consent and she wanted me to write an article about her case, to try and drum up some sympathy in Canada. In the meantime, she said, "I must get hold of Vitaly Korotich to help me too." Korotich, she explained, had a pipeline to Gorbachev. "Korotich was personally put in his job by Gorbachev to do the things he is doing."

The job of Korotich was editor of the most radical official magazine the Soviet Union had seen – *Ogonyok*. Following his nocturnal visits, Gorbachev had asked Korotich to take charge of what was then a conservative organ and turn it into a trailblazer for reform.

It wasn't often that poets got called over to the apartments of Soviet leaders for cakes and ale. "We talked and argued long into the night," Korotich recalled. "He invited me back many times. I kept asking myself, 'Why should he be interested in me?' Some of my friends thought I was a good poet but I was not well known in the party or in Moscow literary circles."

He concluded that his appeal probably lay in that very reason – that he was not a member of the party mafia. When Gorbachev asked him to take the editorship of the magazine, he told the Ukrainian, "My hands are tied, you must be one of my hands."[3]

On foreign affairs, Gorbachev's hands were not so tied. The Soviet public is generally less concerned about external policy than day-to-day matters at home. Most Russians I talked to assumed – unless their boy was in Afghanistan – that the Kremlin was doing its utmost for peace, and left it at that.

Gorbachev's political savvy was on display both with the decision to announce a nuclear-test moratorium and with the choice of date. He announced the policy on August 6, the anniversary day of the United States' nuclear bombing of Hiroshima. With the announcement came an invitation for Washington, which was not amused by the timing, to join the moratorium.

Gorbachev considered the nuclear bombings of Hiroshima and Nagasaki "barbarous." The view of many Soviets was that with the war drawing to a close and Japan on her knees, the incineration of 100,000 Japanese civilians was a needless horror, a war crime of major dimensions. If one atomic bomb was necessary, then surely the second, three days later, was not. But on the other side of the ocean, where the p.r. was entirely different, the nuclear bombings have gone down in the population's mind as necessary for winning the war. Talk of war crimes is not even admissible. The truth of the matter probably lies somewhere in between, but the way the superpowers, particularly the Soviets, can manipulate the thinking of their publics, such a middle ground variant is a rare upshot of East-West disputes.

To no one's surprise, the American side said no to the moratorium. For 19 months Moscow would invite Washington to join the moratorium and for 19 months Washington would have to find alibis to keeping saying no, to keep undertaking nuclear tests in the desert. Alliance partners would have to find reasons for not supporting the Soviets on their unilateral good-will gesture. The moratorium issue became the first of many occasions where the Soviet leader took the initiative and left the other side scrambling. It became the first of Gorbachev's public-relations victories.

Shortly after the Kremlin's moratorium call, Washington attempted what had all the signs of a propaganda counterpunch. The Americans tried peddling a story that the Soviet secret police were using a secret spray dust to track Western diplomats. The spray chemical, the Americans alleged, could even seep into the body and cause death. The story was later proved to be bogus, and the United States, embarrassed, retracted it. But the exercise may have been worthwhile. The initial anti-Soviet charge made headlines all over the world. The retraction, a long time later, was hardly noticed.

Gorbachev wanted to end the Cold War games. In another rare initiative for a Soviet general secretary, he sat down with the editors of *Time* magazine for a comprehensive interview six months after taking power. His call was for cooperation. "So far as we are concerned we are not declaring the United States an evil empire," Gorbachev said. "We know what the United States is, what the American people are and what their role in the world is. We are for a new, better stage in our relations."

The Geneva summit followed in November. Little of the concrete was expected and little of the concrete was achieved. But the atmospherics were important. Gorbachev didn't get far with his opposition to Star Wars but the style was what counted. During past high-level East-West meetings, the Soviets had shown a public-relations gap as wide as their technology gap. They usually eschewed press conferences, briefings, scrums. Instead they would issue a few Cold War bromides and skulk away, while the White House drummed home its unchallenged version of events.

It all changed with Geneva. The Kremlin held more briefings and more press conferences than the super-sell Reagan team. As a result it received much-improved press treatment. It was early *glasnost* and it worked. From his exposure to the outside world before becoming general secretary, Gorbachev knew well that politics was a media game in which the best salesman won.

Ronald Reagan emerged handsomely from Geneva as well. Like many, Soviet officials had never thought much of his intellect. For them, the cocktail-circuit description of Reagan as "an amiable dunce" hit the mark. But following the inconsistency of the Carter years, where one month the moderation of Secretary of State Cyrus Vance was the policy choice and the next month the hard line of National Security Adviser Zbigniew Brzezinski took over, at least now they were dealing with a consistent force. Reagan and Gorbachev got along reasonably well at Geneva, and this in itself made the summit worthwhile. In the pre-Gorbachev period, the Moscow-Washington dialogue had been in a deep freeze, East-West relations stalled, sabre rattling the order of the day. The Afghanistan invasion, the deaths of three Soviet leaders in less than three years, and the hard-liner cabal at the White House led by cold warrior Caspar Weinberger, the defence secretary, had made progress impossible.

Now the dialogue had been reopened in a constructive spirit. As an example, Reagan appeared on Soviet television with a New Year's Day message, and Gorbachev did the same in America. The American president congratulated the Soviet people while getting his freedom message across.

The day after was cold and dreary in Moscow, and outside a bookstore weighed down with Lenin and Brezhnev tomes I stopped passersby for their views on Reagan. For most Muscovites the occasion marked the first time they had seen him. The pre-*glasnost* Soviet press had paid scant attention to any American president. In the case of Reagan, it had him stereotyped as a warmongering capitalist cowboy.

The Russian people were not entirely gullible, however. Many were bright enough to realize that there was another world beyond the shameless distortions of their press. In front of the bookstore on Gruzinsky Pereoluk, they breathed against their fingers for warmth and in the majority spoke favourably of Reagan's appearance. It was obvious he had "an actor's skills," said a middle-aged woman, who was accompanied by a young boy bundled up like a stuffed animal. "He was a charmer. Like a priest before the parishioners." A recently retired construction engineer would not stop talking. "I have a good opinion of him now. The Soviet people will like him much more after this and after his words in Geneva. All the world wants peace. We know he cannot stand alone against the world." A pregnant woman who had just purchased a Lenin book said she and her husband had now changed their minds about Americans. "We didn't expect he would congratulate the Soviet people. It was the first time for a U.S. president to do that."

The positive reviews weren't shared by all. "The policy of Reagan is just to keep the tension between East and West," said a handsome youth from the southern Georgian Republic, who didn't believe what Reagan said. "A strange, very strange performance," said a woman in a gray coat who grew very emotional. "His words were wonderful but his actions are so different from his words."

A young woman with the popular Russian name of Natasha had watched the Reagan performance with her boyfriend and couldn't recall much. She didn't know what the boyfriend thought either. "I think he was too distracted. All he kept saying was 'Natasha, I love you, Natasha, I love you.' "

Two weeks later I returned to my apartment, tired after running all over the city trying to find a store that sold a bed and suffering stomach discomfort after a Russian restaurant meal. I didn't want to watch the evening news, but turned it on anyway, because it was a journalist's duty to do so. The Soviets made many of their major policy announcements on the *Vremya* newscast, and no foreign correspondent could rest easy until it was over. That was often a long wait, because Soviet news had not mastered the idea of the 30-second clip. Instead, entire speeches were sometimes read out by the anchorman, with no accompanying pictures.

This time, January 15, 1986, was one of those nights. The *diktor* began reading a Gorbachev speech to the nation, dashing my hopes for a restful evening. Straining to comprehend the Russian language, I could make out that it was a proposal for a major peace plan involving several stages. To get the details I would have to return to the office to retrieve the Tass news agency's wire.

The streets were snowy and barren, no taxis were in view. In Moscow, cabs would often stop, then pull away upon hearing that your destination was not to their convenience. On this occasion, pressed for time and in no mood for a setback, I started firing packs of Camels at the driver before the door was half-open. He sourly agreed to take me to the office, then wait outside to take me back to the Associated Press bureau, where I could write and transmit the story. I felt lucky I made it, because Gorbachev had delivered his biggest speech to date. He had announced a grandiose 15-year plan to eliminate nuclear weapons from the earth. The Politburo, the Kremlin leader stated, had decided on a three-stage plan. The first elimination stage would extend over eight years and involve a 50-percent reduction in American and Soviet missiles that could reach each other's territory. The second phase, to be completed by 1997, would bring the other nuclear states into the process. In the year 2000 a universal accord would be drawn up to ban such weapons from ever again coming into existence. Gorbachev's proposals, though short on specifics, appeared to drop a previous Soviet demand that any agreement with the United States to eliminate intermediate-range missiles in Europe would also have to include the removal of the British and French nuclear forces.

"If the United States administration is indeed committed to the goal of the complete elimination of nuclear weapons everywhere, as it has repeatedly stated, it is being offered a practical opportunity to begin this practice," said Gorbachev. He sought to negate the rationale for the Strategic Defense Initiative. "Instead of wasting the next 10 to 15 years by developing new, extremely dangerous weapons in space, allegedly to make nuclear arms useless, would it

not be more sensible to start eliminating those arms and finally
bring them down to zero?"

To many in the West this was just pie-in-the-sky Kremlin
propaganda, another Gorbachev p.r. gambit. Some let me know
this by letter after I took Gorbachev by his word on the proposal and
wrote favourably of it. From day one I had taken a highly positive
line on Gorbachev. My instincts told me to believe him and in this
aspect of my work in Moscow my instincts served me well, helping to
compensate for my many other gaffes of judgment on the Soviets.

The speech of January 15 marked a decisive turn in the thinking
of Gorbachev and his policy advisors. They were saying officially
now that the nuclear-arms race had reached a strategic dead end
and that their policy would be dictated by that fact. The attitude
was summed up by their top military man, Marshal Sergei
Akhromeyev, chief of the Soviet general staff. "Today the use of
nuclear weapons is meaningless," he said. "No nation at present can
strengthen its security by nuclear weapons. Mountains of nuclear
weapons continue to grow. However, the security of the nuclear
powers decreases."

This was part of the Gorbachev "new thinking." But it was
hardly new. Gorbachev was only echoing the written words of a very
well-known American.

In April 1956, President Dwight Eisenhower wrote a letter,
remarkable for its clairvoyance, in response to a newspaper
columnist urging him to meet the Soviet threat by a new crash
program in air power and missiles.

"I have spent my life in the study of military strength as a
deterrent to war, and in the character of military armaments
necessary to win a war," Eisenhower wrote. "The study of the first of
these questions is still profitable, but we are rapidly getting to the
point where no war can be won. War implies a contest; when you get
to the point that a contest is no longer involved and the outlook
comes close to destruction of the enemy and suicide for ourselves –
an outlook that neither side can ignore – then arguments as to the
exact amount of available strength as compared to somebody else's
are no longer vital issues.

"When we get to the point as we one day will that both sides know that in any outbreak of general hostilities, regardless of the element of surprise, destruction will be both reciprocal and complete, possibly we will have enough sense to meet at the conference table with the understanding that the era of armaments has ended and the human race must conform its actions to this truth or die."[4]

Three decades after writing the letter, Eisenhower had a listener in the leader of the Soviet Union.

5/Gorky Park

WHILE SIZING up the early moves of Gorbachev, I was, in acclimatizing to my new domestic surroundings, intrigued by the nature of the people. Whatever their other traits, they seemed systematized, hardly ready to break the mould.

After waiting four months, we were finally given a spacious apartment in an L-shaped complex only a ten-minute walk from Gorky Park. Construction was completed on the apartment building in the mid-1970s, but despite the acute housing shortage in Moscow it had sat vacant for a decade. "Various engineering problems" had delayed the opening, housing officials said. The 12-storey building – half for Russians, the other half for foreigners – offered the prospect of breakfast every day with Lenin. Our kitchen and dining-room windows faced October Square, where an enormous bronze of the Soviet Union's founder overpowered its surroundings. Lenin was in an overcoat. His eyes gazed fiercely at everyone. He was a cheerless sight to wake up to, but our fifth-floor apartment did have compensating features, one being a splendid view of the many very Russian activities going on in the square.

Almost every winter morning, for example, I could count on the appearance of the Lenin Monument cleaning brigade. Its 40 or 50 members would arrive in their orange flak jackets at eight sharp, accompanied by trucks, snowploughs and crane. Many of the labourers were older women, all short and very plump. These *babushkas* meticulously cleaned the wide expanse of concrete around the statue, including the thick marble ledges bordering the flower gardens. Some swung the shovels lustily, as if they were chopping down a stand of pines. They cleared away every snowflake, leaving a dark, wet base that made the square look worse than it had with its snow cover.

The men worked on the monument itself. No snow was allowed to remain on Lenin: they kept him immaculate from toe to shining skull. For the cleaning of his great head, the crane would hoist an artisan in a little box about 80 feet in the air. With a small brush à la Michelangelo, he would gingerly sweep the snow away from Lenin's thick eyebrows and the rest of his face. The performance normally took 45 minutes – more if severe weather had left a coating of ice.

Every weekend, newlyweds posed for pictures in front of the monument. Always a Russian was laying a wreath of some kind. And on the big occasions, like Revolution Day, soldiers marched in the square in all manner of formations. I wasn't sure whether the rule applied at this particular monument, but on Red Square, outside the marble mausoleum enclosing Lenin's remains, you were not allowed to smoke. It didn't matter that it was outdoors – smoking, as a friend of mine visiting from Canada discovered, was forbidden.

On a windy, chilling February night, we were standing about 30 feet in front of the mausoleum when a young Russian in an expensive fur hat tapped my friend on the shoulder and told him to put out his cigarette. My friend contested this, citing for one thing the fact that the wind was blowing the fumes away.

"No one in Russia is allowed to smoke in front of Lenin," the Russian objected. "It's the rule."

This youth, Alexander, was not an overzealous patriot doing a duty. I talked with him briefly, during which he levelled complaint after complaint about his country. "Until Gorbachev every leader we have had since Lenin has been a disaster," he said. A friend of his, Konstantin, nodded in agreement. "Maybe there is time to save the country. But I don't know if Gorbachev will last."

As we walked through an underground walkway on our way home, my guest watched a well-dressed Russian stop, pick up a tiny cigarette butt from the almost pristine pavement, and carry it along until the next wastebasket.

I had very consciously chosen the underpass instead of the more scenic alternative because of what had happened the last time I took the overland crossing. I was very late for a reception at the Canadian embassy and couldn't find an underpass across the broad Kalininsky Prospekt. Forgetting what had happened to my editor our first week in Moscow, I ventured out under the yellow street-lights across the dry, snowy road. I wasn't halfway across before a militiaman a block up blasted his whistle and, rage in his voice, ordered me to retreat. I sheepishly backpedalled to the curb, seeking anonymity in the great mass of pedestrians out shopping on that cold winter's evening. But there was no sanctuary. No sooner was I among them than three chastised me in turn as harshly as had the lawman. As if it was their business, they said I didn't know the rules, that I should obey the law, that I must be stupid. I skulked off down the street, only to be admonished by yet two other Russians, who had seen my misdemeanour from a distance. "Don't you know how to cross the road, young man? There's an underpass over there."

I related the story to my Canadian visitor as an example of the collective mentality at work. There was little room for individual behaviour. Everyone was supposed to melt, or rather freeze into the crowd.

The visitor hadn't yet been to Gorky Park. The park, made famous in the West by a novel of the same name, was one of the best places for observing the Russian character, for getting a sense of that collective mindset – the respect for authority, the conservatism, the reflex opposition to individual behaviour – all hallmarks of the Soviet character that anyone trying to bring vitality or enterprising spirit to the Soviet Union would run up against.

One day, while enjoying an ice cream near the oversized archway that was the park entrance, I was astonished to see the collective peace of the law-and-order Moscow day defiled. Two thuggish youths in their late teens were eyeing each other coldly while friends looked on. The taller one, who wore a burgundy T-shirt, fired a long right that struck the other's chin hard. A flurry followed, during which the smaller, more muscular Russian belted his foe with a rising haymaker, speeding him back and over, elbows screeching across the hot pavement in such a way that everyone watching could feel the burning pain.

Now a militiaman ran toward the youths, blowing his whistle fiercely. They abandoned combat and raced for refuge, the short one disappearing into the crowd, the taller one chased by a cop as he headed for the parking lot. The law officer got close, but it was soon evident the younger legs were much more enduring. Slowing down now, the puffing militiaman raised his arm and voice in a call for assistance. Immediately, several civilians responded. Five gave chase across the pavement. The runaway greaser was soon coralled and wrestled over to the grateful officer. A man then volunteered his car in case the lawman needed it to take the offender away. Others picked up garbage that had been knocked from cans during the tumult. Several more stepped forward as witnesses. Collective harmony was soon restored.

Gorky Park was usually more peaceful. Named in 1932 in honour of the Soviet writer, Maxim Gorky, it is an entertainment park where tucked amidst the forests are restaurants, a theatre, a dancing hall, a midway, giant fountains, skating paths, and ponds where black swans glide.

In the winter I went once after a snowfall, when the sun's rays banked brilliantly off the flakes, creating a blinding white light. Skaters shot swiftly down the frozen pathways that ran narrowly through the tall trees. Closer to the Moscow River, on a long, wide stretch of ice, girls practised their figures while boys casually pursued a pick-up hockey game.

My skates were rather old by Western standards, but 20 years younger than anything the Moscow youth wore. The sight of my passing by on Western blades caused a stoppage in play. The Russians stared admiringly at them, discovered I was a Canadian, and asked about their favourite National Hockey League stars. Further along, the ice-flooding machine moved by, throwing up a great cloud of white steam in its train. As soon as it passed, skaters darted into the cloud, laughing, falling, knocking one another over in a rapture of good spirit.

The thousands who wandered through Gorky Park were well behaved, cleanly dressed, uniform in look and style, conscious of their environment (the park was perfectly clean), and not only deferential to authority but also ready to enforce the laws themselves.

In winter once I was walking with my cross-country skis held tidily over my shoulder, minding my own business. On two separate occasions, a Muscovite interrupted to inform me that my skis were not tied together at the end, and should be. I apologized for my deviant behaviour.

In the spring I saw a man crouched with his daughter at the pond where the black swans cruised. They were talking quietly until one of the ubiquitous, plain-clothes law-and-order presences interrupted them. He told them that there was to be no playing near the swans. What struck me was how passively the man accepted the reprimand. With careful nonchalance he collected his child, whose face was expressionless, and moved away in an obedient hush.

More spontaneity that day came from two roller-skating Russian girls who, one could see, had good times on the mind. They passed a tented restaurant, where an immense bearded man seated in the corner belched so loudly he almost blew the tent over. The girls laughed uproariously. They moved along the asphalt path to the boxing ring, where they enjoyed watching two bedsheet-white Russian lads beating blood out of each other. Further along the two brunettes, their long legs in imported jeans, drew some male attention as they skated to the loud music coming through the speakers. It was "Heartbreak Hotel." I found it refreshing to hear music that wasn't classical.

That moment recalled for me the time I flew south with a Soviet official who was acting as my guide. There was some dreadfully sombre classical music mixing with the rattling noise of the Aeroflot plane, and I remarked to my guide that I wished someone would turn the lousy music off. The official, thinking I should be enjoying it, asked me about my taste in music. I delivered a "rock & pop" verdict. He disapproved, saying that his taste lay strictly with the great composers. Then he made a summary comment, quite earnest and quite solemn, that I didn't have to write down in order to remember. "We are a serious country," he said pompously. "We listen to classical music."

At this stage I was just getting to know some of the Russian people. I liked them. It had always annoyed me that in the West, ordinary Russians somehow got lumped in with their leaders, that because they had suffered from Stalin's tyranny they were somehow loathed as a people for it.

I was finding the Russians not only brainy and gifted, but also – as they had not yet been spoiled by the age of technology – closer to the soil, closer to literature, capable of running greater depths of feeling than people in the ersatz-age West.

I was struck early not only by the collective and conservative nature of the people but by a sometimes-cited other aspect of their character. They had a highly charged mix of pride and shame and this to me helped define them. The great pride was in their awesome military power, their sensational space rockets, their land mass, their unbeatable athletes, their greats of literature. But the pride merged so painfully, so saddeningly, with the utter shame of not being able to adequately house or feed their people, with the humiliation of having to stand in line for hours to buy inferior goods, with the suspicion that they were hated abroad. In every Russian I came to know, the contradictory, bipolar nature in their personality – the pole of pride, the pole of shame – sooner or later became manifest.

Gorbachev was determined to remove the sources of the shame. But his gamble that *glasnost* would make them feel the shame more, exorcise their complacency, increase the demand for his measures of change, did not have great chances up against a population so collectively set in its state-secured ways. The comment a Russian policeman made to a travelling American almost a century earlier still seemed to apply. "A Russian," he said, "is too easily contented with his lot."[1]

In an abundance everywhere you went were the true believers: Russians who wanted to listen only to classical music, Russians you didn't think would ever change. An archetype was Sergei Bubka, the world's greatest pole vaulter. I met Bubka one night at the Hotel Sport – a high-class residence by Soviet standards, reserved exclusively for domestic and visiting athletes. We talked for an hour and a half. Then I went to the office and wrote the following lead for my newspaper story: "He jumps for 'moral satisfaction' and 'the joy of the masses.' His goal in life is to be 'in the forefront of the working people.' And he thinks that New York City is 'dull.' He is renowned

Soviet pole vaulter Sergei Bubka and it is a safe bet his next attempt is not going to be over the Berlin Wall."

I had asked the muscular 22-year-old nicknamed "the Cosmonaut" about his chief rival, Billy Olsen of the United States. "Money is his life," Bubka said with a frown as he sat with his coach in a small room. He described how Olsen, driven only by money fever, challenges the bar in now-or-never desperation. "What strikes me when I'm abroad in the capitalist countries," said Bubka, "is how the private interests prevail over the public ones. I look closely at the rich and I see that they don't work but receive a profit from their own enterprises and factories, while the ordinary people who work for them live in need. The contrast strikes me deeply.

"With Olsen, everything hinges on money. He is not sure if he is going to have money in the future and that is why he has to gain as much as possible today. He will live on the money he makes now in the future. The money he gains will be invested in this or that enterprise. But if he fails now I have no idea how he will exist, whether he will be able to find a job."

For Sergei Bubka there was no great pressure: "No matter whether I am a great sportsman or just an average Soviet citizen, I know that I will always have a monthly salary which is enough to live on."

It was a rationale you would hear from many Soviets when they explained why their system was better. In America, they argued, people continually suffered from the stress of not having a job, or of fearing they wouldn't be able to get another if they lost their present one. In the Soviet Union, where work was guaranteed, there was no such anxiety.

Bubka was blind to any advantages in the West, even though as a top athlete he had made several trips over. He was one of the many I met who swallowed what the Kremlin press had fed since birth. He claimed he didn't miss the opportunity to make a lot of money and enjoy America's much higher living standards. "No, what pleases me the most is that I can bring joy to the people with my excellent results. Usually I do my training in my native Donetsk [in the Ukraine] and ordinary people will come up to me and say, 'Okay, Sergei, are you going to beat Olsen or not?' What is more pleasant than to have people who are not engaged in sports knowing about me and looking forward to hearing about good, new results from me? And me trying to justify their expectations and perhaps bring them a small but nice pleasure?"

His outdoor world record had brought him to within four inches of one of sport's breathtaking landmarks – a 20-foot pole vault. But he was in no hurry, he said, to achieve it. "I like to take time to sophisticate my methods. I don't like to do it all at once. I enjoy the challenges of achieving goals bit by bit as part of an overall strategy."

Of more importance to him at this time, or so Bubka said, was getting his Communist Party membership, a privilege enjoyed by about ten percent of Soviet adults. He was already a candidate member; barring a foul-up, he was guaranteed to be blessed with full status soon. "Everybody wants to be in the forefront of the working people," he told me, "and being a member of the Communist Party will enable me to do much more to make a greater contribution to our society."

Shortly after I interviewed Bubka, the foreign ministry invited me and some other journalists on a trip to Poltava in the Ukraine. The city of 200,000 is a food-processing and textile centre of no special attraction except that, like so many cities in the U.S.S.R., it has a bloody war history. It was here, in 1709, that the armies of Peter the Great turned back the Swedish invaders in a historic battle. We knew we were likely to get a tour of the museum commemorating that battle – and we did. One of the disadvantages of these state-run press junkets was that you had to surrender the agenda to chaperons from Moscow. The people we were to interview in Poltava had been briefed. The state farm we were to visit was the area's exemplary one. The day-care centre we were to tour had the floors scrubbed and everyone dressed to the Soviet nines. And the restaurants where we were to eat had food. But while regulated, such trips – which were uncommon before Gorbachev's arrival – provided an important feel of the regions and their people. And as would be evident on later excursions, the surveillance was not so tight as to prevent an enterprising correspondent from slipping out on his own for independent research.

In the February cold of Poltava, we were taken across a state farm where we beheld new tractor equipment. We saw fine stables and learned that Soviets too can ride horses. We visited smiling Ukrainian families who said all was well. Finally, when we met Fyodor Morgun, the torpor ended.

Morgun, 60 years old, was the Communist Party boss for the Poltava region. Everything about him was robust – voice, body language, point of view. He had called a meeting of hundreds of the area's farmers, all of whom showed up at the dark hall in dark old suits and ties to hear his report and ask questions. In powerful bursts of vocal energy, Morgun introduced all the foreign correspondents one by one. There was a hearty round of applause for each – even for the German. Introductions over, he explained that in the 1950s he had read an article in a Canadian magazine on agricultural techniques. He soon determined that Soviet farming methods were wrong. He took the Canadian magazine to a major conference, he said, where he openly rebelled against the universal use of the plough. "I was sharply criticized for it," he said. "The question of my party membership was raised and I was in danger of losing my job."

Morgun described a month-long trip he made across Canada in the early 1960s, then began to talk in glowing terms about the Canadian way, the American way, their pioneering methods, their independent spirit. A group of young Americans, the Communist Party boss said, had recently patented a new wood stove, the design for which he had purchased for the Ukraine. "Look at how the Americans did it," Morgun boomed. "They are enterprising, they are thinking, they are acting. That's how we should do it. Even the Americans, even they who have all the gas, the electricity, the oil in the world, they still work to come up with a new wood stove.

"The Canadians? They have developed a new family of implements and tools and we've brought here 30 pieces of that equipment to copy. . . . And I'm telling you now – there is going to be an explosion of this technology here – no matter how much we have to fight against the conservative forces."

It was obvious Fyodor Morgun wasn't raising these matters for the benefit of the Ukrainian farmers alone. His main target was the foreign press, and his message was that it was time for Soviet society to innovate. In person and in message, Morgun was the opposite of the Sergei Bubkas. The government had taken us to Poltava to show us that Gorbachev had some like-minded people out there.

Morgun, who was as charismatic a Russian as I was to meet in the Soviet Union, decried the enormous amounts of grain his country had to import from Canada. But in five to ten years the country would again be self-sufficient, he predicted. Canada's no-ploughs technology had Gorbachev's stamp of approval; with it and with other sweeping reforms, all would be well. "In Manitoba they haven't known what a plough is for about 30 years. They exclusively use the kind of equipment we are introducing here."

The audience – certainly the journalists attending – was growing most attentive. Now he was on to decentralization. "Our purpose is to untie the hands of local management. We give the farmer the production quota and how he goes about fulfilling it is his own business. But you have to earn the right to be so independent. Show initiative, show enterprising spirit. I know that you like this idea. I like it tremendously. Agriculture used to be like a sailboat in changing winds. You were not allowed to adjust the sail properly to maintain the course." Now, under Mikhail Gorbachev, Morgun emphasized, "the individual adjusts the sails."

From sailboats, it was on to manure. "Now I'm telling you, for Christ's sake, rivet the attention of your people to the collection of horse and cow manure. If there is a cow, there is manure. If there is a horse, there is manure. If there is more manure, there is more for the horse and the cow. That's the key."

Vasilenko Pavlovich, who headed a collective farm, told the journalists more freedom was coming to the farmer. "I used to have seven bosses I had to report to. Now I have only one. Now we don't have to be shuffled before so many committees."

"Decentralization is really worth it," said Morgun. "You've got to trust the local workers. They can feel the market. . . . You cannot plan everything from above."

At dinner the next evening, Morgun, in the presence of many local bigshots, paid tribute to John and Robert Kennedy. He told how they had inspired him in his own career, how their style appealed to him, how their zeal for public service had infected other countries besides their own. The Kennedy eulogy was something akin to an American senator paying public tribute to Lenin or some other Soviet hero. Morgun then invited as many journalists as he could squeeze into his car for further discussion on his way home.

He was indeed, a man of Gorbachev's cloth. Gorbachev had only a passing acquaintance with Morgun. We in the press entourage made bets among ourselves on how soon it would be before the Soviet leader discovered him and moved him to a power position in Moscow.[2]

I returned to the capital encouraged that such party bosses existed and more positive about prospects for change than after interviewing Bubka. Bubka and Morgun lived in the same Ukraine but came from worlds apart. The problem was that while Gorbachev sat in the Kremlin drawing master plans for the overhaul of his society, the Bubkas, the Communist clichés, were in the majority. The Morguns, the new breed, were as yet a radical rump.

6/The Congress

AMONG ORDINARY Russians, the level of apathy toward government was high – comparable to if not greater than levels in the West. The Russians had never had any say in their politics and so had less reason to be caught up in the process. Their interests were more to do with the routines of daily living. Michel Bordeleau, a young Quebecker, spent three years in Moscow studying Russian and playing hockey in a Soviet factory league. Of his Moscow friends, he said, "These people are close to the ground. They work, they drink, they play hockey, they have sex. That's it."

Between periods of every game, Bordeleau's teammates drank good quantities of vodka. Once he noticed a player not drinking, and playing exceptionally well. He complimented him and mentioned something about how a little clean living can pay off.[1]

"I had 200 grams before I came to the rink," the Russian replied gruffly.

In late February 1986, the Communist Party Congress was about to open. These congresses, which are held every five years, chart the country's economic, political, moral, and philosophical course. It being Mikhail Gorbachev's first as leader, this one had special meaning. Anticipation was keen from all quarters – except the man on the street. All that Gorbachev's politics had accomplished so far was to take away his 200 grams.

Instead of simply urging the masses to drink less, which had been tried before and failed, Gorbachev had brought in major cutbacks in alcohol production. It was one of his first acts in power. His idea was to sober up Soviet society in the surest way possible – by making vodka unavailable.

In the Brezhnev era vodka had come to be the opiate of the Soviet masses. But Gorbachev concluded that its impact on the health of the country, on worker productivity, on morale, was staggering. The life-expectancy rate in the Soviet Union, in stark exception to the trend elsewhere, was actually declining. Gorbachev blamed alcohol. He wanted to do to it what Stalin had tried to do to religion, the previous opiate – he wanted to stamp it out.

His cutbacks produced even longer line-ups than had existed before, and bitterness toward him. They produced a headlong rush for substitutes such as drugs, home brew, shaving cream, toothpaste – anything with alcohol in it. Resistance and opposition were both fierce. Though not a big drinker, Gorbachev must have realized the depth of the tradition he was trying to dismantle. He must have known that with such a conservative people, old habits die hard.

Some of the stories coming out of the provinces were close to unbelievable – the mineral-water wedding at Lukovitsi being one example.

In order to show solidarity with the new regime's alcohol policy, some localities were insisting that even weddings be celebrated with mineral water. Party seniors in Lukovitsi noticed this and prepared to get in on the act. The town's next wedding was to be that of Andrei Brownyslavovich. The day after the wedding application was filed, Andrei's father, planning a buoyant wedding, went out and bought five crates of vodka. He didn't know that the party bosses had chosen his son's nuptials to be a showcase, bone-dry affair that would be filmed and used as proof of Lukovitsi's solidarity with the Gorbachev regime.

When the idea was put to Mr. Brownyslavovich, he flatly rejected it. Town fathers then came up with an enticing proposal: in return for having a dry wedding, Andrei and his bride, Irina, would immediately be given their own separate apartment instead of waiting several years, as most Soviet newlyweds must.

So important was the vodka tradition that Andrei's father at first turned down the offer. Under pressure from wife and son, he finally agreed. But by now news of the secret deal was being leaked all over town. Residents who had spent years on the waiting list for an apartment were outraged. A Mrs. Strunnikova, a quarry worker who was next in line, had lived in a crowded hovel for 20 years. She screamed about the sober-wedding scam to local trade-union officials. Public opinion soon began blowing her way.

The dry wedding went ahead as planned, with Brownyslavovich's worst fears being realized – it was the most boring wedding anyone in town could remember. The deed done, he went to claim his son's apartment. But now there had been a change: the town fathers informed him that the apartment had been given to Strunnikova. For their cooperation on the wedding, Andrei and Irina would get a TV set.

Brownyslavovich was incredulous – a dry wedding for a TV set! He wrote a letter to the mass-circulation newspaper *Trud*. *Trud* printed the letter and the entire scam was exposed. Lukovitsi went back to vodka weddings.

At this Party Congress, the 27th, voices of opposition to the anti-alcohol campaign, voices of the average Soviet, would not be heard. This was a Congress in the traditional, authoritarian style, with the party elite dominating the proceedings and blue-collar workers attending as mere tokens.

The city was fantastically lit up for the 27th Congress. Banners proclaiming the glory of Lenin and urging comrades to work harder were draped over the buildings. In the evenings big lights beamed on them as well as on the city's most celebrated architectural heritage.

While on my way to the Aragvi Restaurant, I made note of the unusually large number of Lenin banners and billboards. In a subsequent light-hearted column comparing what was available at the Aragvi with the prospect of being able to get anything you want at Alice's Restaurant, I resorted to deliberate hyperbole. I wrote that I had walked past 11,004 such billboards. A Soviet journalist didn't get the joke. Many months later, at a reception at the Canadian embassy, he approached me. "In your column you said thousands of Lenin posters," he admonished. "I walked that route and saw only a few."

I might have explained that I was suffering from the after-effects of a meal at the Aragvi when I wrote the story. While it may be true at Alice's, you don't get anything you want at the Aragvi. Though one of Moscow's more highly touted eating establishments (many Congress participants could be found there), the Aragvi's dinner menu often consisted of two choices – chicken Kiev and greasy sturgeon. In restaurant terms these two staples rivalled the KGB as a Soviet presence.

On this night, while a rock band of Bulgarian-weightlifter look-alikes made all conversation inaudible, I and another correspondent sought some spirits to cushion the decibel range. To a request for a beer, the waiter said, "No beer." To a request for red wine, he said, "No red wine." To a request for white wine, he said, "No white wine." Moving on to food, an appeal for salad was shot down immediately. Soup was out of the question. Cognac was the evening's lone libation, and at the surrounding tables many Russians were awash in it and latching onto passing innocents for a dance of any kind. My sober table partner got dragged unwillingly into the pandemonium of romp and whirl. Upon his release he immediately ordered chicken Kiev. My search for anything but chicken and sturgeon was rewarded – they had goose. I ordered goose. It arrived shivering in a thin pond of dark gravy, so bony you could almost see through it. I was in need of some quick tea to wash it down but there was nothing surprising in the waiter's reply. "*Nyet cheye*," he said. "No tea."

The historic Party Congress opened with a five-and-a-half-hour speech by Gorbachev, who four days later would call for an end to "windbaggery." The speech was a disappointment to many: he was still promoting "acceleration" instead of *perestroika*. He spoke of the need for, as he put it, "truly revolutionary change," and said "there is no other way." But he provided no blueprint on how to effect it. He criticized Brezhnev's legacy but made no ground-breaking reform proposals of his own. The speech sounded as if it had been written *for* him rather than *by* him. The straight-shooting Aganbegyan met with Western journalists afterwards and made the point twice that "we need more radical measures."

Where the Congress did make a mark was in its advances against the Soviet tradition of secrecy. A spirit of freer discussion and more honesty characterized the proceedings. "Greater openness is a matter of principle to us," Gorbachev said in his opening address. "It is a political issue. Without openness there is not, nor can there be, democracy. . . . Nobody has the right to forget Lenin's stern warning: 'False rhetoric and false boastfulness spell moral ruin and lead unfailingly to political extinction.' "

In defiance of tradition, the leader trotted out a Politburo member, Geydar Aliyev, for a full-fledged press conference. It may have been, someone cracked, the first press conference of his 30-year political career. While an obvious exaggeration, there was truth in the spirit of the remark. The Soviet power elite had long been accountable only to itself; seldom were Politburo members ever criticized in public before their death. It was only now that Brezhnev was becoming an object of scorn; no one had dared reproach him while he breathed. From this cue, one of Aliyev's first questioners, a pubby-looking British journalist from the *Daily Telegraph*, took his lead. He noted in his preamble that Aliyev had made glowing references to Brezhnev 13 times in his speech to the last Congress, and then demanded bluntly, "Tell me, sir, what do you think of him now?"

As the audience snickered in anticipation, Aliyev lowered his chin. His face turned an unhealthy crimson. "Well, this isn't really the subject of a press conference, is it? We're here to talk about social policy. . . . It was natural to speak highly of Mr. Brezhnev in those days. He was party secretary. But we did have drawbacks then. Today we speak of them more critically. The fact that we do shows that we are a stronger country."

Moving on with relief to a question about the alcohol campaign, Aliyev lightened his audience with a poke at the notorious drinking habits of a northern neighbour. The Kremlin campaign was hurting government revenues, but also making progress, he added, and serving "as an example to Finland."

But the Politburo member under the camera lights was back on the ropes fending off a question about the dearth of Soviet women in prominent governmental positions. Aliyev named one female on the Central Committee before adding, "Isn't that enough?" Some of us thought he was being sarcastic, but the look on his face signalled serious intent. Then, as his stretch limousine purred outside, Aliyev said he and the Soviet oligarchy didn't really enjoy any special privileges. He declined to reveal a Politburo member's pay. "I live well but don't go thinking we make very large salaries," he told us. "I don't get more than the directors of some [Western] companies."

His statements on the entitlements of the ruling class were coming on the heels of the Congress shocker – an open declaration by the Moscow party boss, Boris Yeltsin, that the privileges of the elite should be swept away. "The double moral standards in the present conditions are intolerable and inadmissible," said the firebrand radical, who had recently been elevated to prominence by Gorbachev. "Where privileges of leaders of all levels are not grounded, it is necessary to cancel them."

Yeltsin was trodding on sacred turf with these remarks, and Gorbachev or one of his men could easily have ordered that his words be kept behind closed doors. Since the Congress sessions were not open to the press, there would have been little difficulty in doing it. But in one of *glasnost*'s first loud victories, Yeltsin's outburst appeared in the newspapers.

The public outburst was pregnant with meaning: with it, the tall, silver-haired Yeltsin was on the road to becoming the darling of the foreign press, the darling of the Soviet reform movement, and the archrival of the daunting Siberian on Gorbachev's right arm – Yegor Ligachev. The opening salvo in the war between reformers and conservatives had been fired. Before the Congress was over, Ligachev struck back, denouncing the Yeltsin recommendation and receiving backing from the assembly hall.

What Gorbachev was feeling at this moment was a subject for hot speculation on Moscow's cocktail circuit. The Soviet leader was clearly viewed as Yeltsin's booster. Gorbachev had promoted him swiftly because Yeltsin was an outspoken, aggressive radical who could help lead the way. But now, just as Yeltsin was getting started as Moscow boss, they were already chopping at his knees.

Not only were proposals for a reduction of privileges formally rejected, but so was a bid to force a retirement age on Soviet leaders. Like popes and Chinese leaders, the Soviet Union's top men tended to remain in office till death bade them part. Defending the decision, a Congress official explained that some can be old at 40, others can be young at 70. The fact that demands for such change were published testified, he said, to "the democracy of our press."

On foreign policy, Gorbachev announced, "We would like in the nearest future to withdraw the troops stationed in Afghanistan." He added that a schedule for a phased withdrawal had been agreed upon with the Afghan side.

Gorbachev also issued a call for a world congress on economic security. The proposal followed his pledge of January 15 for a non-nuclear world, his call for a five-nation nuclear summit, and his vow to open the Soviet Union to on-site verification. Early in the new year, in another gesture aimed at gaining favour with the West, imprisoned dissident Anatole Scharansky was permitted to leave the Soviet Union.

In the Western capitals there was plenty of talk about the motives behind all of Gorbachev's peace manoeuvring. The belief that he was acting more humanely, more peacefully, than previous Kremlin leaders only because domestic circumstance compelled him to do so. To save his collapsing economy, this thinking suggested, he desperately needed an arms agreement that would allow for a transfer of roubles from guns to butter. Moreover, his charm offensive with the West would bring the Soviets more trade and more technology.

Never mentioned was this possibility: that he was passionately pursuing peace and disarmament because, in addition to the economic good sense it made, he felt that it was simply the correct moral thing to do; that the nuclear-arms race was imperilling the future of mankind and that pragmatic solutions should therefore take priority over continued Cold War posturing.

Whatever his motives, Gorbachev's campaign to change international public opinion was getting a boost from the policies of his adversary. After the promise of the Geneva summit, Reagan's hawks – the Oliver Norths of the White House – appeared to gain the temporary upper hand. Evidence of improved Soviet behaviour wasn't being accepted in the Oval Office. The White House continued to spurn the moratorium on nuclear testing; it threatened to expel a large contingent of Soviet staffers from the United

Nations; it essentially ignored Gorbachev's denuclearization plan of January 15; and in what the Kremlin termed a provocation, it allowed an American warship to sail into Soviet waters in the Black Sea.

During the Party Congress, Vladimir Posner, the Soviet commentator, appeared on the ABC network to discuss anti-Soviet remarks in a recent Reagan speech. The White House was outraged that an American network would give air time to a Soviet "propagandist" without having someone immediately rebut him. A scathing letter from them won an apology from ABC. The Soviets wondered aloud if this was an example of America's cherished principle of freedom of expression.

The Kremlin attributed Washington's post-Geneva hard line to American bitterness over Gorbachev's public-relations gains. Some top Soviets wondered privately whether the president could ever be shaken from his deeply embedded "evil empire" mindset. They wondered openly whether they would have to wait until he was out of office to get an arms agreement. They were most bitter at Reagan's speech reinvoking the Soviet threat with statistics on the arms race they found laughable.

"Now the moment of truth comes," Georgi Arbatov, the director of the Canadian-U.S. Institute, told some of us in the foreign press. "Now you have to say what you really are. Either stand before your people, your Congress, your public as a warmonger, who without reason wants to create deadly weapons and use them. Or you have to go the other way."

The Soviets usually avoided ridiculing Reagan's intelligence, or lack of it. But Arbatov was blunt. "I would prefer in the nuclear age to have a bright opponent, not a stupid one. You need some brains, you know, to understand your real interests."

One of the reasons for Star Wars, he said, was to ruin the Soviets economically. "I think on the way to it, they will get bankrupt themselves. Of course we have a smaller GNP. But we don't have such a greedy military-industrial complex which asks 400 dollars for a toilet seat. We would court-martial such people if they tried to do that here."[2]

Old Gromyko was beside himself with anger at Reagan's

speech. "What is it they are trying to impose on us?" he told the Congress. "We are actually being told, 'Either change your social system, give up socialism, or you are in for war.' "

"It seems someone simply fears the existing opportunity for a radical long-term improvement in Soviet-American relations," said Gorbachev in his closing remarks to the Congress. Militarist, aggressive forces would prefer to "freeze and perpetuate confrontation," he said. "But what are we to do? Slam the door?"

7/First Crisis

AT THE TIME OF the nuclear disaster at Chernobyl – one of the worst and one of the best things to happen to Gorbachev – I was working late on a hockey story and I made my way across the yard to the Associated Press office to file to Toronto. Two AP staffers were leaning over a bulletin on the Tass wire. It said only that there had been a nuclear accident at Chernobyl in the Ukraine. It was past midnight and no more information would be available till morning. I drove home, got a few hours' sleep, and woke up to the worst nuclear nightmare since Nagasaki.

A reactor had blown up. People were incinerating. Radiation was still spewing into the air. Given the Soviets' history of concealing reality, the radiation could have reached Moscow. For all I knew, the invisible enemy was right outside the door.

The frustration – triple frustration for a journalist – was that there was no way of telling. The Kremlin wasn't saying anything beyond a short paragraph. We were living in the country where the calamity was happening, yet most of our information on it was coming from abroad – from Sweden, which had first detected the Chernobyl radiation, and from other countries. Only two months earlier, at the Communist Party Congress, Gorbachev had gone on and on about the importance of being open and honest with the people. But what were the Kremlin bosses doing now? Why were they hiding? Where was the openness? Where was Gorbachev?

My mind went back seven years to my days as Washington

correspondent for *The Globe and Mail*. When the nuclear accident happened at Three Mile Island in Pennsylvania, I had simply jumped into my MG convertible and driven, top down, right up and into the scene of the story.

By that evening Middletown, the closest city to the reactor, was starting to resemble a ghost town. Rumours of a meltdown were rampant. Not many people knew what a meltdown was, but it sounded scary enough, and fittingly, black storm clouds were gathering overhead.

Reporters were arriving from everywhere, and in keeping with the American way, everybody talked to us. The mayor talked, the governor talked, the police talked, the people talked. The police chief, George Miller, was furious that no mass evacuation had been ordered by the state. The mayor, Ronald Reid, was leaning against the pillar of a drugstore, keeping his cool. "The only problem we've had was with three idiots who drove around shouting through megaphones that the plant was going to blow up and that everybody should leave. We arrested them."

In Moscow I had no MG. With or without a car, the authorities were not about to allow me or any Westerner to start driving toward the Ukraine. In Western democracies there are restrictions on the movements of Soviet journalists which make it difficult to scream about the limits placed on us by Moscow. But on the Chernobyl story, April 1986, the news blackout was such that everyone had a right to scream.

The Kremlin had delayed 48 hours before disclosing a word about the accident to its own people and to the world. In the Ukraine the leadership was conservative and anti-*glasnost*, so it was well possible it had been slow in alerting Moscow. But even in the days after the first bulletin, when Gorbachev was fully briefed, the old system of lies and cover-ups prevailed.

Two people had died, an undisclosed number were injured, and the situation was being "monitored continuously." That was all the real news the Soviet people could get. On top of that was piled the hokum. I turned on Moscow Radio and heard an announcer state that it was the first nuclear accident in the nation's history. Besides, he said, other countries had them frequently. "In the United States 2,300 accidents, breakdowns, and other faults were registered in

1979 alone," he explained. I picked up the party newspaper *Pravda*. There were no less than seven pictures from the Ukraine that day – one of the first days of the tragedy. On page one Ukrainians were pictured dancing merrily at a backyard party to welcome a soldier home. On page three Ukrainians were dancing around tractors in a field. On page six there was a photo of nesting storks – Ukrainian symbols of peace and happiness. There were no photos of Chernobyl. But the theme of power and energy was represented: there was a sunlit picture of two beautiful Ukrainian windmills.

Muscovites were largely oblivious to the news. They hadn't heard much, they said on the streets, and therefore it couldn't be very serious. They were preparing for the May Day parade. That celebration, which marks worker solidarity and labour achievements, was one of the big events of the Soviet calendar. No nuclear accident was going to spoil the festivities, even if they were coming less than a week after the tragedy.

On the eve of the parade the Soviets took aim at the Western news agencies for exaggerating Chernobyl. In fact, some did overstate the news. But had the Kremlin been forthcoming on the details of the story in the first place, the inaccuracies would have been far less likely. I met later with a Moscow journalist who explained, however, that the Kremlin couldn't be honest on such a story. If it had been, "the population would have panicked." This journalist, who didn't usually side with the government, said that in this case it was the correct strategy for them to take with the media.

May Day was cool but spectacularly blue-skied. Moscow was festooned in red, the trees and flowers were in blossom and I watched thousands marching through the streets shouting "Hoorah. . . ! Hoorah. . . !" They were joyous. Chernobyl seemed already forgotten. Workers carried banners celebrating the achievements of Soviet labour in all spheres except one – nuclear energy. One big placard read NO TO NUCLEAR MADNESS. But it was a reference to American plans for Star Wars.

Gigantic portraits of Lenin, Marx, and other heroes of the proletariat were paraded through the capital. As the tens of thousands moved along Leninski Prospekt to Red Square, four street-cleaning vehicles followed, meticulously cleaning the pavement on which the marchers had walked. In the square, Mikhail

Gorbachev was all smiles in his top hat. On the evening news the May Day coverage took 55 minutes, Chernobyl less than one.

The irony – that this glorification of the Soviet worker had been staged successfully right after Chernobyl – was all too jarring. If there was ever a justified indictment of worker failure, of buck passing, of laziness, of negligence in the workplace, it was Chernobyl. The Politburo found irresponsibility, indiscipline, and gross breaches of reactor regulations at the nuclear plant. The court judgment cited a worker as saying 12 others at the reactor were playing cards or dominoes, or writing letters, instead of tending to their duties. Between 1980 and 1986 there had been 71 technical breakdowns, but no research into the causes had been done in 27 of those cases. A month before the explosion, Lyubov Kovalevska, a brave young journalist for *Literaturnaya Ukraina*, wrote of basic shortages of equipment at the station, and of mechanisms wearing out. "Problems have multiplied and become overgrown with a massive quantity of unknowns," her article said.[1] No one paid heed.

What happened at Chernobyl's Reactor No. 4, as Gorbachev men would later explain, was an outgrowth of the stagnation in the second half of Brezhnev's stewardship – a period in which no one below would make decisions for fear of what the top would say, a period in which everybody went through the motions and got sated on alcohol. On this count – and on many other counts as well – Chernobyl would become an argument for radical change.

After May Day the *glasnost* policy resurfaced. One Soviet official explained there had been a careful decision to understate Chernobyl until the big day had passed – May Day was too important. With the policy change, a Canadian, the crisp and astute Hector Cowan, became the first Western diplomat in Moscow allowed to Kiev, a city of two million some 130 kilometres south of Chernobyl. Then it was the turn of the Western journalists. Remembering how I had been sick to the stomach after Three Mile Island, I hesitated at the prospect of another possible radiation dose, but went anyway.

On the flight I met a civil engineer from Kiev who had visited Moscow for a couple of days and was now returning. He didn't mind talking about the situation. "About four days ago the health minister told us on television that we should be taking five or six drops of iodine a day." Iodine was deemed good for preventing side effects from radiation. "They also told us to keep the children away from big, open-air spaces." The engineer was not letting his children go to school. He didn't want them breathing the outside air. He and his wife were deciding whether to evacuate the city. Trains and planes out were booked solid, but this fellow, who sounded rather nonchalant about the whole affair, didn't mind. "You have to have special connections like I do. I was able to go to Moscow a couple of days ago."

Kiev is the capital of the Ukrainian Republic. An attractive city at any time, it looked especially splendid in the spring. The Ukrainians were in the streets and bars and restaurants as if it was a normal evening. The only thing different, a local translator said, was that sometimes you could see officials running around with radiation detectors.

We met with the Ukrainian prime minister, Alexander Lyashko, and other top policy makers. They talked at length about how the Western media were hyping the story, and avoided answering many of our questions. The world was late in being notified, they said, because the accident – even though the roof of the reactor had blown off – hadn't looked so serious at first. About 90,000 people had been evacuated but everything was now coming under control. The next day we stopped to see the annual bicycle race through the streets of the city, then were taken to the village of Karalova to meet a group of evacuees from Chernobyl. More than a thousand of them, with their cattle and chickens, had descended to the dirt roads of the town, which seemed to be doing its utmost to accommodate them. Any bitterness we found among the towns-people and evacuees was not toward the authorities but, again, toward Western scribes.

In particular, I remember the menacing look of a young man who followed us around the village, always standing a few paces in back. Just as we were preparing to leave, he stepped forward. "You don't believe us when we say only two people died up there, you people in the West," he said. "You report that it was far worse than it really was. During the last war, we in the Soviet Union lost 20 million people. We did not tell you that we lost only five million, did we?"[2]

"We have all accepted this very calmly," said a woman whose

family of five had left Chernobyl and moved in with a small family in Karalova. On the morning after the explosion, she said, most people in the Chernobyl area didn't know about the accident. Even the weddings went ahead as scheduled. Maria Bakun, who was living just a few kilometres from the reactor complex, said she didn't worry about the radiation. "I just took the dress off I had on, threw it away and had a shower."

From what was visible in Kiev, Karalova, and Moscow, the Kremlin as usual seemed to have the public on its party-line side. The village scene especially was an example of socialists coming together. "Our patriotic upbringing reveals itself during these kinds of situations," said Tamara Dubrotskaya, an attractive middle-aged woman. "We're good at evacuations. We've had a lot of practice at them."

After the initial blunder in not getting the news out, and after being condemned by the world for it, the Soviets were now rallying on the public-relations front. They were holding regular news briefings on Chernobyl and gaining sympathy on account of the exaggerated reports. They brought in an American medical expert, Dr. Robert Gale, who complimented them on their handling of the accident's burn victims. Officials from the International Atomic Energy Agency were invited in; in the main, they substantiated the Soviets' version of the accident.

On May 16, almost three weeks after Chernobyl, Gorbachev himself finally came out of hiding, to demonstrate again that he had the right stuff for the modern-day politician – the Madison Avenue p.r. touch. He had a lot to be defensive about, but his performance was all offence. The Western version of Chernobyl was "a mountain of lies," he said. He alleged that the White House had taken ten days to inform the American Congress on Three Mile Island, and months to tell the world. He was inviting President Reagan to a summit in any European capital – "or, say, in Hiroshima" – to negotiate a nuclear-test-ban treaty. "Let those who are at the head of the United States show by their deeds their concern for the life and health of people."

He was calling for unprecedented openness in the field of nuclear energy with a series of new proposals – a new international early-warning system for communication in nuclear accidents, enhanced powers for the IAEA, and an increased role for the United Nations to ensure the safe development of nuclear energy.

A large portion of the speech was unfairly, in this case, devoted to an attack on the Americans' interpretation of and reporting on the tragedy. His statement that it took months for the White House to inform the world of Three Mile Island was only true with respect to an official report. The press, in fact, had started informing the world from the day that story broke – and far more effectively than foreign reporters or Soviet reporters were able to do on Chernobyl.

In a neat bit of spin, the Kremlin took the stance that if a nuclear-plant leak could render such harm, what might a nuclear war be like? Hadn't Mikhail Gorbachev, the Kremlin reminded us, imposed a moratorium on nuclear testing? And hadn't Ronald Reagan repeatedly turned down requests to join in? Hadn't Gorbachev tabled a plan to denuclearize the world by the year 2000? And hadn't Reagan been cool to that?

Chernobyl also had the propitious effect of putting to bed all talk about what George Bush had once ruminated about – the possibility of limited nuclear war. The despoliation, the ravishment caused by an accident at one nuclear reactor, had convinced the world that only fools could talk of survival after a nuclear conflict. Yevgeny Velikhov, a top Soviet physicist and science advisor to Gorbachev, reported a discussion he had with Soviet army officers after Chernobyl. "I asked how do you wish to survive a nuclear war if you have no possibility to clean this small piece of nuclear garbage?"

The British author Anthony Barnett, building on the thought of Sergei Akhromeyev, the Soviets' top military man, that nuclear weapons no longer served to increase the security of the nuclear states, offered a succinct analysis: "Chernobyl emphasized the twist that has taken place in human affairs. Nuclear power held out the promise of clean energy and national autonomy, but delivered instead deadly pollution and interdependence. There can be no national borders against radioactivity."

Chernobyl provided a nicely timed argument for more serious consideration of Gorbachev's proposals of January 15. It helped win him converts to denuclearization both in his own military and abroad. In the Soviet forces there had been considerable opposition from the hawks regarding Gorbachev's push for nuclear peace and cuts in the military. Now they found those policies harder to oppose.

The tragedy also pushed Gorbachev further along the path of new thinking. He now began to develop fully his one-world policy: the idea that in the interdependent world, where nuclear power knows no boundaries, neither the Soviet Union nor the United States can be an island unto itself; the idea that his country must abandon the old notion of world domination in favour of coexistence and partnership.

For Gorbachev, Chernobyl served as many purposes in domestic policy as in foreign policy. It shook to the floor any old Brezhnevian myths that Soviets still chose to live by. It was a clarion call for more responsibility in the work place, or decentralization. It was unmistakably a boost for *glasnost*. The Kremlin heard the criticisms from abroad on its slow response. The Soviet people saw how important it was that their borders be opened up to those like Dr. Gale, who could help. They saw how the cross-border flow of poisonous radiation necessitated cooperation and openness among nations.

Most Soviets knew that the negligence that led to the explosion of Reactor No. 4 was not an isolated misadventure, but rather symptomatic of a deep malaise. The Chernobyl trial was closed to the press for an obvious reason: the Soviet people and the world would have heard testimony about the run-down, chaotic state of many other nuclear plants besides the one at Chernobyl. Later I visited a reactor at Bilibino in the Soviet Far East. I was told that inspectors had been through it following Chernobyl and ordered millions of dollars' worth of repairs and new equipment before moving on to the next nuclear plant.

In the end, while it was a frightful disaster that brought more shame to the Soviets, Chernobyl played into Gorbachev's hands. From the rubble, from the eerie hush of Chernobyl's ghost towns, the cry grew louder for a new Soviet way.

8/Georgia on My Mind

ON ITS WAY south to Josef Stalin's home town of Gori in the Georgian Republic, the Aeroflot jet dithered for some unfathomable reason before landing in the rain of Tbilisi. I had only just read a report from the city of Kursk: Russian youths there had caused havoc at the airport by stealing the red filters from the lights on the landing strip. They took the filters home to use in turning their basement into a disco.

Tbilisi, the Georgian capital of 1.2 million people, and the former home of Eduard Shevardnadze, is to Moscow what San Diego is to Buffalo. A fine first lesson in the diversity of the Soviet Union, it is where fruit and vegetables crowd the tables, where the sunshine is warm 300 days a year, and where tan-skinned people with dark, romantic eyes speak their own ancient language and try to maintain a non-Russian culture. As a result of the wealth passed down from forefathers, and the capacity to grow food and make wine in abundance, and an ongoing entrepreneurial tradition, Georgia has a significantly higher standard of living than the Russian Republic and most other areas of the world's last colonial empire.

There is the depressing Soviet overlay – the dim, vacant, state-run stores, the bookshops selling Communist propaganda – but it is not heavy enough to mute the abiding vivacity. In Moscow you feel on the verge of saluting, in Tbilisi you feel on the verge of uncorking the wine.

That's what my Georgian guide, Geevie, did shortly after I

arrived. Geevie (pronounced with a hard "g") was a diminutive man, about 60, with a bronze face, silver hair, and a carefree shrug. He whisked me to Tbilisi's finest hotel, sat me down at a table, brought forth bottles of vodka and plates of wonderful hot bread baked in clay vats, and insisted that the party begin. Geevie was the most insistent drinker I ever met. Like other Georgians I encountered, he didn't care much for serious talk about the world around him. The life he sought was a steady succession of banquets.

Upon his declaration that he was coming to Moscow in a couple of months and that we'd all have a big party there, I remarked half-seriously to a Moscow official that at the rate he was drinking, Geevie wouldn't make it to Moscow alive. About a month after we got back to the capital, the news arrived from Georgia. Geevie had died. Natural causes, they said.

The Georgians take more than considerable pride in demonstrating their hospitality. They have a saying, "When guests come to town it's like sunrise and when they leave it's like sunset." It could be amended to read, "When guests come to town they are conscious, when they leave they shouldn't be."

Geevie was insulted when I didn't immediately chug whatever he put in front of me. He would shake his head in disgust and slap his hand through the air in despair. Like other Georgians, he used anything as an excuse for a toast. When I heard that he would continue to be my guide on the trip to Stalin's home town, I knew it would be tough – and at the time I didn't realize our host in Gori would be a guy who could outdrink even him.

The Georgians were not overly mindful of Gorbachev's interdiction of alcohol. In Tbilisi you never heard no from a restaurant waiter if you ordered wine. Instead he asked how many bottles you wanted. Generally, the further you were from Moscow, the less you heard the noise from the Kremlin. Georgia had a long tradition of circumventing the State's authority. The Georgia mafia reputedly ran a show so corrupt it made Al Capone look tame. As the republic's leader in the 1970s, Shevardnadze enjoyed major successes in reigning in the corruption – though he never stamped it out. When I arrived, a former secretary of the republic's Central Committee was facing charges of accepting bribes from his regional secretaries. He operated a system in which either they paid him off or he threatened to have them removed.

Under Brezhnev, corruption had become rampant in all the Soviet southern and Central Asian republics. In the Uzbek Republic, which borders on Afghanistan, investigators found that an estimated four billion roubles had been stolen or misappropriated between 1978 and 1984. Their findings led to the arrest of about 3,000 people, among them Yuri Churbanov, Brezhnev's son-in-law, who served as first deputy minister in the department of internal affairs in Moscow. Churbanov was convicted of taking bribes. The indictment against him detailed 1,500 separate offences over a decade. Citing the widespread moral decay and corruption under Brezhnev, his lawyer argued that "Churbanov is a creation of the system, not its creator."

In Georgia, where he became leader in 1972, Shevardnadze gained a reputation as an innovator in the fight against corruption. One story told of a party meeting at which he asked all the officials to vote with their left hand instead of their right. In this way he could count all the fancy, foreign-made gold watches they were wearing. "Let's give up these expensive watches," Shevardnadze demanded. "Take them off right now, and from now on let's wear reliable Soviet-made watches."[1]

This gift for approaching problems in new ways was one of the things about Shevardnadze that appealed to Mikhail Gorbachev, who was then gaining a reputation in Stavropol as an incorruptible party boss. While tough when it came to corruption, Shevardnadze was liberal in matters of culture, censorship, and media control – an attitude which also twinned with Gorbachev's.

In Tbilisi, Geevie remembered Shevardnadze as "competent, too competent for some." On a bright, dusty morning we weaved out of the capital with a driver who looked about as tight as Geevie and headed for Gori, a textile and food-producing centre of about 60,000 people. As a youth there, Geevie recalled, he had stood thrilled and waved as Stalin passed by. Geevie didn't say much about Stalin but did mention his toughness, recalling his determination never to lose.

"We refuse to be beaten," Stalin declared in 1931. "One feature

of the history of old Russia was the continual beatings she suffered
for falling behind, for her backwardness. She was beaten by the
Mongol khans. She was beaten by the Turkish bey. She was beaten
by the Swedish feudal landlords. She was beaten by the Polish and
Lithuanian gentry. She was beaten by the British and French
capitalists. She was beaten by the Japanese barons. All beat her –
for her backwardness."

Gori looked tired, structurally and economically. Its centre was
dominated entirely by temples to Stalin's morbid might – a
40-metre Stalin monument, Stalin's first home, a large, colonnaded
Stalin museum, Stalin's 84-tonne bulletproof railway car, and a
2,000-metre Stalin promenade, from which visitors stared
blank-faced at it all.

The Stalin museum's tour guide, a woman in her mid-fifties,
lent a touch of the macabre to the place – she looked and sounded
almost vampire-like. "Stalin was very fond of meeting the common
people," she intoned. "He was also very fond of music and he was a
good poet." Most of the museum was devoted to Stalin's pre-1917
career. Mainly a pictorial history, it included photographs of
hundreds of soldiers genuflecting in front of the dictator's Gori home
before going off to battle. No mention was made of his reign of terror
in the 1930s, or of his other "shortcomings," as a Gori party official
called them.

Suddenly the tour guide signalled us to be quiet. We were now
approaching Stalin's mourning chamber – a high-ceilinged rotun-
da, very dark. It had as its altar a lighted bust of the dictator.
Visitors genuflected, prayed, or left flowers. On this day there was
no one in it, and we stood at the entrance for a few seconds of silence
before moving on.

Stalin spent his first 15 years in this city, which was founded in
the 12th century. His small, two-room brick house was opened to
the public as a historic site in 1937 – the year when his repressions
were at their worst. The big museum was opened in 1957, four years
after Stalin's death and a year after Nikita Khrushchev's speech
denouncing his crimes. Groups of schoolchildren visit the Stalin
monuments regularly, and Gori children sing a song about him:
"Little Gori is great/It gave birth to Stalin. . . ."

In Stalin's train car a local party boss who already looked

stewed showed us where the leader used to sleep. Then he took us to lunch at the home of a Gori family he knew well. There, 26 dishes of every meat and vegetable imaginable were brought to the table and the great Georgian tradition of toasts began. The party man, Mikhail, who was young and had a Tony Bennett look, was toast-master. About every ten minutes he would rise, bow his head, in solemn Russian say, "I now wish to drink to . . ." and speak for a few minutes on whatever the chosen theme.

The first toast was to peace. Everyone lifted their big glasses of white wine and, with eye-blinking speed, chugged to the bottom. More wine was poured. Now Mikhail was up toasting world friendship. Then it was a toast to mothers. Then a toast to brothers, then to sisters, then children. Amazingly, as if anyone had had a chance to savour it, compliments were offered on the quality of the wine. Some vodka toasts were thrown in for good measure.

After winding his way through the families, Mikhail toasted the war dead, then crops, then the soil. Special large glasses with bells in them were then brought to the table for a toast to the family who had prepared the meal. No one had to ask the purpose of the bells. As soon as the glasses emptied, the place began sounding like St. Mary's Cathedral. "More! More!" they shouted.

I was fearing the inevitable, and it came when the bell glasses were retired in favour of huge tankards the size of wastepaper baskets. "I would like to propose a toast to Stalin," declared Mikhail, his eyeballs swaying to and fro. He spoke in a particularly subdued tone now, and silence came to the boisterous table. "Stalin was the man who led us to victory in the Great Patriotic War," he began. "Without Stalin we could not have won the war." He expanded on this for a few minutes and then added, "Stalin made mistakes. We acknowledge he made mistakes. All great men make mistakes. Those who work hard make mistakes. Only those who do not work hard do not make mistakes. To Stalin!"

Mikhail toasted a lot of people and a lot of things, but not Gorbachev. His name never surfaced, neither then nor when we moved to a neighbour's home, where we gorged on more plates of food and bottles of wine.

Everyone fell into the car for the return trip to Tbilisi. Before leaving town we stopped at the Stalin monument and beheld it for a drunken while. Two months after I returned to Moscow a rumour began to circulate that Gorbachev's people, who were intent on revealing a closer-to-reality version of Stalin, had ordered the monument removed. For three days and nights dozens of Gori residents formed a protective cordon around the statue. It lasted until they were told the rumour was unfounded.

On the car trip back, Geevie wondered out loud whether the party should continue at a soccer match in Tbilisi or at a restaurant over dinner. I chose bed so that I could be prepared the next day for a Soviet jazz concert. I was intrigued, because in the 1950s Soviet authorities had denounced jazz as "music of the fat." Too bourgeois – like golf. By the 1980s things had changed, though not too much. "Of course," said a young concert organizer visiting from Moscow, "the state is supporting classical music because it is the music of the highest value. It's a great problem to support groups without high social value. But jazz is not considered a threat like pop or rock music." Yevgeny Machavarianni, the festival's director, explained in an interview that rock and pop had become the outlet for social protest in the country, whereas the music developed in jazz did not concern socio-economic questions. At the festival I attended, 50 groups performed, many of them from the Baltic republics. Every one of them was socialist.

From the music of the fat I had a brush with the game of the fat. I had asked Geevie, while he was boasting one day of Tbilisi's sports facilities, why there were no golf courses in the Soviet Union. "Not true," he replied. "There's one right here in Tbilisi."

In my haste as an avid golfer to locate a course, I had inquired about it with the sports authorities in Moscow. They had sworn to me that I would never find a golf course in their country. But a group of Tbilisi businessmen, Geevie claimed, had constructed a small nine-hole club near the city for their use only. Disbelieving, I asked to be taken to the Soviet links before my flight back to Moscow. Geevie made some calls to officials and reported back that it was impossible – my flight home was at three in the afternoon and the club didn't open till four. I didn't know of any golf course anywhere that remained shut until four in the afternoon, and didn't want to play it that day anyway – I just wanted to see it. But

Volodya Grachov, a Tbilisi businessman, said I didn't understand. "We start playing at four," he explained. "Everyone goes then."

"Never mind," said Geevie, promising to bring me pictures of the course when he came to Moscow. "Let's go have a big lunch."

9/Chicken Street

"WHY ARE WE giving all these people so much help, so much money?"

Boris Lebedev, a Soviet author and journalist, both patriot and dissident, was talking about his country's relations with Afghanistan and Cuba. I was on my way to Afghanistan, which, though far enough away from Chernobyl, presented other potential health problems. I had called my friend Boris, who had Soviet army contacts, for advice.

At the cavernous Crystal Restaurant we had just been through the no-soup, no-wine, no-beer ritual with the waiter; this being par for the course, the pale, slender Boris hadn't batted an eyelid. But that wasn't the case when we started talking about the Afghan War – I had seldom seen him so aggravated as then. He said the Afghans were illiterate pagans, unworthy of Soviet assistance, that it was crazy for Moscow to be doing them so many favours.

His view of the war, while so different from the West's, was certainly not unique among Russians. Boris was tired of all the Soviet "help" to other countries – "our Marshall Plans," he called them. He expressed anger that while the Soviets had saved Czechoslovakia from the Nazis and were still pouring millions on millions of roubles into that country, the Czechs, whom he had visited, enjoyed a higher standard of living than people in his own country. Speaking of East Germany as well, Boris said, "We won the war. Those places were in ruin. We helped. Now we are still helping them. And what thanks do we get?"

Same thing for Cuba: "You know how much money we're pouring into Cuba – a million roubles a day. And for what? They're lazy. All they do is spend our money, eat our food, and take women to bed."

As for the "irrelevant Afghans," all he heard from Gorbachev was talk of peace – he'd seen no action. That and Gorbachev's no-nuclear-weapons pledges were getting tiresome. The night before, in his centrally located two-bedroom apartment, Boris had watched his wife "slam the TV off" when the announcer started talking about nuclear peace again. "That's all they ever talk about!" she shouted.

Boris Lebedev had been in the Soviet army in 1980, just as big legions of Soviet troops were being dispatched to Kabul. He was told he might be sent there and deliberately withheld the news from his wife. But he got lucky and only saw his friends go off. "We were all boys at the time," he told me. "I saw them when they came back. I can't repeat what they said about it. It's too awful."

Now Boris was working hard, at a newspaper during the day and on a book at night, and was watching his tax money go to "help" these people. Though he thought Gorbachev was leagues better than any previous Soviet leader, he wasn't confident of a Russian exit from Afghanistan. "He is only one man and one man isn't enough to turn this system around. The whole system needs to be turned around."

As we left the restaurant, Boris made a disparaging remark about the whores at the doorway. Only the West was supposed to have prostitutes, he told me. On the street the traffic lights glistened off the rain-soaked cars and pavement. Boris looked around in disgust: "Look, there is nobody out. Where are they all? There is nothing for people to do. So they are at home."

This was the spring of 1986, and the Soviet-propped Kabul regime was anxious to tell its side of the war story. It was all like a political campaign. The West-backed Afghan rebels, or *mujahadeen* as they were called, had been spiriting Western reporters into the country to give them one version of the war. Now Kabul, in concert with Moscow, wanted redress from these lies, as their officials called them. Afghanistan was a story, much like Vietnam, where so much depended on which side was filling the media's ear. It was claim versus counterclaim, with each camp accusing the other of atrocities. Any examination of the press coverage found two different stories – one from the boys on the rebels' bus, the other from those reporting the Kabul-Soviet version. Nobody could see enough from one side only to do the whole story justice. The hunt was for the least number of distortions.

In Moscow the Afghan embassy was furtively arranging a visit for foreign journalists. Soviet officials quietly told correspondents who had asked to go to the war zone that it was now time to contact the embassy. The Afghans there said to wait for the call. It came less than a day before the Aeroflot plane was to leave.

We flew to Tashkent in the Uzbek Republic and then – still via Aeroflot – over endless barren mountain ranges toward Kabul, aware of the possibility, however slim, that the rebels might shoot the plane down. We touched down at a Kabul airport littered, as was the entire perimeter of the city, with Soviet military equipment. In ancient Kabul itself, however, no Soviet men or war machines were visible. I hadn't gone in believing that a Russian gun was pointed at every poor Afghan's head, but I had expected a greater display of visible Russian might in the capital. I had been warned that when I ventured into the streets I should try to look as un-Russian as possible. Otherwise, I was told, I ran the risk of being taken for a Russian and beaten to death by Afghans.

The heart of Kabul, disfigured by a dry riverbed baking under the sun, was dominated by a sprawling, ancient market hectic with thousands of turbanned Afghans. Veiled women were gathered in separate throngs. More goods were on sale here than in Moscow, and at better prices. Next to the market, serving the illiterate, sat letter writers in the shade of umbrellas. Cars honked everywhere; busses rumbled past with as many passengers dangling from the roofs as crammed inside. At my hotel, airy with high ceilings and spacious balconies, an example of the Afghans' eye-for-an-eye tradition of justice stood before me. The youth who worked as the hotel telephone operator had a black leather paw in place of a hand – a result of his stealing a loaf of bread the year before. He was my key man, my link to the outside world, and it required a bribe a minute to get him to keep the lines open.

I asked where all the Russians were hiding out. "Go to Chicken Street," he and others said. I went to Chicken Street and saw neither Russians nor chickens. The main street was so named because chicken used to be the main produce sold there. Now it was about the only thing unavailable.

"I see the Russians here on the street every day," said an Afghan teenager, Abdul, who was selling food. "They are good people. They give us no problems. They help us fight the war and stop the foreign invaders." At a coat store where exquisite full-length fox furs were selling for $300 American, the owner had a different view: "I hate the bastard Communists. They've ruined our business. No one comes here any more. Before they took over – lots of tourists." He and his three brothers had all had to fight in the war against the rebels, he said. "I wish the Russians would leave. They don't fight anyway. We do the fighting ourselves." Nor did they purchase any of his coats. "They don't buy anything. They don't have any money. They just march around." But another salesman liked the Soviet presence in Kabul. "They took away the land from all the bigshot landowners in our country and they redistributed it. Now the people who are fighting us are these landowners who are obviously angry."

I was about to leave Chicken Street when two young Russian soldiers with rifles across their shirts approached to demand my identity. I satisfied them with a lengthy explanation and then asked them how the war was going. "Everything is normal," said one. "No problems." They said that life was routine for them in Kabul, and that they had a year left before they could go back to the Soviet Union. I mentioned that they could get a good, cheap coat to take back at the store across the street. They showed no interest in that, but when the conversation turned to sport they grew keen. The World Cup of soccer was in progress in Mexico and the Soviets had just played little Belgium. "Who won?" one asked me. When I told him – "Belgium 4, Soviets 3" – he looked grim. "But we still have a very strong team," he said. "Yeh," said the other, "we're still very strong." Then they continued along Chicken Street, sticking their noses in shops, making sure everything was Soviet-okay.

After six or seven years of fighting, the atmosphere was war-business as usual. Though the Russians were not too visible, there were still Afghan guns at every corner, truckloads of Afghan soldiers rolling down the main thoroughfares, and intermittent explosions on the tank-littered perimeter. Afghan school girls in their smart black-and-white uniforms smiled as they drew interested looks from uniformed soldiers. Wedding celebrations burst from crowded hotel lobbies, religious chants emanated all day long from the mosques, donkeys loaded with huge sacks of produce staggered past Toyota dealers' showcase windows.

At ten each night, when the curtain of curfew dropped, all the lights went out. We were at the West Germans' embassy club across town from our hotel one evening when the taxi we had ordered for 9:45 P.M. didn't show up. By the time curfew arrived, we were lost on the streets, hitchhiking with no traffic in sight. An army truck full of Afghan soldiers finally pulled up. The driver let us squeeze into the front cab. When we turned the corner to our hotel entrance, the guards there suddenly jumped to the curbside, brandishing their weapons. It being after curfew, they were obviously shocked that people were arriving. They screamed something we couldn't understand, and for a second we thought the worst was going to happen. But the driver of our truck quickly corrected any impression that we were enemy material.

The next day Afghan officials took us to the small village of Charasiab, 18 kilometres from Kabul and well within the range of rebel mortars. A boy there who looked no older than 11 was holding a rifle almost as big as he was. "I am ready for them [the rebels]," the kid said. "It is my duty to defend the country." We were skeptical that he was capable of firing so big a gun. So he knelt with one knee on the dirt and fired a blast into the open air. Then he smiled.

"Our peasants vigorously defend the revolution," said Ali Zafari, in defence of his child warriors. Zafari was the top Afghan organizer for Charasiab, which was a collection of clay huts, dust, donkeys, and guns. "For the last year and a half, the counter-revolutionaries haven't been able to change the situation around here," he told us. "[But] from very remote parts they fire rockets to create horror among our people." Like other Afghan soldiers, he liked to boast that they really didn't need the help of the Soviet troops. "There are some Soviet army posts along the highway, but they don't participate with us in day-to-day activities. In many cases we don't want to ask them to help us."

"The Soviets can leave today," said Sultan Mohammed, a peasant fighter. "We don't need their help anymore. We can defend ourselves."

In the village of Bagrami, the local head of the Afghan Communist Party, Said Aleed, was sitting on a rug in his clay hut amid eggs, tea, and houseflies. He talked a little about history. Hafizullah Amin, a Marxist, overthrew the reigning Afghan prime minister in 1979 and instigated a reign of terror – opponents were murdered, 100,000 were jailed without reason, religious rights of Moslems were taken away. Millions fled and an internal revolt against Amin began. The Soviets entered and killed him and installed the more humane Barbrak Karmal.

Now, said Aleed, "it is not a party [the Communists] against the religious beliefs of the people. It is not a party against Islam." The refugees were starting to come back, he said.

If the Afghans liked the Communists running their country more under the bronze-faced Karmal than the horrific Amin, it didn't show at defence headquarters. Afghans didn't want to stay in the army with the Soviets in control of the country. They were deserting in droves. Karmal was unable to reduce his reliance on over 100,000 Soviet troops and, in early 1986, the Kremlin replaced him with a moustachioed bruiser whose major qualification for the job was that he had headed up the Afghan secret police.

Muhammed Najib was 39-years-old and massive. He greeted me and two other journalists at his quiet, marbled headquarters away from the heat and tumult of the city centre. We had been driven there by the Soviet television reporter permanently based in Kabul, a figure I frequently saw on the nightly news from Moscow, feeding the viewers what he was told to feed them.

Najib said he had five minutes for the interview but endured our company for about forty, during which time he had about as much to say as the soldiers on Chicken Street. He had only been in power for a few weeks. His orders were clear – end the desertions from the Afghan army and beef it up so that Moscow could start pulling back its regiments. "Desertion has been carried out by what we call traitors," Najib told us. "We give ourselves the right to consider measures against this problem."

The new Afghan leader cursed American stinger rockets as much as the deserters. The missiles, which were supplied in abundance to the rebels, were helping their cause enormously. There was no end in sight to the war or to the Soviet presence, Najib said. The Afghan people wanted the Soviets out but Najib didn't sound like he was in a big hurry. If the Russians did leave, he was probably thinking, he would surely be toppled. On its own, the Afghan army couldn't beat Greenland.

Najib brought forward several of his ministers for interviews and of course they all argued that under the Soviets they were doing great things for the Afghan people. They boasted of taking land from the millionaire barons and redistributing it to poor peasants. They boasted about boosting the literacy rate in the country from ten percent to thirty percent in the seven years of occupation. Lost in the uproar over the Soviet presence, argued Said Ammanadin, a top government economist, was the fact that under the rule of kings in the 1970s and before, Afghanistan had been one of the world's leading basket cases – the seventh poorest country in the world, illiterate, warring, ungovernable and, apart from the élite, poverty-stricken. His description of the earlier Afghanistan was perhaps accurate and some Western diplomats in Kabul did grant that the Soviets had made strides on literacy, land redistribution and education. But he neglected to mention that, under the kings, unlike under the Soviets, tens of thousands of Afghans were not being killed in a seemingly endless civil war.

It was a war which, at least until he came to power in 1985, Mikhail Gorbachev had never been on record as opposing.

The propaganda parade that we were put through by Najib and his men convinced me that if the Soviets weren't intent on staying in Afghanistan in body, then they were in spirit. Afghanistan was maintaining some of its religious and cultural traditions. But it had taken on a Soviet style one-party political system and a five-year economic plan. Russian was the leading foreign language in the schools. Some young Afghans with whom I talked could speak it reasonably well. Russian slogans littered the factories we visited. Kabul conducted about 70 percent of its foreign trade with the Soviet Union. Its foreign debt was taken care of by the Kremlin.

At a Kabul construction factory employing 4,500, plant manager Abdul Raphael told us that "two times a week we come together with Soviet officials and exchange ideas with them." Ammanadin described his relationship with Moscow this way: "If things are running smoothly, there is no discussion. If not, I will go to Moscow." It meant that he was in Moscow much of the time.

The Sovietization effort, the attempt to turn Afghanistan into a satellite like the Eastern European countries, was concentrated on the Afghan youth. A new Afghan democratic youth organization had sprung up. It closely resembled the Soviet Komsomol and Pioneer clubs. Thousands were shipped each year to Moscow for their education. If ever the Soviets left Afghanistan, I thought, they would leave behind more than their horrible battle scars.

At home there was not much pressure on the Kremlin from the average Soviet to get out of Afghanistan. Unlike in the United States, where an anti-war movement could grow, where a David Halberstam could go into Vietnam and report that what Washington was saying about the war was rubbish, in the closed society of the Soviet Union, the war was whatever the government wanted to say it was.

With *glasnost* Gorbachev's intention was to finally start telling the truth about the war. When that happened, Boris Lebedev would have one less Soviet Marshall Plan to worry about.

The Soviets would not be in Afghanistan for long.

10/Challenging the Stereotype

WHEN 33-YEAR-OLD Bruce McWilliams, a Canadian from Vancouver with a sarcastic turn of humour, first arrived in Moscow, he was met by a maze of frozen faces. "They all seemed kind of distant and reserved," he recalled. "They walked by like you weren't there." McWilliams found nothing surprising in this: he had been conditioned by his education, his media, and his government to see the Russians in the robot, enemy image. He didn't accept the cant of the political right – the "We gotta stop these guys, they're going to take over the world" kind of rhetoric. But for him, as for his generation, the word "Soviet" or "Russian" meant dark or sinister.

He and his wife Pat had a lot of travelling blood in them, and they answered a newspaper advertisement that led them to teaching positions in Moscow's school for foreigners, the Anglo-American School. In Moscow one of McWilliams' first priorities was to buy a Russian car. He chose a Lada – or Zhiguli, as it is called in Russian. Acquainted with the Third World reputation of most Soviet products, his expectations were not high. But it did surprise him that the car's first breakdown came so soon – on the way home from the dealer. About halfway home, "not even two miles on her," the Lada seized up and trundled to curbside.

This was downtown during the afternoon rush hour. McWilliams couldn't phone a garage because he couldn't speak Russian. With the hood open, he stood helpless, cursing the Lada's entrails as traffic roared past vomiting heavy exhaust. Quite soon, however, a run-down trailer truck rumbled to a halt and a heavy-set Russian stepped out, smoking a roll-your-own. Now hopeful, but unable to communicate, McWilliams pointed at his engine and did his best. "Maybe *nyet* petrol," he said.

The truck driver nodded and set to work inspecting the gas line. He unfastened the new hosing and peered down it. Then, to the astonishment of McWilliams, he inserted the end of the tube into his mouth and began sucking on it. "He was trying to pull the gas through with the pressure from his lips," McWilliams said. "I stood there kind of helpless, thinking, 'My God, you don't have to do that.' "

The truck driver got one mouthful of gasoline, spat that out, then another and spat that out. Then McWilliams noticed a militia-man pull over. "This was a brand-new car," said the Canadian. "I didn't have any licence, insurance, anything." Visions of the gulag in his head, McWilliams got another jolt. The militiaman greeted him sympathetically, looked under the car's hood, and joined the truck driver in animated conversation. Then he too put his mouth to the tubing and started sucking out gas. Soon he and the driver were taking turns.

McWilliams felt grateful but helpless: there was no way he wanted to take a turn at the nozzle. So, knowing the two words in Russian that mean "thanks a lot," he kept telling them, "*Ballshoy spasiba, ballshoy spasiba.*"

For several minutes the two Russians worked on the car. They took the supposedly brand-new gas pump apart and found a lot of grime. They cleaned out the grime, put the gas line and gas pump together, and got the car started. Then they shook hands with McWilliams and were gone. "The militiaman didn't ask me for ID or anything. He only wanted to help me get the car going."

Not long after that, Bruce and Pat McWilliams travelled to Yerevan in the Armenian Republic. At a market there, strangers, recognizing them as foreigners, filled their bags with fruit and vegetables – no charge. They went to a restaurant, where they couldn't read the menu. The cook escorted them into his kitchen and let them pick whatever they wanted – though the choice was only lamb, beef, and tomatoes. They wanted to take the bus but each time they asked someone how to buy tickets "they would simply hand over their own to us."

McWilliams and his wife were seeing the warm, generous side of the Soviet people. The Soviets were gaining a couple more converts to the notion that they were human too, that they harboured no inner hatred of the outside world.

Mikhail Gorbachev, needless to say, was out to change a few more minds than a couple: he wanted the world to change its mind. It was Ronald Reagan who would tell a group of Russian students, after meeting them in Moscow, that they were just like students he had met in America; if only they could all get to know each other and realize this, added the president, imagine the good that would come of it. Gorbachev, who would certainly agree with the president's thought, was aware that many of the differences between East and West were more perceived than real, and that his task was to change the West's perceptions. To do that required changing the view that the Soviets were a threat, which in turn meant removing layers of Stalinist repression and Brezhnevist rot.

In this connection I got talking one day to a rather young Soviet public-relations man whose eyes were hidden by the overspread of his eyelids and who was on the career hustle. I would have many conversations with him but would never get a good sense of where his real values lay. Sometimes he struck me as a mini-Beria, other times as a progressive. But never would the eyes fully open.

One thing was clear, though – he would do what he had to do in order to make it. That meant that with each liberal gesture on the part of Gorbachev, he tended to sound a little more liberal. No matter how hypocritical, he was going with the new flow. The same could be said for many bureaucrats those days in Moscow. They were peeling off their Brezhnev faces as if they were frogmen's masks. Gennady Gerasimov, the foreign-ministry spokesman who had more wit than eight Larry Speakes jammed together, had been an archconservative while he was editing the *Moscow News*. He had written nothing but party-line clichés. Now, miraculously, he was spokesman for reform, he was another new, liberal Soviet man. "Our generation was waiting in the wings to make these changes," Gerasimov would say later of Gorbachev's revolution. "The only question is why we didn't move sooner." It *was* a good question, but given his performance at the *Moscow News*, he didn't have to ask it.

He knew the answer. Neither he nor the others had possessed the fortitude.

Upstairs, over thick coffee in miniature cups, the career hustler was in a mood to speculate. Gorbachev had announced a withdrawal of 7,000 Soviet troops from Afghanistan – an insignificant number, in that there would still be roughly 113,000 in the country. But this was just the prelude to the real thing, a full withdrawal, the official said. "Afghanistan is next. We'll be out soon. That's the plan."

He had begun by touting the Soviet initiatives on disarmament. Next, he told me, was Afghanistan. Also coming was the liberation of Andrei Sakharov. The human-rights activist was still in internal exile in Gorky for having committed the offence of speaking his mind on public issues. The release of Sakharov, the Soviet predicted, would be part of a larger human-rights package, one that would include the release of dissidents and more *glasnost*.

He was putting forth a scenario for how Gorbachev would remove the spectre of the much-celebrated Soviet threat. It made some sense. If one was going to try knocking down the barricades blocking a better Soviet relationship with the West, one might very well start with those three: the Soviet arms build-up and nuclear threat, expansionism as symbolized by Afghanistan, and the absence of human freedoms as symbolized by Sakharov. To act on them in a comprehensive way would be to significantly reduce the amount of ammunition available for use against the Soviets.

I returned to the office and wrote an opinion column about my contact's surmise, because I knew this man was well connected and because, being the unfailing optimist on Gorbachev, I believed what he was saying. Then, in the months ahead, I watched as the plan unfolded in much the way the young official had predicted.

The process took place as if the Kremlin fathers had sat down, made a list titled "Why the West hates us," and gone about systematic remedial treatment. Indeed, the demands of the Western democracies – the United States in particular – played an integral part in this. But the values of Gorbachev were such that these measures were his top priorities to begin with. They equated with his idea of democratization. Speaking in the summer of 1986 with respect to his foreign initiatives, Gorbachev made the point himself:

"The ruling circles of the U.S.A. and some countries allied to it are trying either to picture our peace initiatives as sheer propaganda or to allege that only the Soviet Union stands to gain from them. Yes we stand to gain from disarmament, just as all people and all governments who now spend billions on the arms race stand to gain from disarmament. But this is only a part of the truth, I will even say, a smaller part of the truth. The main truth is that our initiatives stem from profound concern about mankind's destiny."

His spurt of activity showed no signs of abating. In addition to the small announcement on Afghanistan, Gorbachev had offered a well-received proposal to reduce Soviet and American strategic arms by 50 percent. Now, he unleashed a bevy of proposals for security in the Middle East and the Pacific, some involving new Soviet concessions. With Washington threatening to do the opposite, he promised that the Soviets would adhere to ceilings in the unratified SALT II agreement; and, while Washington vowed to reduce the size of the Soviets' mission at the United Nations, the general secretary permitted 136 members of American families, previously denied emigration rights, to leave for the United States.

At an embassy reception one evening, I heard the "it's all prop-aganda" line from a diplomat in reference to the Soviet leader's talk of letting the Americans verify, on-site, Soviet nuclear tests. Shortly afterwards, Gorbachev allowed private Americans to come to his country to install monitoring devices.

The new face of Soviet foreign policy was not without scars. In the build-up to and the aftermath of the American bombing of Libya, the Soviets blindfolded their public. The American side of the story – that there was evidence the Libyans were sponsoring terrorism – was suppressed. In the Soviet press, Libyan leader Muammar Gaddafi was made out to be an innocent victim, while Reagan was the imperialist demon. This old-style approach to the news came at the same time the Soviet poet, Yevgeny Yevtushenko, was speaking of the need for broader *glasnost*. "The collective opinion of the people cannot exist without the right to one's personal opinion," he wrote in a Moscow newspaper. "The people's opinion is not an instruction passed down from above."

But on Libya it was indeed an instruction passed down from above. While sensible enough not to confront the Americans in the Mediterranean, which would have provoked a world crisis over his Libyan ally, Gorbachev took the rhetorical low road, accusing Washington of bandit crimes. "While declaring that they are fighters against international terrorism," he said, "the United States leaders, in reality, only confirmed once again their adherence to a policy of state terrorism and the aggressive doctrine of neoglobalism."

These were the years of the hard-headed, anti-Communist Rambo movies in America, and the Soviets thought it necessary to respond. They produced *Lonely Journey*. Not a threat to high art, the movie's climactic scene saw six Americans with machine guns surrounding a lone Russian armed only with knives. In an instant, before any of his six antagonists could shoot, the Russian hero fired six knives, each connecting dead-centre of an enemy's forehead. In a reverse scenario in the United States, the moviegoers would have been in the aisles cheering; in Moscow, where the movie played to reasonably good crowds, no one cheered.

But the reaction over Libya, and propaganda efforts like *Lonely Journey*, were becoming more the exception than the rule. After only a year and a half, Gorbachev's peace campaign was already having a broad effect on public opinion outside the East Bloc. The Soviets were not seen as the threat to world peace they once were. Their liberalized foreign policy left NATO countries, including Canada, in a curious if not plainly embarrassing position. On questions of arms control and global nuclear peace, Ottawa was coming face to face with a potential heresy: Canada's policies, it was becoming clear, were now closer to the evil empire's than to those of the United States.

Under the internationalist prime ministers Pierre Trudeau and Lester Pearson, the Canadian government had often taken a more open-minded approach than the United States to relations with the Soviet Union. Trudeau annoyed Washington with his world peace campaign of the early 1980s, and with his statement that the Soviets were showing restraint in their treatment of Poland. However, for the most part, with Brezhnev across the ocean, there were few opportunities for Moscow and Ottawa to see eye to eye. The new situation had never quite come to this – a seeming reversal in the decreed order of global politics.

On SALT II, Canada and the Soviet Union favoured continued adherence; both were strongly opposed to the Americans' break-away position. Regarding a comprehensive nuclear-test-ban treaty, both Canada and the Soviet Union strongly advocated one, while Washington stated repeatedly that testing was vital in order for it to keep its weapons systems modernized. Ottawa had previously con-demned the Soviets' intransigence on verification procedures; but now the Kremlin was giving its commitment to on-site inspection. As for the prevention of an arms race in outer space, Canada and the Soviet Union were again in strong agreement. Ottawa allowed private Canadian companies to assist in the Star Wars project, but the government itself officially opposed it, as did the Kremlin. In order to facilitate development of the Strategic Defense Initiative, Reagan said he was prepared to put a new, looser interpretation on the 1972 antiballistic-missile treaty. Ottawa and the Kremlin advocated continued adherence to the original interpretation of the ABM pact. Regarding the proliferation of nuclear weapons – a highly technical area – Canadian and Soviet positions were in full concert.

This accidental convergence was not something to which either side frequently alluded. Canada's young defence minister, Perrin Beatty, despite the changes in Soviet policy, did not appear convinced of any new thinking. He advocated the spending of new billions for nuclear-powered submarines (a plan the government would later drop). Unlike someone such as Bruce McWilliams, he had never spent much time in the Soviet Union and had no chance to judge for himself. The people who appointed defence ministers and defence secretaries rarely gave enough consideration to the most important criteria of all – how much the candidate knew about the other side, how much time that person had spent there or out in the world gaining a perspective that was wider than that of vested interests. As a result Caspar Weinbergers and Perrin Beattys could appear and could trot out the time-warped bromides. They sounded like masters of old thinking. They were up against the master of the new.

As the months wore on and Gorbachev's peace offensive

continued, the debates were getting hot inside the foreign-policy establishments of Canada and other NATO countries. The Canadian embassy in Moscow had a Friday-night tradition in which a bar was opened downstairs and a volunteer cook became hamburger chef of the week, providing a North American staple not available in the U.S.S.R.

The diplomats were well behaved there, and cautious, as always, with their pronouncements. But enough spirits can loosen anyone's jaw. One Friday night I watched a diplomat growing more and more exasperated with every drink. He was convinced that historic changes were taking place in the Kremlin's thinking. But trying to convince Ottawa was another matter. "Every day we send cables," he said over a platoon of Labatt's Blues. "Every day we tell them. But they won't believe it. They simply won't believe it."

11/The Home Team

GORBACHEV'S good-guy campaign suffered its first major setback in September 1986. The Nicholas Daniloff affair served as reminder that the Soviet Union was still the Soviet Union and that the American right was still the American right. The American journalist's arrest by the KGB on spying charges was a misadventure that brought out the worst in both superpowers, taking their tenuous relationship to the brink of collapse. As the crisis focussed on a Moscow correspondent, it afforded a look at that breed of Westerner. The Daniloff case should have convinced anyone who needed convincing that journalistic impartiality can be most ephemeral when the story involves the two superpowers.

Few groups of journalists in the world are as powerful as the American band in Moscow. Their decisions which stories to report on, as well as their approaches to those stories, have a significant effect on public opinion in Washington and throughout America. Americans have been fortunate in having outstanding members of their journalistic caste on the Moscow beat. Robert Kaiser, Hedrick Smith, Dusko Doder, David Shipler, Serge Schmemman, Gary Lee, and the best American Moscow correspondent of today, Bill Keller of the *New York Times*, have demonstrated a judicious balance and depth as reporters that has made me and many other journalists envious.

But having some of their best there, having some who went in

with open minds, was not enough to surmount the central problem
that correspondents pose anywhere – that they take their value
systems with them and tend to impose them on the society they are
reporting on.

In a 1988 article David Shipler, the former Moscow correspondent for the *New York Times*, shockingly pointed out that
the quality of debate on public issues had become more intelligent
and sophisticated in the Soviet Union than in the United States. He
wrote that his fellow Americans "act as though they have resolved
all the fundamental questions and their role is to teach the rest of the
world."[1] He wasn't referring specifically to American journalists,
but he might well have been. Their attitude is to measure other
societies using their own yardstick as the accepted norm. Tom
Brokaw, NBC's anchorman, broached a theme similar to Shipler's
when, commenting on the puerility of the debate during the
American election campaign of 1988, he said that the United States
had become a country which demanded so much of others but asked
so little of itself.

The inability of Americans to write about problems of other
nations in the context of their own failings is a result, as was the case
with the British of yesteryear, of superpower arrogance. It's an
almost subconscious arrogance which suggests that they are the
beacon of democracy to which the rest of the world should be
aspiring. That there is this conceit by Americans on their democracy
is surprising in the first place, because to others, the notion is at best
dubious. American democracy is little more than a half-spectrum
democracy. It gives the voters a choice of two similar parties – a
centre party and a right-wing party. There is no socialist alternative
– nothing much, practically speaking, to the left of Ted Kennedy. If
such a movement were to spring up, it would run the risk of being
silenced by the American intelligence agencies – who would accuse
it of being Communist infiltrated.

American democracy is such that in the last election 98 percent
of the incumbents in the 435-member House of Representatives
were reelected. The advantage of incumbency has made the House
election process a rubber-stamp affair. American democracy is such
that most of the important government positions – for example, the

entire Cabinet and the Supreme Court – are not elected but appointed; that fully half the electorate does not bother to vote any more; that the elected are in large part a millionaires' club.

These facts seem more apparent to an outsider than to Americans themselves – including the American journalists sent off to judge the rest of the world. Good journalism is good perspective. In the United States 20 million people are still functionally illiterate, millions are homeless, more than 30 million live below the poverty line. It took well into the second half of the 20th century for that country to shed its system of near-*apartheid*. The United States remains one of the last civilized countries in the world that allows its citizens to carry handguns. And "in the richest country in the world," said Georgi Arbatov, "there are ghettos which remind me of Stalingrad or Leningrad after the Second World War."

Moscow correspondents – and not just the American ones – so accurately decry Soviet prison and labour-camp conditions. Yet the impression created by their work would be different if they put their criticisms in the context of conditions in their own prisons. In American jails the incidence of rape, violence, and overcrowding is appalling. The former baseball player, Denny McLain, spent time in Atlanta's jail. He described it as the filthiest place in the world, with outbreaks of violence every day, sometimes five or six times a day. The minorities get the worst of it, McLain said. Describing in *Sports Illustrated* a hunger strike by Cubans to protest conditions, he said that "when a guy was starving the doctors would stick a tube down his nose to feed him. They would handcuff the Cubans – ankles tied to the bottom of the bed, wrists to the top – and then put the tubes in their noses. When the doctors ran out of the right size of hose, they just got bigger ones and shoved them down the Cubans' noses. Guys almost drowned in their own blood."

Perspective, in journalism from Moscow, is often forgotten. When the KGB uses muscle tactics to break up a demonstration in the U.S.S.R., it's reported as if the police never did far worse in the United States, as if there hadn't been a Kent State or Chicago '68, as if – a more recent example – the Philadelphia police hadn't bombed a house belonging to a group of radical black dissidents when they refused to move out of their premises. When American reporters write about the KGB as the "secret police," it's as if the CIA is an open organization; they forget that the American intelligence service had a policy which allowed for the assassination of foreign leaders, as was revealed in Congressional hearings in the mid-1970s. And when they write about the subjugation of Eastern Europe, it's as if there has been no American subjugation of Latin America – no Dominican Republic in 1965, no Guatemala in 1954, no Bay of Pigs in 1961, no Chile in 1973, no El Salvador, no Nicaragua.

None of these examples diminish the guilt of the other superpower, but they make the black-and-white pictures a little grayer.

By the time the Daniloff case rolled around, it had become clear to me that Western journalists had a major contextual problem with respect to KGB surveillance. They failed to see it in the framework of a tit-for-tat game, in the context that in the United States, in Canada, in Great Britain, intelligence communities were doing the same thing to Russian reporters – probably with better reason – as Soviet spooks were doing to them in Moscow.

I couldn't count the number of times I had seen it written, as a comment on the psychology of the Soviet system, that Russians were afraid to enter the apartments of foreign journalists out of fear of repercussions from the KGB. This was undeniably true. Yet how many American or Canadian citizens, having met a Soviet journalist speaking broken English on the streets of Washington or Ottawa, would be prepared to visit that Russian's apartment? Most wouldn't, out of the exact same fear – repercussions from the intelligence agencies. And judging by history, the fear would be legitimate: in the 1970s, 11 Canadians were blacklisted by the federal government for being in contact with Russians living in Ottawa.

When I lived in Washington as *The Globe and Mail* correspondent, the Soviet news agency, Tass, was right across the corridor. None of us would mix with the Russian correspondents. They were monitored so closely by the FBI that it was a standing joke. I was reminded of this during the Daniloff affair. Western journalists were cranking out "poor me" stories on how badly they were treated in Moscow, but Moscow coughed up its best apartments to foreigners at the expense of its average citizens. Tickets to theatre and sport and ballet went first-priority to foreigners, as did restaurant tables, airline tickets, and the like. Compared with Soviet correspondents abroad, Westerners weren't doing badly.

The Soviet press, traditionally weak on fighting back in such instances, did so during the Daniloff case. Iona Andronov, New York correspondent for *Literaturnaya Gazeta*, wrote how she had been beaten the previous autumn by the FBI man who followed her around. The Tass correspondent reported receiving threatening phone calls all the time. "The aim is . . . to frighten and demoralize the Soviet correspondents. We repeatedly addressed it to the local police but in vain." Another Soviet journalist in New York said he once had his car windows smashed in when he was in the car with his children. He said that later on he had his tires slashed and objects hurled at his head. "The FBI agents who follow me, I know by their faces. There are seven of them."

Daniloff was the correspondent for *U.S. News & World Report*. His arrest on August 30 was precipitated by the Americans taking a low-level Soviet operative at the United Nations named Gennady Zakharov. At the time there were good prospects for advances in the U.S.-Soviet relationship, as well as talk of another Gorbachev-Reagan summit, so the timing of the well-publicized FBI move against Zakharov was curious. With spy matters the timing is often flexible. The pick-up and publicity can be set for whenever the government feels the time is propitious.

Zakharov, nabbed by the FBI in an entrapment, was tabbed as a minor spy who had never received classified information. The set-up involved presenting him with some classified material. In these matters Washington usually follows customary practice, which is to release such people into the custody of the Soviet ambassador. This time, even though the man was not a prize catch, the courtesy was not accorded. Indications were that the hard-liners at the White House, wanting to flex a little anti-Soviet muscle, had once again won the battle for Reagan's ear.

Given the trade-off history on these matters, Washington knew the Kremlin would retaliate. But nobody thought the Russians would be so ill-advised as to arrest a journalist. Like Zakharov, Daniloff was entrapped – set up taking allegedly classified documents from a contact in a park. The Soviets accused him of other violations, including working with the CIA agents at the American embassy.

A screaming match ensued between the superpowers, with the

Reagan administration and the American press demonstrating unified hysteria in a way they seldom did. It was team sport. It was like everyone had to get on the bandwagon or they were traitors. For years in Washington in the pre-Reagan era, I had watched American journalists going after their government. I didn't think they could be such homers. But in the Daniloff case the Russians were involved, and it was as if an unwritten rule had been invoked – you played for the home team.

Before the Soviets even tabled any evidence on Daniloff, editorial writers were shouting that their boy was innocent and demanding his release. *So much for reform under Gorbachev*, the rightists bellowed, *this shows it's all a hoax*. It was one of those situations where emotion ran roughshod over reason. When the Soviets released Daniloff to the custody of the American embassy, I went over to see his arrival. There were cheers as he came into view. But the warmth there paled in comparison with the show that was put on during Daniloff's first press conference.

The scene was the embassy's commercial building. Before it began, embassy employees were rushing around in near-frenzy to make sure Soviet reporters had not gotten in to ask him questions. One young public-relations woman, all hot and bothered, told me she had heard, horror of horrors, that a Soviet was in fact in the building, and asked if I had seen him. I said no. What I should have said was, if you're a free society what are you afraid of, what's wrong with Russians at the press conference?

When Daniloff entered the press room, Dominique D'Nombres of *Le Monde* ran up and hugged him. Others crushed around him with admiring words of welcome. The press conference was a collective, loving embrace. Every question to Daniloff, whose performance was monitored by an embassy official, was straight cream-puff. No one asked him to explain any of the evidence the Soviets had brought forward suggesting he was a spy.

No matter how much one believed Daniloff was innocent, there were grounds for some dispassionate research on the story. There was a long history of American journalists being on the CIA payroll abroad. In 1976 the U.S. Congress heard testimony from an editor on the *U.S. News & World Report* who said he had been approached by the CIA. One of the CIA's most important foreign stations was in

Moscow. The CIA director, William Casey, was a fifties-style Red-baiter, so it was safe to assume that the Moscow station would be higher priority than ever, with the CIA boys seeking help wherever they could find it. It wouldn't have surprised many people if an American correspondent had been working with the CIA. Some correspondents could have been cooperating with the agency unknowingly. So many embassy officers were CIA men that American journalists who used them as sources frequently couldn't be sure when they were talking to the CIA and when they weren't.

But none of the possibilities seemed to register with anyone on the home team. The press reported that President Reagan said Daniloff was not a spy. The attitude of editorial writers was, well there you have it, our president says so and therefore it must be right. Reagan, of course, had made so many wrong or misleading statements by that point in his presidency that the White House had lost count. His spokesman, Larry Speakes, frequently had to appear after the president spoke to set the record straight. On occasion he would even speak in the president's name, without Reagan knowing it.

But even if an American journalist had been working secretly for the CIA, would the CIA, which had a history of hiding information from the president, tell Reagan? And if it did, would Reagan – or the leader of any country – come out and publicly admit that the Russians were right, that our boy is guilty? Governments do not identify publicly who its spies are.

Not every single American reporter towed the party line on Daniloff. Henry Mitchell of the *Washington Post* issued a caution, writing that patriotism should not overwhelm objectivity. Dusko Doder, the former Moscow correspondent for the same paper, wrote a piece that did not make Daniloff look good.[2]

In December 1984, Daniloff was approached by a Father Roman, who said he had been forced to serve time in a Soviet labour camp under trumped-up charges. It was a typical dissident contact, and Daniloff took Roman's telephone number. A month later Daniloff received a call from Roman, who informed him that he would receive a package with – according to the *Post* interview – "some material about young people and the Russian Orthodox church." The next day Daniloff got the letter. Inside were two envelopes. One was addressed to the American ambassador, Arthur Hartman. Daniloff took it to the American embassy. The other was addressed to CIA director William Casey.

Many reporters in Moscow, knowing of frame-ups and suspicious of intelligence operatives at embassies, would not have taken the letter to the embassy. They would have told the dissident or whomever it was to send the letter to the embassy himself. They would have said that they were reporters, not messengers. Daniloff chose to be incautious in this instance, and went an ill-advised step further.

Daniloff, who knew the CIA was interested in him, was called to the embassy and chose to go. He was taken to the glass booth, where electronic surveillance is prevented. Doder reported that "they were joined by another diplomat whom Daniloff understood was the CIA station chief. Daniloff was then asked about Roman and was able to provide the CIA with his phone number."

Why would a newspaper correspondent cooperate with his country's intelligence agency in this way? Giving the CIA phone numbers of dissidents, on request, does not qualify one as a spy, and it certainly didn't justify the KGB entrapping Daniloff and throwing him in jail. But it's not something that most Western reporters in Moscow would do.

Daniloff, while maintaining his innocence, suggested afterward that he was likely used by the CIA. "I would like to repeat that when I worked in Moscow I was not a spy and I am sure that President Reagan carefully checked all his sources of information before he publicly stated that I was not an espionage agent. It certainly looks like I was used [by the CIA]."

The first part of the statement, in reference to Reagan checking sources, was humorous. Had the president checked with a source of information such as the CIA, the CIA would have told the president that it had used Daniloff. Then, only telling the truth, the president would have had to announce that his CIA had set up an American journalist in Moscow. Reagan didn't do that.

The Soviets handed over documentation on Daniloff's activities to American authorities. Washington chose for some reason not to publicize all the contents, prompting criticism from Gennady

Gerasimov. "There's a big difference," he said, "between what the documents say and the statements they are making about them."

Gorbachev was on holidays during the Daniloff affair and stayed a good distance from it when he got back. It never became known whether he was informed in advance of the decision to entrap Daniloff. Most likely, considering the nature of the matter, he was alerted. When it was over, the Soviets admitted that they had underestimated the furor that would be touched off by the laying of hands on a correspondent.

If, in fact, Nicholas Daniloff were to have been cooperating with the embassy's CIA men, more than in just some details relating to a dissident, the evidence put forward by the Soviets suggested it would hardly have been of a momentous nature – just as the work of Zakharov in New York was hardly work of a momentous nature.

As Daniloff would write in his book, it was not wise for the FBI to provoke the Soviets at the time they did by taking Zakharov. But that doesn't explain why the Soviets, realizing it was a provocation, took the bait, just as the FBI and CIA planners would have wished. It made no sense. The Daniloff affair was a case of one senseless act following another. In superpower games it can all get quite petty, and the press can get mindlessly towed along.

The Soviets suffered a short-term public-relations pummelling on the Daniloff matter. But the brouhaha triggered no lasting consequences. After Shevardnadze and Shultz met at the United Nations and ironed out the terms of release for the two prisoners, more consequential events, such as the summit in Reykjavik, took over the news. The agenda of East-West relations, mercifully, was out of the hands of the spy agencies.

12/Blockbuster

IN THE REFINED Red Room of the National Hotel on an early November night, we were finishing our leathery beefsteaks when a roaring noise permeated the room, prompting some diners, after two or three minutes of it, to go to the windows. There, through white gauze curtains and a soft rain, the eyes of the startled patrons came upon tanks and other green war machines advancing through the broad, open area that abuts Red Square.

Out of the several streets opening onto the quarter converged soldiers and more armed vehicles. At the foot of Marx Prospekt one phalanx of infantrymen stood motionless, rain tapping against their helmets, for the longest time. The tanks, with arrogant precision, moved into their positions around the stores, theatres, and hotels.

Two hours earlier on this Monday evening, there had been no sign of this, only the usual Moscow-night rhythms. Now the parked cars in front of the hotel had disappeared, including some of those belonging to the hotel guests. At the gauzed windows, they stood mystified, one speculating that a military coup was in progress. Finally, someone explained that the military exercise was a dress rehearsal for November 7 – the Revolution Day celebrations. The day commemorates the birth of the Soviet Union in 1917, the main feature being a display of the country's military might.

Outside in the rain I stood watching with an American student. "It looks like Czechoslovakia, 1968," he told me. "How do you like that power?" Another bystander was more serious. "You see how easy it would be for the military to take over."

Those of us whose cars had disappeared began trying to find out where they had been taken. I rounded the corner to Gorky Street, where I had parked my Volga, and saw tanks moving down the road toward me, five abreast under bright lights. My car wasn't there. I asked a militiaman about it, and he told me it had been moved to a side street. He pointed it out and then told me how to get clear of the battlefield. I drove around endlessly, looking for a road to my neighbourhood, but at every street an army division or military protuberance of some kind was blocking my path. At one intersection I waited for 30 minutes with other motorists for the soldiers to march by; then we were all told to U-turn because the tanks were starting to come. Finally, at close to midnight, with the military occupation looking as if it would never end, I abandoned the Volga under a bridge and, without combat gear, managed to pick my way through the armies of the night to my apartment building overlooking Mr. Lenin.

Rehearsal over, the Soviet equivalent of the Fourth of July or Canada Day began under steely gray skies, with temperatures wavering at the freezing point. On the Soviet birthday they celebrate, not liberty, but military might and economic production. Labour awards are given to the best Soviet workers, loudspeakers boom testimony to the proletariat's greatness, the proletariat responds with shouts of "Hoorah! Hoorah!" and much of the conversation is about serious things – the grain harvest, whether one is meeting the plan.

On a normal day Moscow feels as though it's under the stress of the War Measures Act. On Revolution Day that sense of intimidation is piercing. Along with the rockets and anti-aircraft missiles and soldiers marching in goose steps, the city, as if more crowd control is necessary, sends out thousands of militiamen to line the streets.

War, regimentation, order, the military – they are all such an integral part of Russian culture that the people don't seem fazed by the overabundance of authority. I never heard complaints about it. I once mentioned to a government official that it might help soften the police-state atmosphere if the number of militiamen at every street corner were reduced. "I never thought of it that way," he replied. "I guess you're right. But it's part of our tradition."

While walking downtown on Revolution Day, I cut across a stretch of ground instead of staying on the paved walkway. Several bystanders reprimanded me – a replay of the time I tried walking across the street instead of through the underpass. Sometimes I got the feeling that the Russians didn't need their militia: if they took the police away, the people would keep order anyway.

Into Red Square the masses carried billboard-sized portraits of the members of the Politburo. The portraits were utterly lifeless, the faces looking freshly embalmed and horrible. The spectators cheered as they saw them, and above Lenin's mausoleum, the leaders of the country stood in perfect symmetry, taking in the scene for more than an hour before adjourning to the backrooms for mineral water on the rocks.

In the evening a pleasant silence fell over Moscow. The lighted Kremlin palaces shone magnificently, like castles in a child's fairy-tale book. Some of the military hardware had disappeared by now and snowflakes whitened the streets. At nine o'clock the proletariat moved to the parks to watch the fireworks displays. With each lighting of the skies, everyone went "ooohh" and every time they went "ooohh" the army was watching to make sure the "ooohhs" didn't get out of hand.

Gorbachev would soon begin to moderate the displays of military vulgarity. As well as conflicting with his sense of taste, with his sense of what was modern, the paying of homage to weaponry stood in direct contradiction to his politics. This Revolution Day of 1986 had followed his gambit at Reykjavik. That quickly arranged summit in Iceland had come within a breath of an agreement that would have eliminated four decades of nuclear build-up. While Reagan had arrived for a chat, Gorbachev, who had pushed for the meeting, had come with a sheath of blockbuster proposals.

His three-part package called for the elimination of all the superpowers' strategic offensive missiles within ten years. This was in keeping with his proposal of January 15. The second phase provided for the elimination of Soviet and American medium-range missiles in Europe, with the Soviets making the vital concession of leaving British and French nuclear forces out of the equation. The third phase was a proposed reaffirming of the 1972 ABM treaty, in which each side had pledged not to withdraw from its provisions for ten years. As such the Soviets said it would be a guarantee that during the ten-year period when strategic forces were being eliminated, neither side would seek military superiority.

Remarkable progress was made on parts one and two, to the point where the superpowers were almost ready to sign. But the third phase of the negotiations led to a climactic confrontation over the Strategic Defense Initiative. Reagan demanded that his government reserve the right to test everything that related to SDI. This, in the Kremlin view, was a violation of ABM and would run counter to the spirit of the first two proposals.

Thus the summit where everything was possible produced nothing. A grave-looking Gorbachev explained, in a press-conference tour de force, how, but for the demon SDI, the world could have been changed overnight. Shultz, as distraught as anyone had seen him, confirmed Gorbachev's impression. The American negotiators, who appeared to be the barriers to progress because of their insistence on SDI, sped home to devise a media strategy. In the words of Donald Regan, the president's chief of staff, a shovel brigade went to work to reverse the public-relations damage arising from Reykjavik.

That brigade did its job well. From the Kremlin, Gorbachev watched in wonder as the summit's story line was remade. On state television he charged that everything discussed at Reykjavik was "dispersing in the fog of inventions and fantasies." The administration, he said, was now trying to claim that Reagan did not agree to a complete elimination of all strategic offensive arms by 1996; he added that Reagan was offering one version of what happened, Shultz a second, and Reagan spokesman Larry Speakes a third.

"With all the responsibility of a participant in the talks, I state – the president did, albeit without particular enthusiasm, consent to the elimination of all . . . strategic offensive arms." The campaign against the real Reykjavik story, he said, included preventing the distribution of pamphlets containing the contents of his post-summit press conference and speech. Gorbachev spoke of how Reagan boasted to him in Iceland that Americans enjoy the right to hear any point of view. "Well, the fact is that the pamphlets with these texts have been detained at the U.S. customs house for many days now. They are being prevented from reaching the American reader. There is 'the right to hear any point of view' for you."

The Reagan administration rocked the Kremlin after the summit by going ahead with an earlier plan to expel 25 of the Soviets' UN diplomats. Gorbachev was becoming exasperated. "What kind of government is this?" he asked. ". . . Every time a gleam of hope appears in the approaches to the major issues in Soviet-American relations and to the solution of questions involving the interests of the whole of mankind, a provocative action is immediately staged with the aim of frustrating the possibility of a positive outcome and poisoning the atmosphere." Searching for a rationale, he reasoned that "either the president is unable to cope with his entourage which literally breathes hatred of the Soviet Union and for everything that may lead international affairs into calm waters or he himself is this way."

To Washington's expulsion of Soviet diplomats, the Kremlin responded by sending only five American diplomats home from Moscow. It was considered a rather dovish retaliation; still, the next day the Americans expelled another 55 Soviets. Calmly and deftly, Gorbachev now hit back hard. First he sent another five American envoys packing; but then, in the most telling move of the minicrisis, he withdrew all 260 Soviet employees from the Americans' Moscow embassy, throwing it into immediate confusion and seriously hindering its ability to function. The White House could not respond on this one, since the Soviets' diplomatic offices in Washington and New York did not employ American staff. Reagan ran up the white flag. The consensus, even among the American press, was that Gorbachev had euchred Reagan on a spat that the president should never have entered into.

Come Revolution Day, Gorbachev may not have been savouring all the military might on display, but as he looked down upon the masses in Red Square, he could afford a look of content. He had experienced what many would consider a tough stretch. There had been Chernobyl, the Daniloff affair, the failure at the crapshoot at Reykjavik. He was looking at another unimpressive farm yield and at falling world oil prices that were draining the

Kremlin's reserves of foreign currency – reserves badly needed for the purchase of new Western machinery and technology. But while in the United States they spoke of Ronald Reagan's ability to stay above the fray, to let criticism slide off his back, to be the Teflon man, Mikhail Gorbachev was beginning to demonstrate that, in addition to his other strengths, he had a high Teflon quotient himself. Gorbachev had turned the Chernobyl tragedy into a sermon on the dangers of nuclear power. He had been able to keep himself clear of the Daniloff fiasco, then move it to the back pages with his call for the Reykjavik meeting. And despite not winning the big one at Reykjavik, he had emerged with his image as a world peace seeker well embellished.

Though the preceding months had thrown some curves at him, Gorbachev had emerged firmly in control of the foreign agenda. Now he was ready to turn his revolutionary's gaze on the wreckage at home.

13/Breaking the Chains

IT STARTED WITH a phone call to Andrei Sakharov shortly before Christmas 1986. Until then, while there had been encouraging signs, while *glasnost* was becoming part of the Russian vocabulary, while few could doubt the new thinking on foreign policy, radical domestic reform had been largely in the talk stage. Indications were that Gorbachev was a man of his word, but more evidence was needed. Now, with his phone call to the man considered the conscience of the country, the process of democratization and *perestroika* would begin.

Sakharov had for six years been living an oxymoron: "internal exile," it was called. He was residing with his wife, Yelena Bonner, in Gorky, a major industrial centre 380 kilometres east of Moscow. Under the careful watch of the KGB, he was allowed to make monitored phone calls, write monitored letters, read monitored mail, and go for monitored walks. But he was not allowed to leave monitored Gorky, a city closed to foreigners.

Because of the absence of an honest Soviet press, his sentencing to Gorky for speaking out against the Afghan War had gone largely unnoticed. The average citizen didn't know much about Sakharov. They didn't know that his only sin was to speak out for freedom. They knew only that, as the newspapers stated, he had slandered the motherland.

In the West, however, he was a deity of freedom, the Nelson Mandela of the Soviet Union, a precious symbol of the struggle against repression. He was a man of quiet dignity: a brilliant physicist-philosopher who had invented the hydrogen bomb and won the Nobel Prize for Peace. By comparison, Anatole Scharansky, whom the Kremlin had permitted to leave for the West early in the year, had no career achievements other than fighting bravely against the Soviet system, leaking everything he could find to Western reporters, and getting thrown in jail for his trouble. Many Soviets, including some who were sympathetic to the cause of human rights, didn't like Scharansky. They tended to view the situation in simplistic terms. What would the Americans think, one told me, if one of their own citizens with inside connections went around divulging everything bad about their system to Soviet journalists in Washington? "They'd think he was a traitor."

The occasional rumour that Sakharov might be let go made the rounds. In his baritone voice, Boris Toumanov, a French-speaking Tass official from the Armenian Republic, said over coffee one day in the autumn of 1986 that with Gorbachev promoting open criticism it was becoming increasingly irreconcilable to keep Sakharov in Gorky. At a press conference at the same time, however, officials of the justice department held to the line that Sakharov had disobeyed the law and deserved his punishment. There was no reason to be overly optimistic.

Then, on the night of December 15 at ten p.m., workers arrived unannounced and installed a telephone in the apartment of Sakharov and his wife. The next afternoon, a windy day in Gorky, the phone rang at three o'clock. A woman's voice said, "Mikhail Sergeyevich Gorbachev will speak to you."[1]

"The call was absolutely out of the blue," Sakharov told Ilya Gerol of the *Ottawa Citizen*. "Not only were we prepared to stay in Gorky for the rest of our lives but we, Yelena and I, even had visited the local cemetery and found a spot for ourselves."

Sakharov could barely hear the voice at the other end of the line. The guards outside his apartment were having a party, making a ruckus. Bonner told them to shut up. Gorbachev told Sakharov that "a decision has been taken regarding your return to Moscow." The Soviet leader said Bonner could return too, whereupon Sakharov told him her full name, indicating his annoyance that Gorbachev had not followed the polite Russian custom of using it. Gorbachev then said he understood the couple would have no problem getting set up in Moscow because they already had an apartment from their previous life there. A copy of the decision to release him would soon be sent, said Gorbachev, "so that you can return to your patriotic work."

Sakharov expressed his deep gratitude. Then he referred to a list of political prisoners he had sent Gorbachev earlier in the year and asked him what was being done. "He said he had looked at the list," Sakharov recalled, "and that many of those mentioned would be released while the conditions of the rest would be improved." Sakharov, deciding that the talk might turn sour if he pursued the question further, brought the conversation to a close, said goodbye, and began packing for Moscow.

The Kremlin did not immediately publicize Gorbachev's phone call. At a regular press briefing, among several announcements, deputy foreign minister Vladimir Petrovsky dropped the news that Sakharov had requested a move to Moscow and that the request had been granted. "The request was considered by the appropriate bodies, including the Academy of Sciences and administrative bodies. In particular they took into account that academician Sakharov has been staying in Gorky for a lengthy period of time."

In making the decision, the Soviets may have also been taking into account other developments. First, the contradiction implicit in Gorbachev's preaching openness while keeping Sakharov confined to Gorky. Second, a recent offer by Gorbachev to host an international human-rights conference in Moscow. How could he have credibility as a host while Sakharov was still impounded? Third, Sakharov had indicated that he supported many of Gorbachev's initiatives, including the Reykjavik proposals, the nuclear-test moratorium, and *glasnost*. A release, therefore, would not mean Sakharov would go abroad and, like Scharansky, spend the rest of his days publicly pillorying his former government. Fourth, the release of Sakharov would be, for a Kremlin that was very conscious of its image, a p.r. bonanza.

While it was a small item in the Moscow press, the decision ran on page one around the world. It served as the best substantiation yet that something good was happening in the evil empire. When it was learned that Gorbachev himself had made the call, the triumph for the Soviet leader became a personal one. Some in the West said the Kremlin was making a propaganda show of the high-profile dissident cases without changing its policy toward the others. But Gorbachev soon put that thought to rest with another bombshell – the announcement in the weeks after Christmas that 140 dissidents were being set free and that more would follow.

Most of the cases involved people who had been imprisoned under the criminal code's Section 70. This law pertained to anti-Soviet agitation and propaganda – which often meant making statements the Kremlin didn't like. The government's spokesman, Gennady Gerasimov, announced that a review of this and other draconian statutes was under way and would be "aimed at softening, so to speak, the criminal laws so we have fewer people behind bars and behind barbed wire."

"We're letting all the dissidents go," said my Soviet source, who had predicted Sakharov's release. "That is our intention. They are no longer considered a threat to the Soviet state. They will be free to express their views here as they wish." Within a week of the post-Christmas announcement, Gerasimov had announced that yet another 140 political prisoners would soon be on their way home.

"It's not right to say that it's only propaganda or window dressing," said Sakharov. "Something real is happening here." He criticized the Soviet presence in Afghanistan very soon after returning to Moscow. He had only been gone from Gorky a few weeks when he received an invitation to Gorbachev's forum on international peace. It was held in the grand hall of the Kremlin. The Western press was allowed in. We watched as Sakharov, seated front and centre, surrounded by Soviets who had kept their silence while he was in exile, was given the star treatment. None of the man's attitudes had changed since the 1970s; only the attitude of the system he lived in had changed. One of the speakers before Gorbachev told the gathering how Sakharov had won the Nobel Prize for his striving for democracy and openness, and how special it was to have him present. But how the Soviets had frowned on that Nobel Prize when it was awarded in 1976.

Sakharov estimated that about 600 dissidents were in Soviet jails at the time of the Kremlin's decision on releases. This number was much lower than many in the West had thought. (American and Jewish sources put the figure at 1,000 or 2,000.) I received a letter from a Canadian saying he was surprised, because the impression from reading the media was that tens of thousands of Soviets were in jail for having spoken out against the system. There were many countries, in both the East and the West, where there were proportionately more political prisoners, but the basic point of principle was the same – the Soviet people, at least before Gorbachev's arrival in power, had not been able to speak their minds freely.

The releases came the same week that the urbane American ambassador, Arthur Hartman, was completing his term in Moscow. Hartman had the respect of almost everyone except the hard-line faction in the White House, which had sought his removal. He had not won friends in that group with his lack of enthusiasm, in 1985, for the bogus allegation that the Soviets were using a lethal spray dust to track foreign diplomats. Now, on the eve of his departure, he spoke of the human-rights advances. "*Glasnost* has not been in the spirit of this country since its inception," he said. "The fact that there is a *glasnost* program here is a remarkable fact in and of itself." Were it up to Gorbachev alone, Hartman said, the changes would be much swifter. Gorbachev, said Hartman, "wants to move much faster, but there are counterpressures."

The counterpressures were glaringly on display that same day, only a few blocks from where Hartman spoke. This was the week of the Kremlin's announcement on the dissidents, it was the week preceding Moscow's hosting of the international peace conference. But it was also the week that, just down the street from the foreign ministry, KGB men were out hacking down protesters and journalists on the Arbat mall.

The Arbat is a historic and colourful promenade with a look more Salvation Army than Georgio Armani. On the Monday a small group of Jews came out to protest Soviet emigration policies. Precedent suggested they would be beaten down – the Soviet Union did not allow protests. But on the first day it didn't happen. They paraded for 90 minutes in support of dissident Josef Begun while the Soviet authorities stood and watched. The next day, the day of the announcement that the dissidents would be released, they came again. And again they protested without interference.

But on the third day, the hammer fell. Plainclothesmen moved in, punched and beat the protesters, and cut the cables of Western TV cameras trying to film the protest. The next day the demonstrators came back yet again, and this time the Soviets used bulldozers to disperse them. On Friday, the same thing again. Angry reporters who had been roughed up in the melees addressed the matter to Gerasimov. He replied that it wasn't the KGB but vigilantes taking the law into their own hands. And these vigilantes should be arrested themselves, he said.

In the damp cold of the Thursday I had swayed amid the push and shove of demonstrators and police for an hour. The KGB men, "vigilantes," showed extraordinary physical power. They would silently knock someone to the pavement and inconspicuously move on. Each of them seemed to know what the others were doing. None of the everyday Russian pedestrians showed any surprise or hostility over their actions. At this point Russian citizens generally tended to view protesters as traitorous ingrates – that they got smashed down was fine and well.

No one in the foreign press believed Gerasimov when he said the rough tactics were the work of vigilantes. But nobody believed, either, that Gorbachev and his advisors would willingly let this take place; it was the opposite of the signal they were trying to send. While the Soviet press, to its shame in these supposedly new times, didn't cover the protests, they were front-page news in many countries in the West. The only sensible conclusion seemed to be that the KGB was still strong enough to act independently and had decided, with all the dovish gesturing at the Kremlin, to flex a little muscle.

In the corridors, a Soviet official argued that the CIA had set up the Arbat protest as a provocation. Disruptive tactics of this kind are part of the CIA's mandate, and it was certainly an opportune moment for the agency to blacken the Kremlin's image. One possible scenario would have involved the CIA station at the American embassy promising special help to would-be emigrants provided they staged provocative demonstrations. But if the KGB thought the protests were a set-up, then, as was the question when they arrested Daniloff, why did they play right into the CIA's hands by acting like goons?

For a Soviet Union anxious to clean up its image, the KGB would remain a barrier until Gorbachev slashed its powers and broke its monopoly on policing. Even a cosmetic change – the breaking up of the KGB into different divisions with different names – would make a big difference both at home and abroad. In the United States, the FBI handles internal policing, and the CIA, external. As simple a division as that would diminish the monolithic notoriety of the KGB.

A month before the fiasco on the Arbat, the Kremlin appeared to be making a move on the KGB. The front page of *Pravda* announced one day that action was being taken against certain KGB officials for intimidating a Soviet investigative reporter in the Ukraine. According to Soviet newspaper reports, Viktor Berkhin of the magazine *Soviet Miner* was jailed for 13 days in the summer of 1985 on a trumped-up charge of hooliganism. The arrest followed the publication of articles by Berkhin detailing corrupt practices by officials in the Ukraine's Voroshilovgrad region. Lawyers who won the release of Berkhin determined that the KGB had made the arrest in deliberate response to problems the articles had created for the political authorities.

One high-ranking KGB official was dismissed, and disciplinary action was taken against others. It was believed to be the first time the KGB, an organization long regarded as untouchable, had made public its internal activities in such a way. Soviet journalists were enthused. The government's portrayal of Berkhin as being in the right, one told me, would encourage other reporters to take a bolder approach. Gorbachev himself had been doing some encouraging of that nature. During a tour of the Soviet Far East a few months earlier, he had scolded local media for writing too much puff and covering up the real problems of Soviet society.

With talk in the wind that the freedom-of-speech laws – and the entire legal system – would be reformed, I visited Vladimir Kudriavtsev, the director of the Soviet Institute for State and Law.

This legal expert, who looked like Boris Karloff, was scrambling, like so many of the empowered, to accommodate Gorbachev's liberalism. In an unlit office that looked unchanged for half a century, he explained that the present-day Soviet laws touching on human freedoms were not so bad. In the Soviet Union as in any Western country, he explained, subversion is forbidden by law. The problem, he asserted, was mainly that the laws have been interpreted too harshly. "Maybe there were some errors, some miscarriages of justice. But now they are being corrected. For example, the problem of criticizing the State. Of course, someone who does this must not be in jail any more."[2]

Reinterpretation of existing laws had already begun, and legal reforms were being brought forward. They would either remove Article 70 or make it less severe; the same would happen with the other law that effectively curtailed freedom of speech – Article 190. Among other things, the latter forbade "circulation in oral form" of lies against the Soviet state. What constituted a lie was up to the State to decide.

I asked Kudriavtsev what had brought on this sudden change. "The process of democratization," he said. Now there was a new, expansive attitude in the Soviet Union, one that would "let people criticize and let them improve life at large." The day of this interview, Gerasimov announced that the man at the centre of the Arbat mall fiasco, Josef Begun, had been pardoned by Kremlin decree and would be released to the West. Begun had been imprisoned since 1983 for anti-State activities. Released as well, said Gerasimov, would be the dissident psychiatrist, Anatole Koryagin, 48 years old, who had been accused of anti-Soviet agitation and propaganda after preparing a report about dissidents and their incarceration in mental hospitals.

It was clear from Kudriavtsev's words and the government's actions on dissidents that those appalled by the Soviet legal system could take hope. The abuses in the system were unconscionable. Judges were bringing in guilty sentences to fit the five-year plan's quotas. During preliminary investigations the accused was not getting the right to the presence of a lawyer. At a round-table discussion with Soviet writers and legal experts, it was concluded that jurors, or lay assessors, as they were called, had become total yes men to judges, many of whom were totally unqualified. In theory, the juror had a right to disagree with a judge; but a legal writer, Leonid Zhukovitsky, said it was in theory only. "I know one juror who decided to make active use of this right. Twice he came out in opposition to overly strict sentences for minors." Immediately, he said, the judge took action. "Send me another juror," the judge ordered. "We don't need this kind."

14/The Market Mechanism

"WHY IS IT, Mr. Petrakov, that a Soviet surgeon's wages do not even come close to those of a minibus driver?"

"Because we had decided," said Nikolai Petrakov, the deputy head of an economic institute, "that we had to stimulate the type of work which did not need qualifications, especially heavy physical labour. We were convinced that otherwise no one would want to go and chop trees in the *taiga*. . . . But in so doing we strangled the incentive, the material interests of specialists upon whom the fate of our scientific technical progress depended."

The Soviet Union, he added, can scarcely expect the qualified people to exert a maximum effort when the inventor of a machine tool earns less than the factory hand who mans it. "In this era of computers and robots it is all the more vital to encourage qualifications, knowledge and intellect."

Petrakov had neatly nutshelled not only his own thoughts on labour but those of Mikhail Gorbachev as well. Gorbachev, a devotee of the work ethic, had expressed the view many times that the merit principle must apply in the workplace, that those who give the most to society should be rewarded the most. "What is the main shortcoming of the old economic machinery?" he asked. "It is above all the lack of inner stimuli for self-development." Gorbachev never became an expert in any one field – he was a "generalist" by self-definition – but economics concerned him the most. "In my more advanced years," he told the Italian Communist Party's magazine *L'Unita*, "I have been more interested in economics, read and written on these topics. It can be said that I know a thing or two in this field."

Gorbachev was a keen student of Lenin's New Economic Policy, which the Soviet founder introduced in his last years. Essentially, it meant a lessening of state power and a return to greater autonomy for industry and agriculture. Gorbachev knew well the dictum that without the profit motive, a sluggish economy results. He had so many examples in front of him. Soviets enjoyed an oil surplus; even so, at gas stations Muscovites planned on sitting in line for at least an hour. The attendants, an investigation concluded, seldom bothered to turn on more than one pump; putting out-of-order signs on the other two or three made for an easier workday. It made no difference to an attendant's income; after all, it was a state operation.

The same problem – a lack of incentives – extended right to the grave. The Soviets lined up for coffins like they did for gas. Coffin makers didn't earn any more money making ten caskets a day than they did making five. They therefore worked at the rhythm of men on a permanent slowdown strike. When Viktor Malyshev of Sverdlovsk visited the local coffin bureau to get a casket for his dead brother, he was told he'd have to wait five days. Malyshev protested that his brother was dead now and needed something to lie in. He was told to build a coffin himself. Malyshev went away and built a coffin himself.

The economy, explained Viktor Dashichev, an economics specialist, had been run like an army. "Based on principles of rigid overcentralization, it looked like kind of a giant military mechanism with its battalions, regiments, division and armies – i.e. enterprises, associations, committees and ministries – over which loomed the figure of the commander-in-chief. Everything was subjugated to fulfilling the plan – or orders. But society cannot live and work according to Army rules."

Following a first year in power in which he moved slowly on the economy, Gorbachev undertook experiments and reforms in the economic and political spheres designed to return some incentive and decision making to the people. This was the period – the winter of 1986-87 – when the word *perestroika*, a word that would later be heard around the world, began coming into everyday Soviet usage. Gorbachev's new measures, apart from the human-rights reforms that were also part of *perestroika,* included these:

- An individual-labour law, and legislation allowing private-enterprise cooperatives. The law for individuals specified 29 types of free-enterprise work. It permitted citizens to sell goods or services at whatever price the market would bear and keep the post-tax profits. Students and pensioners could become *chastniks* – as these small-time capitalists were called – on a full-time basis. But others could only engage in private work as a supplement to their regular state jobs. Guidelines for the co-ops were similar.

- A wage-reform package diversifying salaries on the basis of job performance and paying more money to the highly skilled professionals than to blue-collar workers.

- A radical decentralization of the foreign-trade system, authorizing the operators of 70 major Soviet enterprises to strike their own deals with foreign countries, as opposed to having the State do it for them. It meant, for example, that the Lada car company could purchase parts from and sell to the West without working under any quota system or binding Kremlin restrictions.

- Joint ventures. Foreign enterprises could now undertake partnerships on Soviet soil with Soviet businesses. The foreign enterprise was entitled to 49 percent of ownership. Along with this key measure, the Kremlin sought to integrate its economy with that of the West in other ways: by applying to join GATT, the organization governing international trading regulations; by sending out feelers on joining the World Bank and International Monetary Fund; and by promoting the notion of making the Soviet rouble convertible.

- Election reform. Gorbachev announced plans to change the rubber-stamp, one-candidate electoral system, which was farcical, to one that offered multiple candidates and a secret ballot. The changes would affect not only political positions but also those in the workplace. For example, plant managers would be elected.

The economic measures did not represent the deep structural

change that many Soviet economists thought was necessary. But they were signals of a new economic thinking in the Kremlin. The individual-labour law meant that workers could set up their own barber shops, car-repair garages, garment-making houses, home-decorating shops, photography studios, taxi services, and the like. They could become Western-style entrepreneurs in the *little* sense. The genie of free enterprise was being leaked from a bottle jammed shut for generations.

In fact, the genie had long been out – but only in the illegal sense, in the form of the black market. For many goods and services, a highly active black market helped compensate for the great inadequacies in the state stores. The authorities would clamp down on the black market now and again, but tolerated it in good measure. They knew of the shortages. They knew the people had to have the basics. In one of his early and more unpopular moves, Gorbachev had tried unsuccessfully to move against the black market, issuing commands to have moonlighters brought to justice. Now, with the individual-labour law and the creation of the co-ops, he had found a better way. In effect, what the two measures did was bring the black market out into the open – legalize it.

On the streets it was hard to gauge the level of excitement touched off by Gorbachev's announcements. The Slavs were not the type to brandish emotion, particularly in the dead of a winter that was the coldest since the early 1940s. On some days on the Moscow streets an exhaled breath seemed to hang in front of you like a rigid cloud. The Russians had round fur hats called *shapkas*. I often wondered, my first year in Moscow, why they never pulled the earflaps down. One Russian told me it wasn't manly to do so. Another said it didn't look good. But in this, my second winter, I saw a lot of hats with the flaps pulled down. The militiamen maintaining the traffic flow had the best coats – long, black sheepskins, thick as pillows. But in January 1987 those coats didn't help them much. Crimson cheeks against battleship-gray fur collars, they stood so immobile you thought they would never move again.

By the spring Soviets by the thousands were signing up to begin their little businesses. But while some got going in a hurry, a great many were torpedoed by bureaucratic nightmares – the facilities for setting up shop were unavailable, or the raw materials were impossible to get from the State.

The cooperatives experienced many similar headaches, but had more success – especially with respect to co-op cafés and restaurants. The need for these was so desperate that many could charge high prices. Medical clinics, beauty salons, and transport services were also popular new endeavours. With taxes at only three percent, some Russians started to make undreamt-of rouble sums. The Kremlin had to have another look at the tax rate because the unthinkable – the prospect of Soviet millionaires – was becoming thinkable.

The joint-ventures program brought on more Gorbachev-Peter the Great comparisons – the czar reaching West to bring modernization to his backward peasantry. Joint ventures were in fact a direct grab at Western investment and technology, an invitation for the West to come to one of the world's largest untapped markets.

Lenin's New Economic Policy was part of the inspiration for Gorbachev's private-enterprise initiatives. So too could the Soviet founder be seen as the ghost author of joint ventures. In the early 1920s he had invited Armand Hammer, the American industrialist, to participate in Soviet businesses. Lenin died too soon to see the plan through, however, and under Stalin the business gateway to the West gradually narrowed to the point where, with the beginnings of the Cold War, trade was a trickle.

What little was done often required a deep familiarity with the bottle and with bribes, or "gifts" as the latter were called. In the 1960s representatives of a West German firm recalled hiring an expert on Soviet relations in preparations for their first business trip to Moscow. The expert first launched them on vodka-training sessions – rapid-fire, prelunch toasts. Almost all of them failed the test miserably and spent their afternoon in a half-collapsed, woozing daze. The designated best power-drinker among them was chosen to do the lion's share in Moscow. The consultant's second tip concerned how to bribe the Soviet officials with video equipment. Beyond that, the Soviet-relations expert apparently didn't have much else to suggest.[1]

By 1986 foreign businessmen permanently stationed in Moscow were still a rare sight. Canada had one, and he was not faring so well. Carl Axelson, a bearded 49-year-old Albertan, was representing a consortium of 13 western Canadian companies that were trying to break into what they felt could be a billion-dollar market in the oil-equipment business. He lived in a small room by the Moscow River in the International Hotel complex, a modern, gray structure of ubiquitous architecture isolated on the bank of the Moscow River. In late 1985, after he'd commuted between Edmonton and Moscow for three years, the Soviets finally gave him permission to set up a permanent office and employ a Soviet assistant. The three years had cost him 800,000 dollars in overhead, a sum not compensated for by the three small contracts he had landed.

Part of the problem, Axelson told me, was the Japanese, "who spoil the situation with great gobs of gifts." Another problem was of his own making: he teamed up with an American, not realizing, he said, how much more the Soviets distrusted them. But what helped keep Axelson going was his affection for the Russians and, later, the promise of change under Gorbachev. He liked the Russians' spirit, their commitment to friendship, their dedication to the motherland, and their educational system, which he considered superior to North America's. "They're all avid readers here. They are much more interested in the classic arts, and the children know more about other countries than we do. They learn other languages."[2]

By 1987 mineral water and joint ventures had replaced vodka and bribes at the trade table. Joint ventures represented a major change of attitude – from one of Soviet suspicion of foreign traders to one of agreeability. Initially there was confusion over how joint ventures would work. Potential clients from outside the East Bloc worried about Soviet managerial dictatorship in such ventures, and about what to do with their rouble profits. But gradually the ventures got started, and Western know-how and technology flowed. A group of Japanese firms signed a 600-million-dollar contract to build a polyester-textile plant in a city in the Urals. Occidental Petroleum of the United States signed a

six-billion-dollar deal with Moscow for gas and sulphur production.
Soon Moscow was considering about 250 joint-venture proposals.
Even McDonald's, the hamburger chain, was in on the act.

In the flush of all the developments in the areas of human rights
and economic reform, most noteworthy was the news coming out
of the Central Committee meeting in January. It was announced there that Gorbachev was intending to move to a system of
multicandidate elections.

In the past the laughable election system had been controlled by
the Communist Party apparatus. In each electoral district the party
would decide which name would be placed on the election ballot.
That name would be the only one to go on the ballot, and that name
would get 99 percent of the vote.

The purpose of Gorbachev's call for competing candidates and
secret-ballot elections, said Boris Strasheen of the law division of
the Soviet Academy of Sciences, was "to wake up the activity of the
masses and make the leaders feel more responsibility to them."
The new system was to be given a trial run in some districts in the
summer and a debate would then be held on exactly how high up
the ladder of power the new process would reach.

The announcement caused confusion in the Western press
corps. Some reporters suggested that it was a next-to-meaningless
development because it would still be only a one-party system. The
significance, however, lay in the fact that within the one Communist
Party there was a wide range of views. There were the reformers on
the one hand, who supported Gorbachev's plans, and Stalinists on
the other, who opposed them and wanted him stopped. In the voting
system Gorbachev now proposed, men and women with differing
views could vie for voter support. The wing electing the highest
number would be able to exert considerable influence on the future
direction of the Soviet Union.

With the planned expansion of this voting experiment to all levels,
Gorbachev was making his biggest assault yet on the entrenched
bureaucracy. For the tens of thousands who had been secure in their
positions by virtue of rubber-stamp electoral incumbency, that
security was now evaporating before their eyes. It was no surprise that

the Soviet leader found strong opposition to the proposal. An estimated 30 percent in the Central Committee were opposed.

The Kremlin leader laid out the picture clearly during the meeting. "We are talking about a turning point and measures of revolutionary character. We simply do not have any other choice. We must not retreat and do not have anywhere to retreat to." He confirmed that opposition was threatening his plans, saying the start date for the meeting had been postponed three times. (He was quoted as telling news executives that he was close to quitting. "If the meeting had convened and arrived at the conclusion that reconstruction is not justified and should be rejected, I would have said, 'I cannot work otherwise.' ")

The choice for Soviet society is "either democracy, or social inertness and conservatism," Gorbachev told the Central Committee. "There is not a third way. . . . We want to alter the atmosphere in society radically, for we cannot be pleased with how we lived and worked previously."

The general secretary said he could understand selfish opponents of reform. "It is no secret that many were content and some still remain happy to work in a slipshod manner, with unwarranted pay, undeserved bonuses in a mutually undemanding atmosphere. . . . There is however, drama in the situation when even selfless honest people who so far remain captives of outdated notions are among its opponents. There are people who have not realized the acuity and critical character of problems facing society."

Gorbachev's call for real elections began to take effect in the workplace before reaching aspirants to national office. At state enterprises, directors and foremen were being chosen democratically by those who worked for them. In some places, such as the Raf automobile company in Latvia, unusual excitement was being stirred. The directorship of the company had come open, and in keeping with the new Kremlin guidelines, a competition was taking place, with the vacancy advertised in newspapers. "And what happened?" asked Yuri Tikhomirov, a doctor of laws and critic of Gorbachev's new way. "Four thousand applications flew in from all over the country – from milkmaids, schoolgirls, teachers and drivers, and hundreds more from trusting simpletons who believed they had a chance. . . . Should we have deluded thousands of people? After all it was clear as day to the organizers that no bus driver was going to be made director of the car company."

Other critics cited a recent experience in Bulgaria, where industrial personnel – from managers of tiny shops to directors – were elected after a six-month campaign. "Absurd," said a Soviet factory manager. "Just imagine, tomorrow election fever will be infecting every enterprise both great and small. And who will be left to do the work?"

The democracy campaign expanded quickly to the theatre world, where, as the Soviet magazine *Literaturnaya Gazeta* pointed out, democratic passions spilled overboard. Actors and stage assistants moved to usurp the power of some of the Soviet Union's great directors by voting for what plays they should perform and how they should be done. Veterans of the stage, like playwright Viktor Rozov, were beside themselves. "This," he said, "is naive and laughable."

15/Getting Out

HE WAS FRAIL underneath his thin, dark coat, and the cheap metal of his prison-capped teeth glared against the early Moscow sun. He had spent 34 years in Soviet prisons and labour camps and in internal exile. Now, in the spring of 1987, the Kremlin was letting career-dissident Danylo Shumuk emigrate to freedom.

At the airport, before the final tension of clearing customs, he was showing me and another reporter a maimed arm and reflecting, "I was in Poland until 1939. I was a deeply committed underground Communist then and was ready to die for the ideology. It was an ideology that came from within me. But then later when I faced the reality of Communism it was not meeting my hopes at all. My expectations were betrayed."

He then began his long journey of activism for human rights and Ukrainian nationalism, most of which was spent in some form of incarceration. The 73-year-old's most recent sentence was for anti-Soviet propaganda. He spent 15 years in isolation in the Kazakh Republic, ten of them behind bars.

Joe Clark, now Canada's external-affairs minister, first took up the Shumuk case in 1974. The matter was of symbolic importance to the 600,000 Canadians who are of Ukrainian background, Clark felt. On a visit to the Soviet Union in 1985 he met with Alexander Lyashko, the Ukrainian premier, who dismissed the matter as unimportant. In turn, the Soviet foreign minister Andrei Gromyko did the same, gruffly rebuking the Canadian minister for raising matters of internal concern.

This was always the Kremlin's line on emigration – it was a matter of internal concern. When pressed further, the response was that the applicant for emigration knew state secrets and therefore would have to stay. Early in Gorbachev's term, the policy – a bitter clashpoint in relations between the Soviets and the West (particularly the United States) – remained in place. Freeing Sakharov and the dissidents from incarceration was a major human-rights advance. But the question of emigration rights for the tens of thousands who wished to leave the Soviet Union was equally important.

A year and a half into Gorbachev's stewardship, in October 1986, I met to discuss the emigration policy as it affected Canada with Viktor Sukhodrev, head of the Canada desk at the foreign ministry. Sukhodrev was one of the smoothest Russians of them all. His specialty was linguistics. He had served as translator for Khrushchev at the Kennedy summit, for Brezhnev at the Nixon summits, and later as one of Gorbachev's translators with Reagan. Sukhodrev could not only speak fluent English, but he could do so in the accent of his choice and with the matching look, in whatever style – British, American, or European – the occasion required. Depending on the tenor of the times, his demeanour in Russian could be that of an iron-faced Stalinist, a decadent Brezhnevite, or an open-minded Gorbachev man.

Sukhodrev was still waiting for his wish to become ambassador to Ireland to be fulfilled. He had established such close ties with Soviet leaders over the years that I was surprised the system's entrenched patronage and cronyism had not bequeathed him a reward at least as modest as that. I had put the question to a close relation of the former, long-time Politburo member Anastas Mikoyan, as we roared through the Ukraine in a train one night. "Gromyko didn't operate the foreign ministry that way," he said.

As we talked in the dim chill of the gargantuan, banana-coloured building that housed the foreign ministry, I expected a more progressive signal from Sukhodrev on emigration, but right away he opted for a Stalin-era demeanour. He made clear there would be no loosening of the rigid, no-exit policy. He stated, for example, that Canadians now trying to get their relatives out of the Soviet Union had taken up residence illegally in Canada in the first place. Some are war criminals, he added. "We will not give prizes to people who have contravened the laws of our land." He referred to the importance of state secrets, then explained how lucky it was for Canada that the Soviets even addressed matters of emigration. "It is only as a sign of goodwill that we talk about these things with a country which basically has no legal right to call for or demand, if you will, a discussion."

But it wouldn't be the first time I would get one message from one senior Soviet official and then see a different story emerge. The hard line didn't hold. When Eduard Shevardnadze visited Ottawa that same week in October 1986, he dodged the demands of protocol and walked over to a group of Canadian human-rights protesters. He listened patiently to their complaints and took home with him, along with their words, a list of 40 prominent cases of divided families and another plea on behalf of Danylo Shumuk.

By early in the new year, in a sign of things to come, 22 of the 40 cases had been solved and Shumuk was on his way. Canada had never enjoyed that type of cooperation from the Soviets. "This shows how much things have changed here," said Vernon Turner, the Canadian ambassador.

Shumuk, like almost everyone else, was encouraged by Gorbachev's actions, but not sold. "The changes are not as radical and will not be as radical as I would like them to be," he said. "This kind of democracy they are talking about here is only partial democracy. There is an absence of an opposition party and therefore there cannot be a real democracy. Only when the government knows it can be replaced in four or five years can there be real democracy."

As he prepared to board the West-bound plane for the first time in his life, he added, "I love the Ukraine deeply. It is not easy for me to say farewell to my motherland. . . . But I have serious motives."

Shumuk left the Soviet Union in 1987. So did Josef Begun, who had spent 17 years trying to emigrate, and so did Ida Nudel, the mother of the Jewish emigration movement, whom many thought would never clear the curtain. Jewish emigration, which had reached a peak of 51,000 a year under Brezhnev in 1979 before falling to a few hundred a year, was suddenly shooting upward again.

"We have hopes," said Vladimir Slepak, a radio engineer who also spent 17 years trying to get out. "But as the German chancellor Bismarck once said, 'There are two things you can't predict – what God will do and what a Russian will do.'" Slepak had spent five years in internal exile along the Mongolian border for hanging a banner from his apartment balcony that read, "Let us join our son in Israel."

But this time you could predict what the Russians would do. Not long after Begun and Nudel left, Slepak was permitted to join his son in Israel. Anatole Scharansky barnstormed around the globe suggesting that new Soviet emigration policies were worse than before. But each month, Jews left the Soviet Union in ever-increasing numbers.

Margaret Thatcher of Great Britain came to Moscow early in the thaw and, in tribute to Gorbachev, quoted England's greatest poet: "There is a famous passage in which Shakespeare speaks of a tide in the affairs of men, which, when taken at the flood, leads to fortune. Perhaps Mr. General Secretary you have already caught that tide." She declared that "the greater your readiness to release prisoners of conscience and to allow those who wish to do so to leave the country freely . . . the greater the readiness that you will find in the West to believe that peaceful and friendly relations with the Soviet Union can be maintained and extended."

As was often the case when faced with foreign leaders who confronted him on human rights, Gorbachev couldn't resist a "how about your own backyard" dig: It was fine to talk about the Soviet infringements on the Helsinki accords, he said, but what about the situation in Western countries? What about "the millions of unemployed and homeless and destitute, those beaten by police . . . those whose civil rights and human dignity are subjected to glaring discrimination simply because of the colour of their skin." The concept of freedom in the West, he argued, did not permit any choice beyond capitalism. "When this or that people – in

Nicaragua, Africa, the Middle East or Asia – actually reveal a desire to look for a different road of their own, something that will suit them better, they find their way immediately barred with dollars, missiles or mercenaries."

As a sign of the new times, Thatcher was allowed on Soviet television to preach her capitalist wisdom. That would have been unthinkable in the era before Gorbachev. After the Iron Lady got through demolishing three Soviet interrogators with rapier thrusts, many Kremlin officials probably wished it had still been unthinkable.

While Gorbachev chose to dispute her on emigration and human rights, it was obvious he was changing his mind on his government's draconian policies. He had taken over the leadership sounding all the old Kremlin lies on emigration, which included not just the state-secrets rationale, but also the argument that the West was trying to organize a Soviet brain drain. One of his officials in the foreign ministry, V.N. Sofinsky, went even further, appearing before the Western press to say that the Soviet Union had to bear in mind "increasing the military potential of Israel" by letting so many Jews go home to join the army.

The Russians I met had strong racist tendencies. Peoples who have been sealed off from the rest of the world as much as the Soviets are more inclined to find fault with different colours and creeds than peoples with a more open history. Even the better-educated Soviets I knew verbally abused blacks and Asians. The Soviets regarded these people as primitive. As a general rule, they tended to look down on many minorities, including the Jews.

The Kremlin's attitude toward Jewish emigration fired anti-Soviet passions among the world's Jews and among politicians in the capital of Israel's biggest ally, the United States. The treatment accorded Soviet Jews was not the worst of Soviet sins by any objective appraisal. But because of the intense pressure placed on politicians and the media by the Jewish lobby, it was always near the top of the priorities list when it came to affairs Soviet in Washington.

While many Soviet Jews had to go to the West for better medical treatment, the majority of them were seeking better living standards. Most did not go to Israel but to the United States or another country. When Yelena Bonner visited Ottawa with Andrei Sakharov in February 1989, she angered the Jewish community by saying, with Sakharov's agreement, that 90 percent of the Jews leaving the Soviet Union were economic refugees. Washington by this time had begun denying some Jews refugee status because they could not demonstrate "a well-founded fear of persecution" in the Soviet Union.

The Soviets were embittered by the desire of the Jews to leave their country. The reason came down to the old saw about the Soviet motherland as the great provider. Russians had fought for the motherland; 20 million had died to save it, along with the rest of the world, from the Nazis. And hadn't the motherland given these people free housing, free education, free medical care, and a guaranteed job? So how could all these tens of thousands want to turn their backs on the motherland?

The Soviets argued that Israel had no right to complain about other countries on human-rights issues, given its treatment of Arabs in the occupied territories. It further angered the Soviets that an emigration protest by a handful of Jews could automatically draw half the Western press in Moscow for blow-by-blow coverage.

The Soviet arguments helped put the emigration question in better perspective – a perspective that Western journalists usually failed to provide. But no matter what the rationale, there was no escaping the bare inhumanity of their keeping up bars around their country, of their forcing people to stay in the Soviet Union. There was no defence. The secrets argument was a lie more than 95 percent of the time. The organized brain-drain lament was also a lie.

I went to the Moscow apartment of Elizar Yozefovich, a refusenik. He said he had been on a hunger strike for 27 days to try to draw attention to his bid to leave the country. He said his wife needed medical care in the West. Their apartment was fine by Soviet standards. He worked as a computer technician, and was no longer harassed by the police for teaching Hebrew to the Jewish community's children. So I thought, why the hunger strike, why the passion of Yozefovich to leave? It was "not because of any strong feelings against the Soviets," he said. Rather, in addition to health care, it was primarily because he was a Jew and wanted to live in

Israel. The mistake made in the West, he said, was to confuse dissidents with refuseniks. "The dissidents want to change the system here. They are Russian patriots. We are Israeli patriots. It doesn't mean we don't think a lot about this country. We want all the best for this country."

That Gorbachev swallowed his Russian pride on the question of Jewish emigration was an important factor in advancing the prospects for East-West harmony. There had been no indication that he was any different from other Russians brought up to detest those who turned their backs on the motherland. But he chose to reverse his own stated policy, and in so doing went to battle once more against the country's conservatives. In this case, his fight was with those who controlled the bars along the border, and who very likely had acted against his will in busting up the Arbat mall demonstration – the KGB.

Speculating on a Soviet leader's relationship with the KGB is a difficult venture. But evidence suggested that between Gorbachev and the Soviet security force, considerable tension was developing. The KGB was the very symbol of the conservative, law-and-order society, of the totalitarian way. Gorbachev was pursuing a dovish liberalism abroad, and his liberal *glasnost* policy at home was, in effect, cutting into KGB power. While he didn't appear to be forcing reforms on the KGB itself, the Berkhin case, in which the organization was embarrassed on the front page of *Pravda*, was not a vote of confidence. A new emigration policy was only one more signal for the KGB to mull over. If it wasn't becoming clear to the security force that Gorbachev was intent on dismantling the old order – an old order in which the KGB was at the top – it should have been.

It was at this time that I met my first KGB agent (though I had probably met several of them unknowingly). I had asked for an interview with the infamous British turncoat, Kim Philby. Failing that, I wanted to speak to someone in touch with Philby. The result was that a KGB agent who worked the Philby file agreed to be interviewed on the subject. We met downtown at the courtyard bar of the Intourist Hotel. He was tall, strong, and cool, with a young Clint Eastwood's eyes and an effortlessly furtive manner. He eased his way through four scotches, smoked cigarettes like he was in a

Camel commercial, and was very much Mr. Control. In our 90-minute conversation, during which he allowed notes but no recording, he wished only to talk about Philby, but I decided to risk a question on Gorbachev.

When I asked what he thought of *glasnost* and *perestroika*, his facial expression gave me the answer. He had nothing positive to say about Gorbachev's policies throughout the interview. "You understand of course that the KGB is a conservative organization," he said. Its members would continue to be conservative, he added. At the same time, however, "the KGB is not only a most conservative organization. It is also a most loyal organization."

Yes, there was opposition to certain of Gorbachev's moves, but that did not mean the loyalty would wane. "Our organization consists mostly of clever people, you know, very clever people." Gorbachev's reputation was aided, he allowed, by his affiliation with the earlier Soviet leader, Yuri Andropov. Andropov had been KGB chief before becoming general secretary. Gorbachev had been one of Andropov's men.

Shortly after the interview, a Toronto advertising agent named Kirby Inwood arrived in Moscow to do battle with the KGB one on one. On a tourist trip to the Soviet Union in 1985, Inwood had met a woman – the tall, dark-haired Tanya Siderova. He fell in love and she got pregnant, and they were married in the Soviet Union in July 1986. A son, Misha, was born in September of the same year.

In December, Inwood was planning on moving his wife and child to Canada when he was told that they would not be able to join him. Tanya had worked previously as a radar technician. She knew defence secrets, the Soviets said.

No shrinking violet was Kirby Inwood, and he began a blistering, attack-dog p.r. campaign to have the Moscow decision overturned. He fired off letters to cabinet ministers, to the prime minister, to the editor of *Pravda*, to Mikhail Gorbachev. He followed up with newsletters to all media with capsule accounts of what was transpiring: "Glasnost is a fraud"; "Prime Minister condones violations to appease Soviets"; "Canadian baby world's youngest refusenik"; "30 cabinet ministers refuse to help."

Sensitive to the rage of publicity, Joe Clark and the Canadian embassy went to bat for Inwood. Initially they came up dry. These things take time, they told Inwood. But the Toronto man was in no humour for patience. He arrived in Moscow and, tornado on his heels, began hammering on KGB doors. He saw KGB agents in Moscow, in Leningrad, then back in Moscow again. He telephoned me to brief me on what had happened, and I joined him and Tanya for cognacs at a little bar on the tenth floor of the Intourist.

I had already spoken to Tanya Siderova on the telephone. She struck me then, and later when I met her, as one of the many Soviet women who had too many things going for them to want to stick around Russia. She was tall and reasonably attractive at this stage of the proceedings, and seemed intelligent and resilient. Soviet society didn't have much to offer someone like her, who also had the big plus of being able to speak English. The best way out for her kind was to hook up with a foreigner. It turned out to be her misfortune that her choice was Kirby Inwood.

In the Intourist we walked down a corridor, with Tanya leading the way and Kirby checking out her long legs from behind and saying, "Now you see why I want to get her out of here." In the bar he could hardly wait to tell the story of his jaw-to-jaw encounters with the KGB. None of them could promise much help in getting Tanya to Canada, and as the frustration built, Inwood finally shouted at one, "But what's all this stuff about openness and *glasnost* and a new climate under Gorbachev?"

The KGB man, according to the Inwood version, stared at him coldly through gold teeth and the smoke of a cigarette and countered, "*Glasnost* may be *glasnost*, Mr. Inwood. And Gorbachev may be Gorbachev. But the KGB is the KGB." Then, as the movies would have it, the spook pulled the cigarette from his mouth and stabbed it into the ashtray.

"I'm telling ya," said Inwood, "this guy was a dead ringer for Stalin."

Inwood really enjoyed telling that anecdote. He said he was convinced that the Kremlin would let Tanya and Misha go but that everything was being blocked by the security arm, by "the guys who are KGB right down to the bottom of their plastic shoes." Tanya Siderova agreed. Despite Gorbachev's efforts, she said, "the KGB still has the power."

Dealing with the secret police and the Soviet bureaucracy, said Inwood, "has been worse than dealing with the Mexican post office." He had been led to believe, at his first meeting with KGB agent Smorodin in Moscow, that all would be well. "He said he had all the papers necessary to make a decision and that it would be made in a week. He was very positive. He talked about how our case broke his heart and how he loved Canada and how everything would be okay. It was all suck, suck, suck. I mean, he conned me 100 percent. I believed him."

Inwood's on-the-record tirade lasted more than an hour. Every insult to the KGB was in *The Globe and Mail* in a front-page story the next day. If ever Kirby had overstepped the bounds of prudence, I thought, he had done it now. Now, I thought, there was almost no chance that he would get his wife and child out.

But these were indeed new times in the Soviet Union. A few months later the Soviets decided they'd had enough of Inwood's ranting. They decided that Tanya suddenly no longer possessed state secrets and that she and Misha could go home to loving Kirby in Toronto. The wife and son arrived to a triumphant welcome in Montreal, Quebec. The Canadian media, which put out so many sob stories about the separation of this loving couple of Tanya and Kirby, gave the homecoming front-page coverage. The politicians patted themselves on the back for a job well done. Tanya Siderova had been rescued from the Soviet dungeon and could now enjoy happiness everlasting in the land of silk and money.

Within two weeks of the landing, however, the story came to a tragic, tabloid-style end. Kirby Inwood, a man whose history with women had long been suspect, flew into a rage and beat up Tanya and the child. He was charged with assault and, in one of Canada's most notorious court cases, convicted. In Moscow, the newspapers ran the story, and the Soviet emigration authorities – the guys who were KGB right down to the bottoms of their plastic shoes – got the last laugh.

16/Telling It Like It Is

HE DIDN'T HAVE any background in journalism. His experience was limited to the overseer's role, which he had exercised as first secretary for the Stavropol region. But in the business of the media, as in many aspects of life, Mikhail Gorbachev demonstrated unusually good intuition.

Being a correspondent, I was struck one day by the message he was delivering to Soviet journalists. He was telling them not to regurgitate dry facts but to get underneath the story, to bring across the emotion of the Soviet people, their depth of suffering. It was the type of advice a reporter might hear from a good newspaper editor – not from your average politician, especially a Soviet leader.

"It is impossible to write of the people's destiny in a formal, bureaucratic, soulless way," the general secretary had recently told a group of journalists. "Sometimes a true to life picture is presented, but the author writes it in such a way as if the pain of the people is not sensed.

"If you remember your people always, if you write with an anguished heart of the grimmest things, then surely something will emerge which in the long run will contain a lesson. [There will be] a sense of involvement in the destiny of the people and the care that their life should be better. I am not going to teach you. I simply address your hearts and minds."

I read this aloud in my office one day and then praised it to Valya, a Russian acquaintance. I had known her for some time and remembered particularly her summary comment on Soviet history: "Stalin kept the masses at bay by fear, Brezhnev by vodka and Gorbachev by high-sounding ideas and promises." Valya was involved in various artistic endeavours. Though not a dissident, she shared the Russians' deep cynicism about the future, about whether Gorbachev could really change their lot. Many Russians would talk as if all was well, but deeper down they despaired. After what they'd been through, optimism didn't come easy.

In her snappish, pointed way, Valya objected to my praise of Gorbachev. "Yes, you say that, but you don't know about these people and how we have been treated. When I was starving and my son was starving, those bastards were eating caviar!"

I argued against forming a judgment of the Kremlin's present leader by forever dredging up facts of long-gone history. This is where the weakness lay in the analyses of too many Western historians. Among the leading Sovietologists in the United States, only Stephen Cohen of Princeton and Jerry Hough of Duke had propounded the view that substantial liberalization of the type Gorbachev was undertaking was possible in the Soviet Union. The other Russian experts had become too closed-minded to imagine that a new Soviet man could arrive and could succeed. In their analyses all Russians were inextricably trapped by their past. None could escape or start anew, as Lenin himself had done. For the longest time these experts would refuse to believe that Mikhail Gorbachev was a reality, because to admit as much would be to say that they had been wrong for most of their lives.

While Valya acknowledged that Gorbachev possessed greater human values, she also felt, as did others, that one man was not enough. "What we need for there to be real change in this country is to spill some blood," she conjectured. "There comes a time when the status quo reaches the point where more than good minds are needed." She and her intellectual friends didn't want too much bloodshed – only enough. "For fundamental change anywhere, there usually has to be some."

I went back to reading Gorbachev's advice to the journalists, recalling that he was not a late convert to *glasnost* but had, in fact, demonstrated a new attitude to the press during his Stavropol days. "You should reform yourselves," he told them now in Moscow.

"The media is an instrument of *perestroika* and to be an effective instrument, it should undergo restructuring just like the entire society. We say that there is no monopoly on criticism. Therefore the press itself can't be exempt."

Gorbachev had made substantial progress by this time in moving the Soviet media away from its post-1917 role as the State's public-relations agency. In 1917, when the government was taking over everything, it was decided, after impassioned debate, that the press had to be included. "The rule of democracy which is being established in Russia," Trotsky argued, "demands that the domination of the press by private property must be abolished, just as the domination of industry by private property [must be abolished]." If there was any sanity in that kind of reasoning, it was ravaged by Stalin and subsequent Kremlin leaders, who made the press their servant.

Gorbachev invited criticism not only of his society but also of himself. He told the writers that he needed it and had to be prepared to react maturely to it. "Nothing can compromise a leader more than repudiating a person for criticizing him," he said, in direct refutation of the Stalin creed. But despite his apparent willingness to be censured, the Soviet journalists weren't prepared to test him, even in the new era of *glasnost*. The only criticism I had seen of Gorbachev by name in the Soviet press was in a newspaper, in a letter to the editor, and concerned the outcome of the Reykjavik summit. The reader wrote that he should have compromised on the question of Ronald Reagan's SDI in order to gain something from the summit. It stood out because as a rule, *glasnost* or no *glasnost*, the Soviet press didn't question the Kremlin's foreign policy. The only other time I saw them do so was in another letter to the editor: an American youth wrote in accusing the Kremlin of subjugating Eastern Europe – this while all East Bloc leaders were in Moscow to celebrate the 70th anniversary of the Bolshevik Revolution.

In the late 1980s the country's scribes were leaving behind the days when, according to Mikhail Nenashev, a former editor of *Sovyetskaya Rossiya*, one-third of an editor's time was taken up receiving instructions from his Communist Party first secretary. These calls, the purpose of which was to upbraid the editor for any criticism run in his newspaper, had almost completely ceased by

1986, Nenashev said. By 1987 Soviet newspapers, in particular the central papers, were unleashing a daily barrage of criticisms of their society's domestic failings. The media was becoming what Gorbachev wanted it to become – the engine of change. The journalism was investigative, blunt, and, in many cases, of a highly professional calibre. Given that decades had been spent covering up the society's afflictions, the possibilities for ground-breaking stories were endless.

The *glasnost* press was not a free press, it was still state-owned and for that reason subject to the whim of the politicians in the Politburo and Central Committee apparatus. The opened valve of criticism would soon be shut, most speculated, if a conservative like Yegor Ligachev came to power. It was the hope of the Soviet intelligentsia, therefore, that Gorbachev could last long enough to make press freedom an integral part of the culture, too deeply entrenched to reverse.

As it stood, *glasnost* was defective in many ways. It can be argued that a state-owned press, such as Canada's CBC, can report freely; but the Soviet press was no CBC. Politburo members were never criticized by name in the Soviet media. The focus of most press criticism was on the failings of the previous regime; and as I have mentioned, Soviet foreign policy was practically immune.

Gorbachev wanted a more honest press so that the Soviet people could see themselves and their country in a realistic light. In addition, he wanted the Soviet people to have a more realistic view of other peoples. This latter goal required a reversal in media thinking. Soviet correspondents had always looked at the world through a filter of negative, anticapitalist stereotypes, and reported it that way. The United States, according to their guiding perspective, was an imperialist haven of racism, unemployment, homelessness, drugs, and record crime rates. Each superpower emphasized the negative when reporting on the other. But the Soviet press, at least until well into Gorbachev's stewardship, was far less objective than the American one.

With the media reforms came Soviet criticisms of their own foreign correspondents. In the spring of 1987, Fyodor Burlatsky, a leading Soviet analyst and policy maker, argued that the Soviet media's misrepresentations of the West had been damaging to their own country – that the Soviet Union's backwardness in matters technological was partly a result of having kept the news of the West's high-tech revolution hidden from the Soviet people.

"We did not inform the public about the new technological revolution which was rapidly developing in Japan, the U.S.A., and Western Europe since the mid-1970s," he said, "and of the revolution in minicomputers, new means of communication, new centres of economic power in Brazil, Argentina, Singapore.

"We cannot effectively solve the problems of our economic development until we break out of our isolation with regard to information . . . until the Soviet people are given the opportunity to compare their own work and their own professional skills with those of the workers, farmers, scientists in the West. While we were frequently patting ourselves on the back . . . the whole world was rapidly developing all around us."[1]

Burlatsky recommended more articles from foreign correspondents on the employed instead of the unemployed, on culture instead of cults, on progressive Western figures instead of reactionary ones. His words, and those of others, soon had some impact. The West began getting a more positive Soviet press than ever, while at the same time the Soviet domestic reporters were painting their own country black. The enemy was getting some credit, the home side was taking a beating. It was Gorbachev-style realism.

Whatever the limits of *glasnost*, the changes that policy had wrought in little more than two years were startling. The thaw under Khrushchev hardly approached the one now being inspired by Gorbachev. One of the world's most sycophantic presses was suddenly open and adversarial. Protests on the streets, in the republics, were now possible. On television, foreign leaders could lecture the Soviets on the joys of capitalism. Fewer and fewer foreign radio transmissions were subject to jamming. Politburo members such as Eduard Shevardnadze held press conferences. Soviet authors finally got their *Dr. Zhivago*s published. Dissidents were set free. Great figures of history, denied their true place by Stalin, were rehabilitated.

Vitaly Korotich, the Ukrainian poet whom Gorbachev had invited over for late-night discussions, became the kind of publisher the Soviet leader had envisioned. As editor of *Ogonyok*, Korotich published Pasternak's *Dr. Zhivago*, he published *Children of the Arbat*, the great novel of Stalinist terror, he exposed privileges of the Soviet leadership, he exposed how Soviet police tortured a criminal suspect, he exposed corruption. About the only things he wouldn't touch were issues of national security and the works of Aleksandr Solzhenitsyn, who, in Korotich's view, was "a fool. He is not a writer but a political opponent."

While the print media experienced a renaissance, changes came a little more slowly at first to the outmoded Soviet television system. (In the late 1980s the Soviet population, which was fully literate, was still old-fashioned enough to cherish the printed word – it was one of the things to be admired about the country.) It being state television (as opposed to commercial), the purpose of Soviet programming was not to entertain but to educate. That meant no mindless sitcoms, no sex, little heavy-duty violence (except in films glorifying the war), and virtually no commercials.

The average North American, raised on a heavy TV diet, is told every 15 minutes in a battery of TV commercials to want something. To want new clothes, to want new cars, to want, want, want. Commercial-free television means the Soviets do not have the theology of materialism pounded into them with such relentlessness. There is more room in the mind for other values.

The Soviet TV staples were political discussions, history movies, classical music, sports programs, and ballet. In 1987 on a typical day, the TV viewer in Moscow would find the following: a documentary on agriculture, a discussion show called *The Human Being and the Law*, a Soviet symphony, a hockey game, a folk-dancing concert, a program called *Our Garden*, a show on science-prize winners, highlights of Lenin's speeches, a talk show called *Searchlight on Perestroika*, a night story for children, a short on Angola, a rock-music special, and a report on the World Chess Championship from Spain. Livening up the fare would be the beautiful female program announcers, who introduced the programs with utter elegance and faultless vocal precision. By 1988, with the modern world moving in, many males, of equal perfection, were doing that job as well.

By this time Gorbachev's media reforms were beginning to have an impact on television. On Friday nights a public-affairs show called *Vzglad* ("Viewpoint") was at its best a *60 Minutes*, at other times a *Geraldo*. Different episodes exposed corruption scandals in the Central Asian republics, provided an objective portrait of the lives of Soviet soldiers in Afghanistan, examined AIDS, focussed on demonstrators fighting police in Pushkin Square. To do this type of television had been the career dream of *Vzglad*'s producer, Anatole Lysenko. Fifteen years earlier he had proposed to do a show called *In Your Kitchen*. The kitchen was where Soviets talked about the things that concerned them most – money, politics, sex, life, death. Lysenko wanted to reflect their views. But this was the Brezhnev era. His proposal was rejected.[2]

By 1988 live satellite hook-ups showed American families talking to Soviet families, and American legislators talking to Soviet legislators. Public-affairs programs showed citizens debating Politburo figures at a Party Congress, and protesters waving anti-Kremlin posters at a demonstration in some far-off republic.

The nightly Soviet news hour, which began at nine p.m., was the most important telecast of every day. All the major channels across the country showed the one-and-the-same-program – *Vremya*, or "Time."

Though modernizing quickly, *Vremya* was not a North American-style news hour. When I arrived in Moscow I could count on virtually every *Vremya* telecast beginning with the same lengthy segment – the farm segment. Nothing but shots of tractors and threshing machines working the fields. After a few seconds of "vrooooms" and "whrrrrs," the camera would zoom in on Boris or whomever and show him working up a frenzy. The heavy-voiced reporter would talk about how Boris was building socialism, meeting the plan, providing an example to everyone. Then, after a couple of minutes of discussion about the fields and more tractor close-ups, it would be on to the lesser news of the day.

After months of witnessing these monotonous lead-ins, I telephoned a *Vremya* producer to ask him about it. "Why, every single night. . . ?" The producer took offence. "This is a tactless and rude question," he replied. The news on agriculture was the most important news of all for the country, he explained, and merited top billing all the time.

With time, the prevalence of tractors diminished somewhat and *Vremya* started to take on a more Western-style format. But it was not about to go American in a big hurry. Unlike in the West, where leaders' speeches are usually reduced to 20-second clips, Soviet viewers got the full gavel-to-gavel rendition whenever Gorbachev went to the podium. No matter that the speech might run for an hour or more – it was the lead item on *Vremya*, upstaging even the farm-belt segment, to which *Vremya* would cut directly after. When Gorbachev was touring the countryside, the TV news carried his streetside chats and his town meetings as well as his speeches. Sometimes it would be almost two hours before the rest of the news came on. As well, the full transcript of his address would be in almost every newspaper the next day. As for Politburo figures, the newscast would often carry five or ten minutes of their speeches. But here it was harder to predict.

One night, having hurriedly switched my dial away from *The Human Being and the Law*, I saw several leading literary figures paying tribute to Vladimir Vysotsky, the late poet, singer, and actor. The gravel-voiced Vysotsky was an anti-establishment champion who exposed deception, corruption, repression. Alexei German, the Soviet film director, called him "an antidote to every falsity." Vysotsky once wrote a song with a line referring to himself: "Look now, there he goes again without a safety net." Predictably, he ran afoul of Brezhnev's authorities, who no longer published his poems or produced his records. Then Vysotsky died, at only 43.

Now, on Gorbachev-era television, he was getting the full state-rehabilitation treatment and being awarded a posthumous prize for his art. The TV show was a splendid tribute. Soviet times had changed. A few days later, however, Vysotsky's widow said she was disgusted by the hypocrisy of those who now were praising him. When he was out of favour, she went on, they wouldn't touch him.

Another night a Soviet censor, Vladimir Solodin, appeared on the screen. He confessed to his role in banning all great books and works of art that didn't support Kremlin thought. The restrictions had been put in place under Stalin, he explained, out of fear of independent thinking.

"I took a very active part in this work," he said. "We looked for anything that did not correspond to an official view at the time. Often the instructions came down from the offices of the [Communist Party] Central Committee." Solodin said that tens of thousands of titles had been barred from release to the general public. Under Gorbachev, he said, more than 90 percent of those titles were now being made available; most of what was still being prohibited was either anti-Semitic or violently nationalistic.

"I often felt sad," confessed the censor, reflecting on a life of saying no. "It wasn't pleasant work."

All the reforms Gorbachev had introduced in the preceding few months – human rights, media reforms, decentralization, the proposal for multicandidate elections, and the like – could be listed under the catchword that Gorbachev was now beginning to use frequently – democratization. He wasn't moving toward democracy in its Western, multiparty sense, but the thrust of his reforms was toward freedom and choice.

It was as if Gorbachev had read a memorandum that had been written in the spring of 1970 by three eminent Soviets – Roy Medvedev, Andrei Sakharov, and Valery Turchin. This astonishingly prescient memo, uncovered by the British author Anthony Barnett in *samizdat* (the underground press), was an analysis of the decline of the Soviet Union complete with prescribed remedy. It was written to Leonid Brezhnev, Premier Alexei Kosygin, and N.V. Podgorny of the Presidium of the Supreme Soviet. In part, it read as follows:[3]

> *Dear Comrades,*
> *At present there is an urgent need to carry out a series of measures directed toward the further democratization of our country's life.... Without democratization our society will not be able to solve the problems now facing it, and will not be able to develop in a normal manner....*
>
> *Over the past decade menacing signs of disorder and stagnation have begun to show themselves in the economy, the roots of which go back to an earlier period and are very deeply embedded. There is an uninterrupted decline in the rate of growth in the national income. The gap between what is necessary for normal development and the new productive forces actually being introduced is growing wider.*

In addition to many mistakes in industry and agriculture, there is intolerable procrastination about finding solutions to urgent problems. . . . Signs of corruption are becoming more and more noticeable in a number of places. In the work of scientific and scientific-technical organizations, bureaucratism, departmentalism, a formal attitude toward one's tasks and lack of initiative are becoming more and more pronounced.

The memo discussed the tumbling productivity of labour and how the Soviets were being vastly outstripped in computer technology by the Americans.

Our stock of computers is one percent of that of the United States and with respect to the application of the electronic computer, the gap is so great that it is impossible even to measure it. We simply live in another age. . . .

What is wrong? Why have we not only failed to be the pioneers of the second industrial revolution, but have in fact found ourselves incapable of keeping pace with the developed capitalist countries? Is it possible that socialism provides fewer opportunities for the development of productive forces than capitalism? Or that in the economic competition between capitalism and socialism, capitalism is winning?

Of course not! The source of our difficulties does not lie in the socialist system, but on the contrary . . . the source lies in the antidemocratic traditions and norms of public life established in the Stalin era, which have not been decisively eliminated to this day.

Non-economic coercion, limitations on the exchange of information, restrictions on intellectual freedom, and other examples of the antidemocratic distortion of socialism which took place under Stalin were accepted in our country as an overhead expense of the industrialization process. . . . But there is no doubt that since the beginning of the second industrial revolution these phenomena have become a decisive economic factor; they have become the main brake on the development of the productive forces in this country. . . .

These problems cannot be resolved by one or several persons holding power and "knowing everything." These problems demand the creative participation of millions of people on all levels of the economic system.

. . . However, we encounter certain insurmountable obstacles on the road towards the free exchange of ideas and information. Truthful information

about our shortcomings and negative manifestations is hushed up on the grounds that it "may be used by enemy propaganda." Exchange of information with foreign countries is restricted for fear of penetration by an enemy ideology. Theoretical generalizations and practical proposals, if they seem too bold to some individuals, are nipped in the bud without any discussion because of the fear that they might "undermine our foundations." An obvious lack of confidence in creative thinking, critical and energetic individuals is to be seen here. . . .

Limitations on freedom of information mean that not only is it more difficult to control the leaders, not only is the initiative of the people undermined but that even the intermediate level of leadership is deprived of rights and information, and these people are transformed into passive time servers and bureaucrats. The leaders in the highest government bodies receive information that is incomplete, with the rough spots glossed over; hence they are deprived of the opportunity to utilize effectively the authority they have.

. . . An overwhelming part of the intelligentsia and the youth recognize the need for democratization, and the need for it to be cautious and gradual, but they cannot understand and justify measures of a patently antidemocratic nature. And indeed, how can one justify the confinement in prisons, camps and insane asylums of people who hold oppositionist views but whose opposition stands on legal ground, in the area of ideas and convictions? In many instances there was no opposition involved, but only a striving for information, or simply a courageous and unprejudiced discussion of important social questions. The imprisonment of writers for what they have written is inadmissible. . . .

Democratization, with its fullness of information and clash of ideas, must restore to our ideological life its dynamism and creativity – in the social sciences, art and propaganda. . . .

Carrying out democratization is not an easy process. Its normal development would be threatened from one direction by individualist and anti-socialist forces, and from the other by supporters of a "strong state". . . . But we must realize that there is no other solution for our country.

There followed a proposal, in draft, of a program to be carried out over a five-year period. The program's measures included the halting of interference in foreign radio broadcasts, a broadening of international communications, amnesty for political prisoners, public supervision of all prison camps and psychiatric institutions, and multicandidate elections.

Sakharov, Medvedev, and Turchin argued that democratization would have beneficial consequences for the Soviet Union internationally:

> *The possibility for peaceful co-existence and international cooperation would grow, the forces of peace and social progress would be strengthened. . . .*
>
> *What is in store for our nation if it does not take the course toward democratization? Its fate would be to lag behind the capitalist countries and gradually become a second-rate provincial power. . . . Economic stagnation, lag in our rate of growth, coupled with an unrealistic foreign policy on all continents, can lead to catastrophic consequences for the country.*

The memorandum was ignored by Brezhnev and his high command. Its authors were later incarcerated or put under special watch for speaking out in the vein represented in the memo. Seventeen years later, however – maybe too late – its contents were coincidentally appearing in Gorbachev's speeches. The memo's analysis, from the description of economic stagnation to the observation that socialism itself wasn't to blame, paralleled the new leader's thinking; its recommendations became, in most cases, Gorbachev's recommendations.

It is unlikely Gorbachev ever saw the memo, but right down to the last line, it inadvertently had become his manifesto. "Dear comrades," that last line said, "there is no other way out of the difficulties now facing our country except the course toward democratization." Or, as Gorbachev later put it, "we need democracy like we need air."

17/Eleven Time Zones

INA, MY SOVIET secretary, would always tell me to get out of the office, get out of Moscow. "There are 11 time zones in our country. You can't base your judgments only on what the people are saying in the capital." Ina had an ulterior motive for all this: she wanted the boss out of town. But her point was well taken, and I drew up plans for a grand tour of the heartlands and hinterlands of the country twice as large as any other.

I would go on a car trip, driving south through old Russia, through forests and antiquated villages where the great writers had lived. I would journey to Central Asia to Dushanbe, where in January it was warm enough for the Soviets to sit outside and drink tea. Following that, an excursion beyond Siberia to the very far reaches of the northeast, where the Soviet Union almost nudges North America.

Ina was delighted, while the driver of the office car, Valery Vasechkin, was not so keen. He had to do the tour of old Russia with me, driving the icy, deteriorated highways, competing for space with an endless caravan of dark, swaying trucks. As a rule, Russians didn't drive outside the cities much in the winter. It was too dangerous. The car could break down because of the desolate cold or the bad conditions, and the risk of serious accident was too high. Elizabeth Todd, a Scot who taught kindergarten at Moscow's Anglo-American School, discovered the dangers of driving outside the city centre one night when her little car was humming along and suddenly dropped several feet into an unmarked pit. It left her barely conscious. Fortunately, the workmen had left a ladder in the ditch, and she was ultimately able to climb to safety.

Valery always felt sad that *The Globe and Mail* had purchased a domestic Volga instead of a sleek foreign product. By Russian standards the Volga was a fine automobile, but that didn't mean much. In the 1980s the Soviets, who could build magnificent rockets, had not yet learned to produce a car that ran much better than a stagecoach. The *Globe*'s was a dowdy, cream-coloured sedan which had a distinct growling sound. By the time Valery started revving her up for the trip south, it was only a year old but already had made almost as many trips to the repair shop as to the office. I had bought it spanking new in the mid-winter of 1985, off an outdoor lot where I had to scrape away the snow and ice for 20 minutes to determine its colour. The Volga survived its first week on the road nicely. But in the second Valery presented me with a long list of desperately needed repairs. Even the knobs on the dashboard were starting to fall off. The radio knob fell, the windshield-wiper knob fell, the plastic air vents fell.

For Valery, as for most other chauffeurs, the car was his life, his symbol of status in a society which, under its egalitarian cloak, was exceedingly status-conscious. While Valery choked along in the Volga, the other correspondents' drivers would tear by in their megahorsepower products with undisguised conceit. Valery kept telling me, "We need some *perestroika*, – a new car." A correspondent, he argued, was a man of prominence, someone who deserved only the best, "a Mercedes." I agreed, of course, but advised that he would either have to arrange for the Volga to be stolen or else crash it into a telephone pole. Then head office would have to get us a new car.

Once we had driven beyond Moscow's grimy perimeter,[1] we were greeted by the Russian rural landscape I had read about – an immense expanse of winter white, snowflakes shining like a billion diamonds, stands of tall silver birches, seemingly ready to march in formation, proudly saluting the day. We were soon driving through ancient hamlets where the Volga's wheels threw up water over *babushkas* in horse-drawn carts. They were taking milk to the villagers. They glared with disdain at technology's intrusion.

At the town of Chekhov, where the famous Russian playwright wrote *The Seagull* and *The Man Who Lived in a Shell*, our entry was blocked by a highway militiaman, who said we needed written permission from Moscow. After phone calls to the foreign ministry solved the problem, we drove past a tank monument, a Lada repair shop, a church with peeling domes, and a billboard that read, *Decisions of the 27th Party Congress – Let's Fulfill Them Comrades*. At the entrance to Chekhov's residence a foul-humoured policeman turned us around, pointed us down the highway, and then followed us to make sure we got out of his territory.

We drove further into rural life and further into the 19th century. We saw Russians walking slowly to their cottages, carrying pails of water from poles across their shoulders. Little children wrapped in thick brown fur coats – they always dressed better than their elders – trundled along like bear cubs, faces red from the frost. The homes, collapsing log cabins that sloped with the terrain, were painted charmingly in peacock blues, mustard yellows, and a variety of greens.

Valery didn't enjoy my remarks about the backward look of the countryside. A strong patriot, he wanted me to see the modern things, and was relieved when we came to an area where new brick houses were under construction. "Look at that," he enthused. "Look at the beautiful homes they are building in our country."

The further we drove, the more distant seemed the news from Moscow. In the villages, peasants said they had heard talk of big change but that big change was for the cities, not them. In Kromy, founded in 1147 and now beginning to make its break with the Middle Ages, the horse still seemed to be the main mode of transport. "This is the good life," said Valery, smoking a Yaba, his favourite Russian cigarette. While looking for TV aerials, I asked him what people did at night. "The club," he said. "They go to the club, or they read books, or they talk."

When Yasnaya Polyana, the estate of Leo Tolstoy, came into view, it reminded me, with its servants' quarters and tree-lined pathways, of George Washington's estate at Mount Vernon, Virginia. It was here that Tolstoy wrote *War and Peace* and *Anna Karenina*. His grave is on a hillock on a lawn, marked by no monument, tombstone, or plaque, only by flowers and fir branches brought by visitors. On this day the entire splendid property was deserted except for a Russian woman who asked that I take her picture with a camera that looked vintage Louis Daguerre. She talked of the great Russia of Tolstoy's time and how everything had changed for the worse.

It was only about three hours by car from Moscow. Tolstoy walked the distance many times, but our Volga was already showing signs of stress. When Valery sounded the horn, it refused to stop blowing. Finally he got it under control, but after that it sounded off whenever so disposed.

At the hotel in Orel, a city founded by Ivan the Terrible, Valery paid three roubles – about six dollars – for his room because he was Russian, and I paid 60 dollars for mine because I was a foreigner. Tired, and wanting a quiet meal, I found my way to a dining lounge that looked peaceful enough. But within five minutes the battering-ram sound of the band began, and all the diners were up between the tables, bounding around like football linemen in training. After an anemic salad, a slab of meat arrived at the table wearing a look that said, "If you eat me, you're crazy." I ate it.

"The food's not as good here as in Moscow," Valery warned. In the morning we waited in the hotel restaurant for a breakfast that never arrived. Enough people were staffing the kitchen, but they were all quarrelling too intensely to notice us. Outside the hotel Russians talked derisively of Gorbachev's alcohol restrictions and showed little enthusiasm for the highly touted reforms. "Things don't change here," one man said. Then he added, despite the surrounding evidence of low living standards, "People aren't in a hurry to change. They're used to the ways." In the small towns, it seemed that way: everything was backward, self-contained, sheltered from the technological revolution. The pressures of modern living hadn't touched these people yet; they went about their business quite oblivious to any different life and quite undemanding of one. When Valery said, "This is the good life," he meant it. When I asked one villager about the reform talk back in Moscow, he was puzzled. "Oh, that stuff," he said. "That stuff is for the intelligentsia."

On the highway, conditions worsened. The trucks bounced and wobbled and relentlessly spewed their heavy black exhaust. The cracks in the pavement got deeper, the road got narrower, and the sun played blindingly off the snowbanks. While going down an incline, the Volga bounded so high off a series of mounds and holes that it almost flipped over. The remains of three accidents were visible ahead. Standing off in the snow was what looked like yet another war monument. Actually it was the skeleton of a bus.

Valery wanted to stop at the site of the Battle of Kursk. Here, in 1943, the Germans and the Soviets fought what is regarded as the biggest tank battle in military history. It involved more than 1,500 tanks and armoured vehicles and resulted in a Soviet victory. Wearing only a thin windbreaker in a desperately cold wind, Valery stood silently for minutes on the battlefield, smoking a cigarette and looking as proud as I ever saw him.

He stopped for gasoline a few kilometres down the highway. Someone in the station told him that the attendants had gone home for dinner. It didn't surprise him. He drove around for another hour till he found a station where the men manning the petrol were on the job. Soon the Volga was at the Ukrainian border. The first building in view there looked modern, warm, and cozy. "That's it," said Valery, even though Kharkov, our destination, was still a long way off. He meant that we were out of old Russia and back in the 20th century.

The Kursk battlefield was one example of the Russians' pre-occupation with war history. But the city of Voronezh, 700 kilometres southeast of Moscow, was a better lesson in that, and in the region's conservative nature, and in how difficult it would be for Gorbachev to forge any kind of real change.

After I returned from the car journey I flew to Voronezh, a city of almost one million which is bonded to war history. Peter the Great's flotillas were constructed here; Voronezh played a major role in stopping Napoleon in 1812. After the 1917 revolution it was one of the first cities where Soviet power was proclaimed. Then came the Great Patriotic War – as the Russians call the Second World War – with its unimaginable devastation. Before the war the population of Voronezh was 275,000; after, less than 1,000. Forty-five thousand residents were killed, 75,000 injured, and the rest evacuated; 90 percent of the city's buildings were destroyed.

The war was now more than four decades past, and Mikhail Gorbachev had begun a self-proclaimed revolution, but in Voronezh those things didn't seem to matter. In Voronezh, Topic A was still the war. I took a tour of the city from Pyotr Pavlovich, its energetic architect, who had helped rebuild Voronezh in the model of so many Russian cities – clean, perpendicular lines with broad, tree-lined boulevards; a cold, empty central square dominated by a bronze of Lenin.

Pavlovich was full of life, but his tour turned into a toast of the war dead. "Now here's the Valley of Death," he said, pointing to the bank of an artificial lake where the bodies had once been stacked four high. Of the 150 mass war graves in Voronezh, it was the biggest. "And here's the line of glory. This is where the Germans were finally stopped."

His car wheeled up to a big marble monument, on which the names of all who died in the war were inscribed. A local woman who was accompanying us almost broke down here, and Pavlovich spoke of how good the people of Voronezh were at mourning. He recalled watching his first Victory Day in the city: "Almost everyone carries flowers to the graves. The emotion I saw here on the streets that day almost frightened me. I hadn't seen anything quite like it before."

Voronezh was steeped in the values of the past. At the city's newspaper offices I asked the editors about the changes and planned changes under Gorbachev. None had stirred much excitement among the public, they reported. As for Gorbachev's freeing of the political prisoners, the people of patriotic Voronezh were categorically opposed. After all, these dissidents had criticized the motherland, hadn't they? In reference to Sakharov's release, one editor told me that "nobody was enthusiastic." Not one letter in favour, chimed another: "The measures that were taken against Sakharov by the government were fair. If a person allows himself activities against his motherland it is not correct."

Another prominent dissident, Yuri Orlov, had just been released, and when his name came up it set off a scornful buzz around the editors' table. Orlov, a 62-year-old physicist, had been allowed to leave the country the previous autumn, after seven years in a labour camp and a period of internal exile. He'd been charged with anti-Soviet agitation. "Orlov gave secrets to the West," said one of the men. "Our country must defend itself." These were sincere newspapermen of middle age or older. They had spent their lives in the provinces, far from Moscow, and had been highly susceptible to the only view of the dissidents the pre-*glasnost* press allowed – the old Kremlin view.

As indoctrinated conservatives, they were having difficulty coming to grips with Mikhail Gorbachev's new-deal Communism. On media policy, the general secretary had stated that no zones should be closed to criticism. Yet when they had finished disparaging the dissidents and I asked if they were questioning Politburo decisions and debating Kremlin foreign policy in their pages, they looked rather puzzled. The editor-in-chief said their criticism didn't extend to the top level. "And what our government says on foreign matters, we support it." Remembering Gorbachev's move to have democratic elections spread to plants and businesses, I asked him if he would be opening his position to elected challenge from the newsroom. He told me he didn't think so.

In the evening a plump young schoolteacher named Olya talked about how treadmilled her life had become. Yet she couldn't get excited about prospects for change. Being able to criticize the system more than before didn't really interest her. "But why would we want to criticize the foreign policy of our government?" she asked. " . . . The foreign policy of our government is peace. How can we criticize that? We all want peace."

I went to the opera with one of the city's party bosses and a couple of other officials. At intermission, while the regular folk lined up for tasteless beverages in the foyer, we made our way to a special chamber reserved for the elite. Cognac, vodka, and other delicacies were served to us. At the next intermission our private party continued. The next night, over dinner, we spent many moments toasting the war dead of Voronezh. One of the party bosses had travelled West and spoke of how deeply he had been impressed. He saw the Gorbachev changes as a bid to put an end to the sloth ethic. "We know that in the West they've been working harder than we have here. Now we have to change that."

In the Russian heartland people were taking slowly to the winds of change. In the hinterlands it was worse. On the country's southern edge, in Dushanbe, capital of the out-of-the-way Tadzhik Republic, the god was neither Lenin nor Gorbachev but the prophet Mohammed.

Ancient-looking men in turbans sat on cots in the big, open tea houses sipping herbs all day long. Many not so old did the same, leaving one to wonder who was working in the fields. It was January, but beneath the mulberry and the poplars, Dushanbe had the look of a lazy, hazy Asia day. Anyone dropped here unknowingly wouldn't have guessed he was in the Soviet Union. Among the buzzwords rising from the mosques, *perestroika* was not one.

The Tadzhik Republic is tucked in close to China, Pakistan, and Afghanistan. It was once the conquered ground of Genghis Khan, Tamerlane, and Alexander the Great. It passed from Persian to Soviet hands in the 1920s but has remained Farsi in speech, and Moslem in religion, and non-Russian in population. Only ten percent of the people are Russian, some of them are the militiamen, who patrol Dushanbe's streets in big coats, looking jarringly incongruous against the backdrop of turbanned tea drinkers.

In these days of January 1987, tension was spreading across the Central Asian republics owing to a rare outbreak, weeks earlier, of violent protest in Alma-Ata, capital of the Kazakh Republic. It was a forerunner of what was to become one of Mikhail Gorbachev's most critical problems – nationalism in the republics. The rioting in Alma-Ata, which saw more than 200 people injured in street fighting between Kazakhs and ethnic Russians, had been touched off by a decision of Gorbachev's to replace the Kazakhs' corrupt native-son leader, Dinmukhamed Kunayev, with a Russian. Some reports suggested that Kunayev supporters, thriving off his corrupt regime, had organized the outburst. Others suggested that drunken students were behind it. Still others presented a more ominous scenario – Moslem nationalism boiling over.

The population of the Central Asian republics was predominantly Moslem, and expanding rapidly due to a birth rate much higher than that of the rest of the country. In the wake of Alma-Ata, Moscow expanded its pro-atheism campaign to counter the growth of Islam. The Moslems' leader in the Tadzhik Republic, Khodzi Kolonzada-Kazi, said he would fight back. Outside his mosque, in dark robes and black patent-leather boots, he spoke to me while two assistants took notes to make sure I got what he said straight. The new atheism drive was aimed at religion generally, he said, rather than specifically against the Moslems. "But if the atheists, who do not know our religion, start saying things against it, we will protest and we will call for countermeasures against such actions."

Everyone I interviewed attested to the growing strength of religion in Dushanbe, but none foresaw it getting out of control. The threat to the stability of the Soviet empire in Central Asia was tempered somewhat by the relative absence of poverty. The Tadzhiks, while suffering from a shortage of schools and hospitals, had only to look at the turmoil in some of the nearby Islamic states to know that in terms of shelter, employment, food, literacy, and stability, they were not doing so badly.

I stopped Irina Kolosova, a Russian student attending university in Dushanbe, while she was strolling down a main street. All was normal between the Russians and the Moslems in Dushanbe, she said. "It was a great surprise to me to learn about what happened in Alma-Ata, to learn that the action was against the Russians there. I couldn't understand it."

Like other Western correspondents, I was barred from entering Alma-Ata at the time. By visiting a neighbouring republic I was trying to get more on the story than I could from Moscow. In this respect I considered it good fortune when I was seated one night at a crowded restaurant with a group that included a Russian army officer.

My three companions were the officer, an attractive, blond Russian woman, and another Russian with a gentlemanly smile. The demeanour of the latter suggested that he was out to break the Soviet drinking record. To accompany his Soviet *haute cuisine*, he had in front of him a pitcher of beer, a bottle of red wine, and the biggest bottle of champagne I had ever seen.

The army officer, late twenties, had arrived with a bit of

swagger. He was handsome and cocky, with wavy black hair, the odd well-placed pimple, and sure eyes. When by mistake I alluded to him as a *soldat*, or soldier, he brazenly countered, "*Offeeetzair!*" and demanded to know who I was. In a jesting tone I told him I was a spy from the West. He picked up on it right away: "And yes, I'm with the KGB. I know that all you in the West are told by your propagandists that every Russian works for the KGB." He threw up his chin in disgust. "Huh!"

While he was turning his attention from me to the women on the dance floor, the gentleman Russian was preparing to make a big to-do about opening his gigantic champagne bottle. But while lifting it with both hands, which almost caused him to lose his balance, he noticed that the restaurant had already loosened the cork. He looked remarkably sad to discover this. Then the blond lady, who was drinking beer, gave him a curt rebuke. When he offered her some champagne, she replied testily, "I'm sorry, beer and champagne are a terrible mix."

I was more interested in speaking to the officer in my clumsy Russian, so I offered him a cigar, even though I knew there was no smoking in the restaurant. Looking pleased, the officer got up and signalled me out to the reception hall, where patrons were smoking their brains out between courses. Once he'd lit up, I didn't waste much time. "What really happened at Alma-Ata?" I asked. "Students, kids, they got out of control," he said. "Just a bunch of drunks. It's all over." Not wanting to talk more on that subject, he started asking me about Canadian hockey. What was Phil Esposito, the great scorer of the 1970s, doing now? Back at the table, under the restaurant's yellow lights, he started motioning with his fists. "Your hockey," he said. "You were the ones who made the game this way. You are the ones."

I turned to our pleasantly tanked neighbour and asked him about Alma-Ata. "Moslems," he said. Islamic nationalism, according to him, was on the verge of breaking out elsewhere as well. "In Alma-Ata they almost took over."

Annoyed with this, the officer signalled me out to the reception hall again. There we found the coat-check attendant smoking the remaining inch of the cigar the officer had stubbed earlier. The officer looked at him as if he was crazy. Then he told me that the other guy, the gentleman at the table, didn't know anything. "Everything goes by rumour around here. How would he know what happened in Kazakhstan?"

After that, the officer got in an argument with him. Before long, however, the gentleman drinker had neatly shifted the conversation over to me and hockey. Then he got up and without saying a word to anybody – which was uncharacteristic of him – walked out into the night.

I had been expecting it all evening and the officer now tried moving on the middle-aged blonde. She rebuffed him, suggesting that he was getting drunk, and took her leave. The officer followed.

The next morning I left Dushanbe for the mountaintop town of Nurek to see whether *glasnost* and *perestroika* were alive and well there, or never heard about. The city has the biggest hydro-electric station in the Soviet Union. Its long-time party boss was Anatole Malinov. He revealed that in his 14 years of running the show he had not been criticized once in the local media. "No, not yet anyway," he said. "There are no questions on which I should be criticized."

On other matters Malinov, who even looked a bit like Gorbachev, was not disposed to change. On Gorbachev's new individual-labour law? "Our town is rather small so we don't consider this significant." On the proposed multicandidate elections? "I don't think there should be any changes. In my opinion there will be no changes in the selections of party bosses." On economic reform generally? Some helpful decentralization in the decision-making process had taken place, he said. But "there have been no economic changes for so many years and it's very difficult to get some of these things through to people."

It was the same reaction to reform as I'd heard in Dushanbe and other parts of the Tadzhik Republic: Mikhail Gorbachev was talking a big new game but not many were listening.

18/Mischief in Magadan

WHEN I INITIALLY made plans for a long drive through rural Russia, my hope was to head due east through lesser-known areas. That would have taken me through a land mass bigger than Canada. The difficulty for the foreigner, though, is that so much of the U.S.S.R. is off limits. "Yes, you can drive east," a Soviet official told me, "as far as Yaroslav." Yaroslav is 260 kilometres from Moscow. The rest of the way – all the way to the Pacific Ocean – is barred for security reasons.

Paranoid about defence, the Soviets didn't want any foreigner driving past military installations of any kind. By comparison, restrictions on travel for Soviet correspondents in the United States and Canada were not nearly as severe.

Gorbachev, however, began to address this aspect of his closed society as well. To begin with he substantially increased travel opportunities for foreign correspondents – though not by car. In 1986 they started travelling alone on a regular basis – something that hadn't often been possible in the past. As evidenced by his willingness to open the Soviet Union's armaments installations to on-site inspection, Gorbachev had little of the xenophobia of previous Soviet leaders. In the summer of 1986 he vowed to open to foreigners the Far Eastern seaport of Vladivostok. Seven months later I and other journalists were invited on a tour, not of Vladivostok – which would be opened in due course – but of a more fascinating Far Eastern region – Magadan, site of Stalin's dreaded labour camps.

Except for the occasional reference to the labour camps, I hadn't heard much about desolate Magadan. Ina had mentioned it once. She said Chekhov had been there. I had also read that it was one of the world's great gold-bearing regions and, as such, home to a group known as the Golden Boys. The Golden Boys weren't gold diggers but gravediggers. But somehow they were still among the richest people in Magadan. They had a capitalist-style monopoly on the entire graveyard business – plots, caskets, service. They operated on the bribe system, with the highest bidder – bids being in roubles or vodka – getting the best service. The Golden Boys also ran a booming bootlegging business. They were reputed to be near-millionaires. Unfortunately, my plan to do a story on them had to be scrapped. Just weeks before our trip began, a taxi driver named Igor Baranov, armed with a rifle, went to see the Golden Boys and put a bullet through each of their heads.

With a group of about ten reporters, I flew straight across the Soviet Union for nine straight hours in an Aeroflot plane that smelled like most Aeroflot planes – like bananas. In the daylight hours, the last five of the trip, I didn't see anything remotely resembling life, only mountains of ice and frozen lakes. When Averell Harriman was the American ambassador to Moscow in 1943, he travelled to the then-nascent Magadan to see if the Russians had enough gold to pay for the weapons they needed in their war against Germany. "Nobody in the world," Harriman told the city fathers, "could ever succeed in building a real city in such a god-forsaken place. Why do you bother trying?"

We landed in a blast of sunshine, and as we made our way across the desolation to the city of 170,000, a frail, mustachioed man with a high-pitched, eager-to-please voice explained that "there is a psychological problem of isolation here. But if you have good friends and a hobby you can survive."

He was our guide, a heart-on-the-sleeve type in his mid-thirties whose name was Grigori Visenberg. A schoolteacher, he was married with one child. Two or three were wanted but he had to share a tiny, one-room flat in Magadan with his wife's grandmother. The grandmother rarely stepped out into the subarctic temperatures. With only a thin curtain separating their living space from hers, Grigori and his wife never had a chance to spend much time alone.

Nine months of the year, Magadan is reachable only by airplane or by icebreaker through the Sea of Okhotsk. To us, it looked like a frozen Wild West town minus the horses and handguns. The cheap prefab buildings did nothing to adorn a treeless dirt landscape that sloped toward a harbour where two icebreakers sat wedged. The low rise structures looked so rigid and uninviting on this late March day that you wanted to stay on the bus.

Stalin's prison camps had long ago been torn down. To the surprise of none of us, the people of Magadan did not want to talk about them. Most even chose not to criticize Stalin. We met 88-year-old Ivan Lokin, who had lived in Magadan for 55 years. Looking through the window of his downtown apartment, he pointed out a hospital, and said of the main prison, "It was right there." From there the frozen prisoners were sent out to work in the gold fields. But Lokin said it was too painful to talk about the conditions, the deaths. He had written a book about the development of the Magadan region without mentioning the labour camps. At first the camps were inhabited by real criminals, who apparently were not treated inhumanely. In 1938, however, at the height of the Stalin purges, when innocents were being carted away to Magadan, the Soviet leader had the boss of the prison system shot for alleged disloyalty. His replacement ran a barbarous operation, one which most of the Soviet Union and the world did not learn about until 1956, when Nikita Khrushchev opened the windows on Stalin's reign of terror.

Not many details about Magadan were known, and we weren't about to find out more from the region's Communist Party leader, a stereotype Brezhnevian named Alexander Bogdanov. The old party bosses of Russia had a habit of tapping or banging something when they grew impatient and wanted to demonstrate their authority. With the first question on the labour camps, Bogdanov began curling his sheaf of papers into a scroll. With the second he began tapping the scroll against the desk. With the third the tapping turned to banging. "This period of history is shut," he reprimanded

us. "It is not necessary to speak about this." In Moscow, Gorbachev
had stated that there could no longer be closed pages in Soviet
history. But when I reminded Bogdanov about the new *glasnost*
policy, he paid little heed. The fact that we were in Magadan was an
example of *glasnost*, he said. "I think you know the answers to these
questions [on the camps] yourselves. It was all said at the 20th
Party Congress."

Mention of the prisons could be found in books selling in
Magadan, but their author was a Canadian – Farley Mowat. The
first thing I noticed in a downtown bookstore was a stack of
Mowat's books translated into Russian. The clerks assured me
that in Magadan, Mowat, a veteran of Siberian travels, was a star.
They also advised that the spot to go in town was the Hotel
Magadan.

The Magadan Hotel was not a four-star threat. The patrons,
gold miners out to do some Friday-night stompin', seated themselves in a pink and lime-green baroque-style dining room that had
not seen a fresh can of paint since Harriman's visit. These Russians
faced the barrier, even in the Hotel Magadan, of the no-drinking
edict. The administrator, a big, busty woman in black dress and
black bunned hair, patrolled with intent. But the Russians found
ways to get their drinking done.

The long skirts of the red tablecloths gave diners the opportunity
of pouring from their own bottles under the table while pretending
to tie their shoelaces. They took advantage of that opportunity. But
we noticed also a constant stream of weather-beaten Magadanians
to and from the dining hall. In the mens' washroom downstairs, I
found out why.

Soviet washrooms are among the filthiest in any country calling
itself civilized. When I picked up my visa to come to the Soviet
Union in 1985, a lower-level Soviet diplomat at the Montreal
consulate warned me about the lavatories. "They are a disgrace,"
he said. "Nobody in our country will clean them. No one wants that
kind of work."

None I found were quite as putrid as the Hotel Magadan's. The
odour wafting from the men's room was so pungent it hit me a good
30 feet from the entrance. The washroom floor was a minilake. Not

one of the turn-of-the-century toilets was in working order, but they were all used anyway. Most remarkable was that this washroom was used as an unofficial storage room for the diners' spirits. A ledge extended across the top of the urinal stalls. On it, as if in lockers, stood uncapped bottles of vodka and wine, some fuller than others. Every minute or so a restaurant patron would make his way through the stench, take a haul on his bottle, and head back upstairs a little happier.

The administrator was especially friendly, turning a blind eye to the libations of myself and the other correspondents. The other matrons of Magadan were also friendly. When the pounding rock music started up, two of them headed toward our table. One grabbed Bill Keller of the *New York Times*, while the other, who was not far shy of 250 pounds, came in my direction. I resisted. "No thanks, maybe later," I said. But she held her ground, and when her lips started to turn a fierce purple and her bulk began to stiffen, I decided I'd better oblige. The Magadan custom was not to say no.

The dining room got progressively louder and happier as the evening wore on. The administrator valiantly continued her patrols, but she was fighting a losing battle. She blew up at one point when champagne corks soared from a corner table, ricocheting amid the chandeliers. But she could not keep a serious face and soon joined in the laughter and the merriment. Even in Magadan the Russians could have a good time.

Occasionally on trips like these, the chaperons from the foreign ministry would set up visits to local families for the journalists. The families were usually among the most well-off, and had been forewarned about the types of questions reporters would ask them. Keller and I were taken to the apartment of Dmitri and Valentina Mityushin and their two children, Dima and Natalia. Dmitri, a dock worker, had travelled with his family to many Soviet cities but settled in the Magadan icebox primarily because of the wages – three times higher than in cities with normal climate conditions. At first the Mityushins had to live in a one-room apartment in Magadan. But life improved. Now they had three rooms, a black Volga car, a fur coat for Valentina, and enough cash to go for a long vacation every year on the Black Sea coast.

Their dining room, while tight for space, was typically Russian.

A carpet hung on one wall, a heavy dark wall board covered another. A big table flush with food and alcohol took up most of the floor space. The big, silver-haired Dmitri worked the docks; the devoted Valentina, who wore a black dress with prints of bright flowers, was a clerk in a meat store. "Where the husband is, I must be," said Valentina about coming to Magadan. There was no doubt who was in control. When Dmitri, talking about sports, mentioned skiing, he looked over to his wife and added, "She skis awfully, of course." Valentina didn't flinch.

One would have expected the officials to choose families for these interviews who liked the general secretary. But Dmitri was not overly enthusiastic about Gorbachev. He said he had been compelled to use his under-the-table contacts to get the very spirits we were drinking that evening. "Life is tough here," he said. "Why not let the people drink when it is the proper time, when they have guests? I don't understand this rigid law."

We asked him to compare Gorbachev with Stalin and other earlier leaders. "What's the difference?" Dmitri asked. "It doesn't really matter. All the leaders work for the betterment of the people. The most important thing is that there is no war." In his view, Stalin was a determined man who had no choice but to act the way he did. And his prison camps at Magadan that had swallowed tens of thousands who had committed no crime? Dmitri wasn't sure about that. "Perhaps there were camps here. I don't know."

After the visit we were taken on board the icebreaker *Makarov* for a cruise. Then everyone gathered in time to meet the Iron Lady of Magadan – Major Angelina Osinov. It was rare to find women in boss positions in the Soviet Union, but Magadan and the even more remote town of Bilibino, which we were about to visit next, both had tough-minded 40-year-old women in charge.

The red-haired Osinov looked like Margaret Thatcher and spoke with equal clarity and force. She quickly explained Magadan's major problem – the people have so much money that they don't know what to do with it. The average family saved over 2,000 roubles a year, an exceptional amount in Soviet terms. Many Russian families earned only that much in a year. Magadan offered nothing in the stores to spend much money on, and the lady mayor was enforcing the anti-alcohol edict so strictly that they couldn't drink it away either. The only big hole in the wallet came with the annual 42 days' leave, when families like the Mityushins flew all the way across the Soviet Union to a warm vacation spot.

Most of the year they worked the mines or the dock, walked the cold, moon-like landscape with pockets stuffed with roubles, and squeezed into their small apartments at night. From a life of such routine, they plucked whatever joy they could find. A sad irony was that they could do nothing to upgrade either their housing or their living standards, which were deplorable. In the socialist society, the raw materials to improve their conditions were not available. The miserable living standards were chiefly responsible for a divorce rate of over 50 percent, Osinov said. She was divorced herself but didn't want to talk about it.

Gorbachev had not visited Magadan specifically but had been in the region the year before. He demonstrated little sympathy for the social problems, saying that the solution for them lay in people not waiting for the State to do everything. "I will say frankly that the opinion of the Politburo is this: those who are given to sponging and complaining all the time that they have too little of this and too little of that, that they want this, that and the other thing, that the builders and everyone else are to blame, that there are fac-tors beyond their control preventing them from working better – these people must make way for new forces who understand the demands of the times and are ready to shoulder the tremendous responsibility."

Osinov had recently dismissed 160 Communists who had not lived up to the proper work discipline. While she had plenty of the old style in her blood, we sensed that she was a deter-mined champion of reform and, potentially, a strong ally for Gorbachev.

In the evening we went to Magadan's disco, where the girls wore four-inch heels and danced in the styles of bygone decades. Grigori Visenberg came along and, emboldened by a drink or two, spoke under the music's din about how life was passing him by. "I am a simple man, I have a simple job. There were times when I thought I could do something important. Those years in Gorky when I was a student, they were my best years." He told me about the trying circumstances in Magadan, about his tiny flat, about how he dreamed of visiting the West again some day. He had been outside the East Bloc only once, to Vienna. "I had read about the great architecture and the music and the castles there. And when I went I found it was all real, true, like fairyland. Everything was absolutely beautiful."

He was beginning to have some hope now – hope that with Gorbachev the East-West schism would mend so that he could return to places like Vienna. "You know I never used to read the newspapers at all here. Only the sports I read, because everything else was always the same. But now I am reading. There are developments. . . . There are possibilities. Sometimes I get excited, I get hopeful that my life will turn."

The next day we travelled north, closer to the Arctic, to Bilibino. Grigori had lived and almost died there. He was out driving one night on the desolate glacier land with the temperature around normal – 40 below. His motor went dead and "for the first time in my life I was scared." The temperature in the car was soon as low as the temperature outside. Grigori panicked and started running to and fro over the dark ice, looking for a light, looking for anything. Soon he could feel parts of his body going numb. He knew he didn't have much time left, and since no cars had come by for an hour, he held little hope. But finally he saw lights in the distance and frantically waved down the approaching truck. He got a ride home, but his body was so numb that he had to apply the Siberian cure. He drank the first half of a bottle of vodka, then poured the second half all over his body and rubbed it in. In Siberia it's considered a surefire treatment. Soon Grigori began to feel warmth – from within and from without.

Bilibino was all stillness. The nuclear plant that sat on a promontory grimly overlooking the town was the main employer. The oft-repeated line in Bilibino was whether the odds were better for death by frying or by freezing. For many of Bilibino's 25,000 citizens, the highlight of the year was a trip to the big city – Magadan.

"It sounds like you wonder why we stay here," said the fat editor of the local newspaper, Yevgeny Goncherov. "Are you a patriot of your country?" he asked one journalist. "And are you not a patriot of yours?" he asked another. "Well, I'm a patriot and we who live here are all patriots. That's why we stay – to build the country."

"You have to watch this man," interrupted Valentin Blinov, a geologist gesturing at the editor. "With all this *glasnost*, he has the power now." But that was okay, he explained. "Before, we in the Soviet Union lived in a different world. We had to. We had so many enemies and we had to protect ourselves from outside influence. But we want to live in a real world now. And that's what the new policy of our government is about."

The citizens of Bilibino were proud. Alexander Bartchenko, 47, was the town's construction chief. Over a long dinner he boasted about the quality of his housing. Long after midnight, when the feast had ended and he was walking correspondents home in the unbearable cold, he brandished a set of keys to all the buildings. "Here, pick one," he asked. "I will show you how good my housing is." Bartchenko and scribes marched to the chosen apartment, roused the startled couple who, on command from the builder, gave a tour of their three rooms. Bartchenko wasn't finished. He led everyone to another apartment block, but when a sleeping couple appeared at the door, Bartchenko was convinced it was time to go home.

The young people of Bilibino were not as patriotic as he and Goncherov. At a grocery store I asked a Russian girl of about 16 how life was in Bilibino. "Boring," she replied. What do you do at night, I asked. "Sit at home." And what do others do? "The same." You want to go and live somewhere else? "Yes." When? "As soon as possible."

The last stop on the trip was the Omolon reserve, where a clan of native people, the Chukchees, herded reindeer. That's about all they were given the opportunity to do, and that's about all, the Soviets argued, they wanted to do.

"A curious thing about the Chukchees," explained Grigori. "They have difficulty walking on flat land." He wasn't trying to be insulting: he explained that plains are a problem for them because by heredity they are used to moving over hills and mountains. "There, they go at marvellous speeds." At the reserve *I* was being moved at marvellous speeds – across Siberia's outer reaches on a reindeer sleigh. The Chukchee driver finally stopped whipping the beasts, and we skidded to a halt in front of a hut where some of the clan were busy eating reindeer tongue. I asked them if they knew about Canada's Inuit. "Yes," replied reindeer herder Gavil Takaya. "I hear they have their own private reindeer herds." He sounded excited. Would he, Gavil, like a private herd? "No, the state herd is enough. It keeps us busy all the time."

Inside the hut, posters of Lenin peered down on the Chukchees, most of whom spoke reasonable Russian as well as their native language. There was talk of the number of reindeer – 1,100 – that had to be killed during the year to fulfill the plan. I wondered aloud what would happen to the Chukchees if the plan wasn't filled.

"Well, it can't be Siberia," a Russian official cracked. "They're already here."

19/Internal Resistance

THE MESSAGE OF the travels was that the word at the centre was slow to be heard in the far-flung Soviet provinces and regions. A deeper quandary for Gorbachev, however, lay in the fact that where the word *was* being heard, it was meeting considerable resistance.

My initial notion, and the inclination of many, was to presume that the Soviet people would react with excitement to the democratic reforms. That notion was anchored in the West's reflexive conceit that its own style of government was the ideal to which the world's other, less fortunate nations aspired.

But that was forgetting a lot. It was forgetting the deep animosity many Russians harbour to the Western way. In Soviet eyes it was the West that produced Hitler; it was the West, in the person of Britain's Neville Chamberlain, that had first appeased Hitler (Stalin's deal came later); it was the Soviets, at the cost of 20 million lives, who more than anyone had borne the burden of bringing him down.

Despite the surrounding evidence that the socialist-Communist experiment had failed, many Soviets still believed in their system. Its lack of success lay, they maintained, not with the Leninist model itself but with the disastrous way it was being put into practice. They still considered their own system morally superior in its ideal form, in its ethic of equality for all. The Soviet education process and the Soviet media – particularly in the period before Gorbachev – strongly reinforced this belief.

Capitalism was admired by the more materialistic Russians, principally the youth. The young people wanted the clothes, they wanted the hot cars, they wanted the porno. One of my close Russian friends, an accomplished and mature writer, would ask me each time I went West to bring back some magazines featuring naked women. Later, in earnest, he started including porno videocassettes to his requests, which I didn't deliver. But even though he very much desired the evil fruits of capitalism, he did not want to see this stuff for sale in his country. His attitude was that the Soviet Union was too good for such decadence.

Gorbachev's new-deal socialism, which in a curious way paralleled Reaganism in pushing for less government interference in people's lives, was not an easy sell. Gorbachev was aware of what had happened to the last two notable moderate leaders in the great white land. In the czarist days Alexander II was assassinated; more pertinently, in 1964 Nikita Khrushchev was overthrown, in large part because he tried to tinker too much with tradition.

Many months earlier I had put the question of Khrushchev's experience to a distinguished professor of economics, Andrei Anikin. For our talk he escorted me into a barren boardroom with an oak table the size of a swimming pool. We sat on different sides and chatted for an hour – the echo extending to the Baltic republics. It was the Russian way of doing interviews – the decidedly uncosy Russian way.

"The difference between Khrushchev and Gorbachev," the aging professor emphasized, "is that Gorbachev has a greater mandate for change." In the early 1960s there had been more prosperity, and so less need for innovation. The present stagnation of the economy and of life in general offered Gorbachev a better chance to make reforms. In addition, Anikin, as did everyone, considered Gorbachev better educated, more polished, and more politically astute than Khrushchev, the country bumpkin.

Soviet society, however, had not become any less conservative in the years between Khrushchev and Gorbachev. Indeed, it had become *more* conservative. Not to be underestimated in Gorbachev's Soviet Union was a lassitude of heart and of body – the residue of too many decades of crushed incentives and other repressions. Over so many people I met there hung a pall of resignation, of relinquished hopes. Their complexions were chalk, their spirits the same. They were ghosts with bodies, and I wondered if any leader could revive them.

While the Soviet intelligentsia and the Moscow foreign community were very enthusiastic about events, on the street the news of great reforms was greeted coolly. Some said they'd heard good things from the Kremlin before, too, "and what happened then?" Others felt the reforms were not needed, and opposed them. Still others felt that Gorbachev was too daring and would be toppled.

In a spasm of *glasnost* in April 1987, the newspaper *Literaturnaya Gazeta* filled up pages of space with readers' views on reform. Almost half the readers were against it. Some were of two minds, the rest were in favour. "We must fight the psychology of private owner-ship," said a writer from Kiev who was opposed to decentralization. A man from Odessa warned against any tendency to follow the liberal lead of Hungary, the East European neighbour to which some in Gorbachev's Kremlin looked as an economic example. "We are in a different situation," said the letter writer. "Our peasants are used to a commune and collectivization. It is in their blood."

A survey of 120 enterprises carried out by the Institute for Sociological Research showed that for most Soviets, *perestroika* only meant having to work harder with no corresponding increase in return. "The worker's job has not yet undergone any radical change in character, organization or pay," said Professor Vilan Ivanov of the study. "The consumer market is the same as before. Moreover the production growth rates for consumer goods were lower last year than in 1985."

In Moscow only one in five managers believed reform was working well. Half the shop foremen surveyed said that *perestroika* was having absolutely no effect; the other half said it was turning out to be a slow and complicated process.

I often made my own soundings of public opinion at the hockey arena on dark winter nights. When I suggested to Russians that they must be excited about all the developments, the response was often a blank stare. I soon found out that the people measured change by what was on the shelves, in particular the grocery-store shelves. Their bottom-line assessment of Gorbachev came down to that.

"Have you been in the stores?" they would say. "If you have, you will see that nothing has changed."

The average Soviet – in this he is much like voters everywhere – tended to assess the government on the basis of pocketbook issues. Less tangible changes – liberalization, détente, and the like – followed far down. After availability of consumer goods, the second priority was living space – getting a separate apartment or getting a bigger apartment. Any leader who did well on these two counts would be highly popular.

Though Gorbachev's more meaningful economic reforms had only just begun, results were expected quickly. But by mid-1987, more than two years into his governance, the ledger showed no notable gains in living space, a somewhat worsened food supply, and drastically reduced availability of alcohol. The foreign-policy successes and major advances on human rights did not compensate for these failings.

Even his *glasnost* campaign was finding opposition. The institute's survey showed that in the Kazakh Republic, many believed that publicity of shortcomings did more harm than good. The country's military establishment was appalled that the free-speech trend was leading to less-than-stirring appraisals of the Great Patriotic War. General A.D. Lizichev was finding artistic works that contained "tangible echoes of abstract pacifism," and stated that "it is alarming that tracts like this about events of the last war sometimes find support among critics. . . . There can only be one truth. That is the truth of victory, the truth of heroism and the steadfastness of the Soviet people." Marshal Sergei Sokolov, the defence minister, was bold enough to publicly question Gorbachev's *glasnost* creed just as it was getting off the ground. "We do not have the right to allow books, films or plays to see the light of day if they portray events of the Great Patriotic War tendentiously. . . ."

As for the Soviet elite, *glasnost* was threatening to open their lifestyle to public scrutiny, which in turn threatened a revocation of privileges. Gorbachev felt that those leaders who worked enormously long hours had the right to certain perks. He was a believer in the principle that good socialists should be rewarded according to the contribution they made to society. At the same time, he would not brook anything that smelled of corruption and was opposed to flashy displays of elitism. In keeping, he rescinded limousine and chauffeur privileges for hundreds of Moscow administrators in 1987.

For this, the common man cheered him. Only the most conservative Russians were happy to make way on the streets for the limousines. Most cursed "the bastards." Russians who could speak English liked to use that word, especially when it came to the privileged set. The day the cutback in chauffeured cars was announced I talked to a friend on the phone. "The bastards will have to make their own way now," he exulted. "Just like the rest of us."

It wasn't long before the elite responded to Gorbachev's decision. The wife of a Soviet minister wrote a letter to a major newspaper:

"I am writing to you from inside the 'pack,' "[1] said the woman, whose name was not published. "It's my husband in the black car. It's our family which uses the special shops. It's me they're proposing should stand in an ordinary queue."

She worked as a school director, she said. Her husband's hours were so long she hardly ever saw him. Yes, there were special shops, but she claimed that they didn't remove her need to queue at the market and drag home heavy bags like other housewives.

"Yes, I sometimes use his car but it's not to lead the good life. And yes we have a state *dacha* [cottage]. But in four years my husband hasn't spent more than one day there. We, or our old parents, only use the *dacha* one month a year and, by the way, we pay for the whole year."

"Socialism's chief precept is – from each according to his ability, to each according to his labour. His labour! I consider that for all these years as a minister my husband has not been paid according to his labour. What hellish responsibility he has, what stresses, what a psychological overload. Do these meagre 'privileges' compensate for his wasted health?

"Dear comrades, believe me, it is not the fear that we might be deprived of our privileges that guides my pen, but resentment. Resentment of [the treatment of] a man who has achieved everything himself because all his life he has worked like a man possessed. And the overwhelming majority of our leaders are like this."

It seemed that for every initiative from Gorbachev there was a corresponding threat to some segment of the population. And as the threats mounted, so did the opposition. *Glasnost* meant that those who had been above public criticism were now publicly accountable. The launching of a multicandidate election system meant that those in safe positions might soon find those positions challenged at the ballot box. The individual-labour law was threatening the black marketeers. More independence from Moscow meant more pressure on enterprises to survive on their own. New wage structures threatened to leave the lazy, the easy riders, with lower pay than anyone else. Most alarming was the threat felt by the legions of bureaucrats who, as a result of Gorbachev's radical slashing of the state bureaucracy, were suddenly facing the prospect of being turned out on the street – unemployed in the no-unemployment society.

Gorbachev was aiming to reduce the Soviet bureaucratic apparatus by a phenomenal 30 percent. Three million would be fired over the next two years, another 16 million by the end of the century. A Canadian diplomat visited the Ministry of Fisheries one day and saw the usual assemblage of about 400 workers. An official told him to look closely now, because the next time he came there might only be 200.

Full employment had always been the Soviets' biggest propaganda weapon when it came to boasting of its moral superiority over other systems. Providing jobs was considered a sacred trust. "Can one really talk of having democracy and human rights," asked Tass in reference to the United States, "when the jobless number eight million and when millions upon millions of people suffer from the afflictions of racism, hunger and poverty?"

The Soviets' claims to full employment had always been something of a farce, in that so many of the jobs were of the redundant, do-nothing variety. I entered the Praga Restaurant one drippingly hot summer day and was surprised to see the same two men who had been hanging up overcoats in January still doing the same work in July. They stood there sweating, not a coat in sight, waiting for business that never came.

But they had a job: the guarantee of one was always there.

Anyone who wanted to draw a salary could sign up for a so-called job and do so-called work and draw a so-called income. If there was a difficulty in the Soviet Union before Gorbachev came along, it wasn't for those trying to find work, it was for those trying to lose it. I read somewhere that the number of jobless drifters in the Soviet Union was increasing. Rather startled to hear that such a species existed under socialism, I went to see an economic specialist, Sergei Zinchuk. The militia, he explained, would sooner or later find out about a citizen who was willfully unemployed. This person – say Ivan – would be notified that he had a month to start work. If Ivan was still loitering after a month, the militia would arrange an appointment for him with the labour bureau. If Ivan didn't report there to get a job, the constabulary would take stronger measures – remove his permit to live in the city and take away his social-security benefits. Once that happened Ivan would become a drifter, moving jobless from town to town – a bona fide Communist bum.

While Gorbachev wouldn't say so in such terms, in effect, he was removing one of the system's chief tenets – the job guarantee. The sacked millions were not automatically being transferred to new posts. Many had to go to job retraining programs to find another métier. Many had to shed their white collars and leave for faraway regions to take the only work available – physical labour. Some went for months or more without finding any work at all. Gorbachev wanted meaningful productive labour out of everyone. But at the same time, his economy wasn't producing at anywhere near a rate that would make such a goal possible. As for the unfortunate millions being dismissed, an official of the Soviet labour committee explained, "It is time to calmly accept the fact that a person's profession is not necessarily for life." Of course the dismissals are a tragedy for many, the official said. "But is it real? You have to agree that hanging onto a position that no one needs is also a tragedy."

No one seemed to be arguing against reducing the Soviet bureaucracy by a great percentage. But the measure was inflicting more misery on a society already laden with it. Gorbachev promised again and again that there would be enough work for everyone and that the dismissed would soon find other employment. But the rhetoric was turning increasing hollow.

There were certain sources of stability in Soviet society,[2] and it was becoming apparent that Gorbachev was threatening them all. One source was the massive police-state controls. *Glasnost* threatened them. Another source was the providing of the basic necessities of life, such as food on the table and a job. Economic reforms threatened full employment, and, contrary to high expectations, food supplies were dwindling. A third source of stability was calm in the republics. But the Kremlin's freedom-of-speech call was triggering a series of nationalist flare-ups.

By mid-1987 the people – at least those who weren't apathetic – were beginning to choose sides. The reformers found a leader in Boris Yeltsin, the Moscow party chief who had railed against privilege at the 27th Party Congress. The conservatives could look a good deal higher for leadership. They could look to the Siberian who had beaten down Yeltsin on the privilege question – the Kremlin's number-two man, Yegor Ligachev. Ligachev, who was a decade older than Gorbachev, was the focus of rumour after rumour that he was plotting against the Soviet leader. At almost every diplomats' or journalists' cocktail party, one could be sure that the talk in one of the four corners concerned speculation about the infighting between Ligachev and Gorbachev. No one knew for sure, no one had the inside story. So the guessing wars raged on.

In his heart, Ligachev seemed to be an old-school Communist. His speeches, while recognizing the need for economic change, revealed a deep belief in the inevitable victory of Marxism-Leninism over capitalism. Gorbachev, by now, had come to discard that idea. For him, times had changed: in this world of interdependent nations, the struggle between ideologies had to be abandoned in favour of peaceful coexistence. That was the new reality of the nuclear age.

Ligachev, by occasionally sounding on board, kept making it difficult for observers to categorize him, to nail him down. It was Ligachev, for example, who gave final approval for the release of *Repentance*, a film which harshly portrays Stalin's repressions and which, as a powerful work of art, some critics have compared to Alexander Solzhenitsyn's ground-breaking novel *One Day in the Life of Ivan Denisovitch*. In some speeches Ligachev twinned his rhetoric with Gorbachev's. "The process of change which has begun in this country is revolutionary," Ligachev said. "It is not cosmetic repairs in our socialist building, but the overhaul of the basic structures of the economy and political and social spheres." On *glasnost*? "The development of democracy is openness. Broader openness is a matter of principle, just as is honest criticism of those who deserve it. It contributes to the process of cleaning society of everything that is alien to it."

But in July 1987, the guessing on Ligachev came to a halt when he briefed newspaper editors on which direction to point their copy. He told them to start taking a clearer ideological position, to assert Communist Party principle, and to maintain vigilance against Western bourgeois culture. "Unfortunately," he said, "we have a number of examples where the principle is not followed." In some new works "you'll never meet with the word Communism." Of the artists, the ideology boss admonished, "They say give us more rights. But they don't know what to do with these rights."

His speech was a clear call for *glasnost* to stay within the bounds of Communist ideology. But Gorbachev would have none of it. A few days later he came before the editors himself and instructed them to continue along the critical path they had been following previously, to air all past and present controversies. He was accompanied by Alexander Yakovlev, whom he had recently promoted to the Politburo. Foreign analysts suspected that Yakovlev had been brought into the inner circle to cut into Ligachev's ideological turf. His appearance at Gorbachev's side advanced that perception. What we were seeing was the drawing of the battle lines.

20/The Rockers

"WE'RE NORMAL human beings. We like freedom, speed and risk." –
Sergei Turmenev, leader of the Rockers, a Russian motorcycle
gang.

In these days of change and uncertainty, the fight for self-
expression in the Soviet Union was taken up by the young. The fight
was lower-key than in the West in the 1960s, but had an edge to it.
The elements were there: a burgeoning drug-and-rock culture
similar to the American one two decades earlier; growing
disillusionment with a war, in this case the Afghan War; an
intensifying resentment of traditional parental values; and a
visionary leader who, like a Robert Kennedy, demanded that peace
and freedom ring. The Soviet Union, at least in the 1980s, was still
too much an authoritarian state for a protest movement to flower on
a vast scale. But the times of Gorbachev were becoming less and less
predictable.

The Rockers rode, the rock bands played in open fields, the
druggies shot up, the hair grew longer, and they all mocked the
Komsomol, the State's orthodox youth organization.

The Rockers motorcycle gang, formed shortly after Gorbachev
came to power, was making the news in 1987. Not for rape or
murder or violence, but for making too much noise. These were
tame bikers. They congregated, sometimes hundreds of them, in the
large parking lot at Luzhniki Arena at midnight. They wore black
jackets with studs made of rubber and rode roaring, low-quality,

175

Czech-made bikes that woke up too many neighbourhoods. They didn't have much purpose: only, as Turmenev said, freedom, speed, risk.

They loved engines, the wan-looking Yasmin Karpon told me. Karpon was a Yugoslavian photographer. He and I were sitting in the dining room of the Belgrade Two, the cockroach champion of Moscow hotels, just across the street from Eduard Shevardnadze's office. A journalist had recommended I meet Karpon because he was a wheeler-dealer with good contacts in the Soviet underground.

The first thing that struck me was his smile – about the fastest smile I had ever seen. When I asked about the rockers, he didn't hesitate. "Yeah, I know them. I already have great pictures. You want to interview them? I can line it up. You'll be the first Western journalist to see them."

I wanted to see them. I offered Karpon 200 dollars for the pictures and he accepted. The next day he gave me the Rockers' telephone numbers. The day after that the interview was set. On a wet afternoon my driver Valery drove me to the downtown theatre where I was to meet them. Valery was as nosy as a cat. I didn't really want him to know I was interviewing the Rockers. For one thing, being such a stalwart patriot, he loathed them. "People have to work. They can't go around like that waking up everybody. They should be arrested." For another, I didn't want him telling his security friends downtown about the interview – something I guessed he would do in order to score points, and something that wouldn't help the Rockers.

Predictably, Valery lingered after I climbed out of the car instead of pulling away, and was watching when I met two of the Rockers. They escorted me through some back streets and up a flight of stairs to a third-floor apartment. We passed a girl – a Rockette, I imagined – whose expression was blank and immobile. The Rockers ignored her, I said *drasveetye* ("hello") and she said nothing. With the others, I made myself uncomfortable in the typically Russian apartment – stale air, run-down furniture, obsolete appliances, and empty bottles.

I pulled some beers and American smokes from my bag so that the bikers – now three in all – would think I was okay, and listened to Turmenev.[1] He was a tall 24-year-old, handsome à la Tom Cruise. He had real studs on his leather jacket and, unlike his prototypes in North America, was reasonably articulate and clean, as were the two bikers at his side. Besides drive motorcycles, Turmenev didn't do much – just the odd job. He had organized the bikers two years ago, with few limits on admittance to the club. "You have to be courageous, free and drive well." I asked him what he meant, in this Russian context, by the word *free*. He told me it was kind of like the difference in attitude between a Yeltsin and a Ligachev.

It didn't take him long to get to the point – Ligachev had to go. He wasn't concerned, as my tape-recorder rolled, about ripping into the number-two man in the Kremlin. "People should have the right to live the way they want to," he said, "not the way Ligachev thinks they should. Who is he to know and dictate what we should do?" The problem, Turmenev explained, was that Ligachev types were all over the place. Gorbachev was on the right track but "in real life not much is changing. There are bigshots in small towns and villages who don't want to change. . . . The trouble is these older people here. You know, these types who lived in the times of fear, in the Stalin era. Well, they just can't get used to freedom." The Rockers wanted to speed up democratization, said the Leader of the Pack, because "if we wait long enough for everybody to get used to it, we'll be too old to enjoy it."

They had recently taken up the defence of Alla Pugacheva. Alla was the wild and famous Russian rock queen who had some Janis Joplin heat in her big Slav body. One night heavy-lipped Alla stormed into Leningrad's Intourist Hotel, the one overlooking the gray Baltic, and raised four-letter-word hell because they didn't have the biggest suite in the place for her. Soviet newspapers pounced on the story, berating the zany lady's Western-style bull-headedness. En masse, the Rockers drove to the local Intourist office, beamed their lights on it, and chanted, "Leave Alla alone . . . Leave Alla alone. . . ."

Usually the Rockers didn't get much heavier than that. But they had recently been in a brawl with the Moscow militia, said Turmenev's Rocker buddy, Valery Tagankov, and "a lot of heads got broken." The police ambushed them, Tagankov claimed, after they had made a noisy run past Red Square. "They say we are noisy, but a motorcycle happens to make noise and it happens to be legal to drive one. If they want us to be quieter, let them import some quality American bikes and we'll buy them."

After I assured him that Western bikes weren't too quiet either, easy rider Tagankov, a 26-year-old who worked in a theatre, quoted Lenin. "Lenin said the minority should not be oppressed by the majority. But the youth are oppressed here because only the opinion of older people is taken into consideration. They don't care about the youth. There's nothing for the youth to do at night. Young people want to apply their energy, to find their way out of stagnation, but there's no room." What was needed, he said, was a multiparty system in which politicians would have to compete with each other.

They talked a lot about democracy and freedom, notions familiar to them not from school-time readings of Locke or Hobbes but from the sporadic arrival of Western news via friends, or from foreign radio or Soviet newspapers. In the early 1980s Turmenev had been mocked by the authorities for growing his hair long. They had called Turmenev a Beatle, and "to be labelled a Beatle was a real curse."

On my way out I passed the girl again. She was still sitting erect and comatose. The Rockers started bidding for my tape recorder, getting up to about 600 dollars. I made a mocking reference to the rubber studs on Valery Tagankov's jacket, then mentioned that I had a leather jacket from the West. The bidding went higher and higher.

The Rockers were fans of Mister Twister, an underground rock group that *glasnost* had drawn to the surface. With Karpon's help, I lined up an interview; the band also agreed to a picture session with a visiting *Globe and Mail* photographer, Zoran Milich, who met them on a side street running off the Arbat mall. For Milich, they cooperated for almost any type of photo. Soon they had their Soviet passports out and were making funny faces at them. Milich, feeling this was extraordinary, was clicking away in a frenzy.

Soon a green minibus arrived, delivering assorted security officers. They took the three band members into custody. Soon after that they also found Milich, who had been shooting from the window of a vacant second-floor apartment. They took his passport, carted him off with the others, and sat him down in the station under a big picture of Lenin. One militiaman sat in front of him, the other behind. What seemed like hours went by. The officers spoke Russian, which Milich couldn't understand. But at last relief came. "Finally a guy came in, stamped my passport, and saluted me. Everyone started speaking in English. They even returned my film. I couldn't believe it. I thought they would want to keep the film because of the passport shots."

Meanwhile in another chamber, Mister Twister himself, a 27-year-old named Oleg Usmanov, was also being released. One of the militiamen asked him for an autograph for a member of his family. None of this surprised Usmanov much. He explained that some in positions of authority were ignoring Gorbachev's signals while others, such as these security men, were paying heed.

"Three years ago," he explained, "you couldn't even play. The militia would come and take you away. What we did was cram into someone's apartment and do it there. You know how small Moscow apartments are. Well, we'd get 200 people in there and you could hardly breathe. But you wanted to hear the music." This was when Konstantin Chernenko was the Soviets' big-band leader, when rock music and the like was considered a pernicious influence and only classical music was thought suitable for the young.

But now, under the new rules of the game, Usmanov could play the "Unsinkable Double Bass Blues" in public and collect a few roubles a show and sign autographs for the KGB. The state record company, Melodiya, still wouldn't produce their songs – life hadn't yet reached that point. Mister Twister was still distributing its music on underground tapes. Still, Usmanov was more upbeat than the Rockers. "You see new rock groups popping up all over town these days. There's a great release of energy here and some of the sound is good – getting as good as in the West." Where the release of energy would lead, he wasn't sure. "But something's catching, I can feel it."

Since he had no way of getting a private apartment, Usmanov lived with his mother. For quality instruments – the Soviets didn't produce any – he went the underground route. He was on his way to Murmansk, a port city in the north. "I've got a relative up there who might have a way of getting me a new bass guitar from the West."

For a long time Usmanov had wanted out of the Soviet Union forever. But the new climate was changing his mind. "I love to play with Westerners. I've played with travelling Americans. I've played with finished groups. It's great. Their equipment is super. But I want to develop Soviet music. I want to be part of it here."

The film *Is It Easy to Be Young?* was being shown at this time, having made stunningly quick passage through the censor's office. Soviets across the country were turning up to see the question in the title being answered with a cheerless negative, and to understand better the despair of having grown up under Brezhnev and Chernenko.

Using documentary techniques, Yuris Podnieks, the 30-year-old director from the Baltic republic of Latvia, let the youth speak loudly. At the film's beginning, teenagers at an outdoor rock concert in Riga bounce up and down wildly, arms linked above their heads. They are still under the music's power as the concert ends, but the militia steps in to contain the raw emotion. On the train leaving the park, however, passions rekindle, and the youths rampage through the train cars, vandalizing them. Seven of the 100 involved are jailed and break down in the courtroom. Some years later, the camera follows those seven again. One youth says he wants two things in life – to be loved and not to have an empty head. A third is seen at a morgue, commenting on his work on dead bodies: "It doesn't matter to me what I chop up." On the whole, the job is "not my cup of tea." A woman enters, hands him some extra roubles, and asks him to do an especially good make-up job on her dead mother.

The film left no doubt where the Soviet youth stood on Afghanistan. In it, teenagers asked why they were being criticized for spraying their hair red when the country might soon ask them to go off and fight in that war. A mother whose son had been in the war spoke of how she trembled every time the postman came to the door. Finally her son returned – with a blown-up leg. First he would only drink every day, but then he became a fireman. Being a fireman offered the same extremes as being in a war, he explained.

In *Is It Easy to Be Young?* a Soviet punk summed things up.

"Whether you want it or not, everything comes down from adults. But for me to follow their views is impossible."

It seemed strange that the Western word "hippie" was seeping into the Soviet vocabulary at this time. But one could see them in the parks: long-haired youths gathering under trees and playing guitars, doing some drugs and looking contemplative. More prominent, however, were the punks and the heavy-metal types. The latter were a bizarre sight, parading by statues of Lenin and other heroes wearing chains, medallions, bracelets, iron bars, and leather gloves studded with an assortment of bullion. The way some of the *babushkas* froze in their tracks and glared, it was as if they were going to have heart attacks.

The heavy metallists lived in basements, read the West German magazine *Metal Hammer*, and spray-painted walls with thoughts such as WE WILL DIE FOR METAL. One metallist named "Brick" complained in a newspaper one day that he could get nowhere in school because of his teachers' prejudice. "[They] pay more attention to what my head looks like," said Brick, "than what is in it."

The search of Soviet youth for the "whatever" extended to musical groups like Chudo-Yudo, who broke furniture on stage, blew up condoms, and poured out the filthiest Russian language imaginable. There were so-called fascist youths who opened fire with handguns on cherished war memorials, and there was a group of young toughs called the Lyuberites who, operating on the principle of purifying the capital, came to town every so often to beat up the long-hairs.

Fuelling this antisocial behaviour, according to *Ogonyok*, was "the endless eulogizing of our achievements, the constant incantations about the boundless worth of Soviet man." The increasing rebelliousness was a reaction against "these backslapping lies, this hypocrisy, sanctimoniousness and endless assurance that people in our country are always comrades and brothers to one another, that the militia are there to look after you. The reaction is an atmosphere of cynicism and almost open, trampling underfoot of all moral laws." More and more Soviet young people were deciding to become negative heroes, the magazine said, because they had been overfed with positive ones.

The malaise at home spawned an ever-increasing desire to get abroad. Considerable enthusiasm greeted two of Gorbachev's reforms – one that loosened emigration restrictions, another that made it easier to travel overseas. Most Soviet youths I met looked up to foreigners – as long as they were Caucasian – in a big way. The Soviet film maker Stanislav Govorykhin wrote in disgust of the time he asked a Russian boy what he wanted to be when he grew up and the boy answered, "foreigner." This attitude was prevailing all over the country, the film maker said, and was not simply the result of a young Russian's dreams of Western wealth. A contributing factor, said Govorykhin, was the Soviet state's blatant discrimination against its own citizens in favour of foreigners. "From early childhood the youth see what an exclusively excellent attitude is displayed to the foreign guests in our country."

Visitors to the Soviet Union might not agree with Govorykhin's assessment, but compared with the way the Soviets treated their own travellers – like cattle – visitors went first class. Too frequently I saw hundreds of Soviet citizens standing in ice-box conditions on an airport tarmac waiting for a minibus to pull up with a couple of tourists. Some rule said the guests had to board first; then and only then could the Russians get on and thaw. In vacation spots like Yalta, Soviets received a coloured card permitting them access only to the weedier beaches. It would be more than hard to imagine Soviet tourists in Canada or the United States being given the favoured treatment while the home-country people got shoved to the back of the bus. But Soviet youth grew up watching and feeling the subordination, and seeing in the strangers from abroad what appeared to be a higher class.

The counterculture groups represented only a small proportion of Soviet young people. Evidence of a more general malaise could be found in the falling popularity of the very symbol of dedicated Soviet youth – the Komsomol. Its membership was dropping; so was its spirit. The Komsomol is the youth arm of the Communist Party, the builder of Communist orthodoxy, the testing ground for high Communist ideals. A high standing in that group was essential to anyone's future career; it was from its ranks that Gorbachev launched his move to the top. But beginning in the mid-1980s, great numbers of young people began rejecting the organization on the basis of the very things for which it stood. Between 1985 and 1988 its membership dropped from 42 million to 38 million.

The Komsomol chief, Viktor Mironenko, said an important reason was the number of youths becoming involved in religion. The Komsomol, which is open to young people between 14 and 30, towed a strictly atheist line, banning all believers from membership. Gorbachev meanwhile was liberalizing the Kremlin's attitude to religion and, in the process, overseeing a noticeable religious revival. Instead of recitation of Communist dogma at Komsomol meetings, Soviet youth who cared were increasingly turning to substantive issues such as the environment and the war. The Komsomol was a relic of old-fashioned Communism, the kind that Gorbachev was steadily turning his back on.[2]

Most of the young spoke positively about Gorbachev but more enthusiastically about Yeltsin. Many didn't care. It was not clear whether Gorbachev was radical enough to bring the lost generation to his side.

"We grew up in an atmosphere of loud slogans and high-sounding reports," said Alexei Novikov, a freelance journalist. "Up to the age of 20 I never suspected there was anything wrong. We are so powerful that we can reverse northern rivers, we were told. . . . And then suddenly the word is out that many of these gigantic projects were not needed at all. . . . We were constantly told that truth is the most valuable thing in the world. And I guess that must be the reason why they kept it safely away from us."

Novikov saw, for example, how his country officially scorned "professional" sport in the West. At the same time, he noticed that the only time Soviet "amateur" sportsmen took time off from training was to pick up their paycheques.

"We have lost our faith in many good things – in justice, in goodness, in equality for all before the law," said Novikov. Now there is *glasnost*, he said, "but I am afraid that someone will suddenly decide somewhere that there has been more than enough truth . . . and that this campaign has been going on for too long."

21/The Gospel Goes East

FOR ALL HIS rhetoric and his initiatives, Gorbachev entered 1987 without an arms agreement with the United States. Early progress on arms control was critical for the Kremlin because scaling down the defence budget would release money to revive the dying economy. But with the near miss at Reykjavik, Washington and Moscow were starting to snarl at each other again. Gorbachev was holding to the line that he would only pursue arms negotiations in the framework he had put forward there: the elimination of medium-range missiles in Europe, a radical reduction in long-range strategic weapons, and an extension of the ABM treaty that would block further development of Star Wars.

Though the feasibility of creating an impenetrable defensive shield had been more or less invalidated, Reagan was standing by his commitment to it. If there was going to be progress, someone was going to have to compromise; and as was usually the case throughout the Gorbachev-Reagan period, that compromise came from the side wanting the deal the most – the Soviets.

But first, and perhaps as a way of preparing for another conciliatory measure, Gorbachev, under pressure from his military, finally called a halt to his nuclear-test moratorium. The 19-month moratorium ended on February 26, 1987, with a 20-kiloton blast on the dirt plains near Semipalatinsk in Soviet Central Asia. "A historic chance for ending nuclear tests for once and for all has been missed," Major-General Gely Batyenin sombrely told the Soviet and international press.

During the 19 months of the unilateral freeze, the United States had recorded 22 tests. While the Soviets put on some sad faces when they renewed their own explosions, in their hearts they were anything but gloomy. They knew that this round in the East-West propaganda war had been all theirs. Throughout the entire period of the freeze, Reagan's policy makers had been on the defensive, compelled to offer a series of excuses for not joining the moratorium.

First they charged that the Kremlin had deliberately hurried through a great number of tests before calling it and therefore were so far ahead in testing they could well afford a moratorium. This charge was soon proved untrue. The more general "it's all propaganda" line withered because the Soviets kept extending the moratorium, thereby showing that they were serious about it. A third American rationale suggested it was unwise to join the Soviets in such a venture because the Kremlin could never be trusted when it came to verification procedures. Gorbachev scuttled this thinking with some of the most liberal commitments for on-site inspection ever made. Yet another justification was required. The State Department now argued that they needed to test their nuclear weapons regularly in order to be sure of their quality as a deterrent. The unspoken corollary was that since the Soviets weren't testing, the quality of their nuclear arsenal was no longer reliable.

"The U.S. is changing reasons as quickly as gloves," said Yuli Vorontsov, the first deputy foreign minister, in response to all the alibis. "Events are showing that the king is naked after all. The U.S. simply does not want to stop testing."

In the United States the public-relations damage from the moratorium was limited. The art of disinformation, depressingly well developed in the Soviet Union, was becoming almost as advanced in the United States under Ronald Reagan. With his gift for reading scripts persuasively, the president could say whatever he wanted to say on television and find a huge audience wanting to believe him. His audience, when all three networks covered him, was 80 or 90 million. Any newspapers or other media daring to point out the distortions of fact the next day had a far smaller public. The net gain was always the president's. And as was noted by the *Washington Post*'s editor, Ben Bradlee, Reagan also had the good luck to be facing one of the most compliant White House press corps in decades. America was caught up in an era of chauvinism, of flag waving. To criticize was to be unpatriotic.

In Europe and other parts of the globe where the president's voice resonated less strongly, the Soviets scored well with their moratorium. It was a significant step in a series of charm offensives that led to a striking result – polls in Europe showing that the Americans under Reagan were considered a greater threat to world peace than Gorbachev and the Soviets.

Magnifying the moratorium's public-relations bang was Gorbachev's follow-up announcement: his intention to sign an agreement with the United States that would remove medium-range missiles from Europe. The two sides had agreed to such an accord at Reykjavik, but the Kremlin had only been willing to sign it as part of the package plan. Now, in the spring of 1987, Gorbachev was saying the other parts of the package weren't necessary. In essence, he was setting aside Soviet concerns over SDI.

While he had failed to get American support on his moratorium, his offer on European missiles was virtually fail-safe. It was almost an exact copy of the zero-option proposal that Reagan had put forward in 1981. The Reagan plan stipulated that the allies would not deploy their Pershing IIs and cruise missiles in Europe, provided the Soviets withdrew their existing SS-20s. As almost everyone expected at the time, the Soviets declined. Now Gorbachev had resurrected the zero option. His doing so left the president with little room to manoeuvre: rejecting it would have meant vetoing his own proposal. Gorbachev was good at making offers the other side couldn't refuse or would look dumb in refusing. This was one example, the moratorium another, and his proposal to eliminate nuclear weapons by the year 2000 a third.

His offer on medium-range missiles was greeted with happiness in the West. Gorbachev would get his arms deal. The Americans liked the terms. They were also impressed by Soviet behaviour in other areas, particularly on human-rights questions. George Shultz came to Moscow to work on the missile agreement and spoke frankly at a press conference. He had talked to refuseniks, dissidents, and ordinary Soviets about a range of matters. "It's quite clear," he concluded, "that there are some important changes taking place in the Soviet Union."

Gorbachev prepared visits to Czechoslovakia and East Germany to consult on the medium-range accord. He also wanted to sell *glasnost* and *perestroika*. Gorbachev's reform campaign was reverberating throughout Eastern Europe, with potentially dramatic consequences. Since the early postwar years, Moscow had acted as the barricade to liberal change in that part of Europe, as the tightener of the totalitarian knot. The invasions of Hungary in 1956 and Czechoslovakia in 1968 were two examples. But now it was becoming the proponent of liberal reform.

Gorbachev was urging the same freedom-of-speech reforms and economic reforms on Eastern Europe as he was on his own country. He told the East Bloc leaders that Moscow was no longer in the business of dictating what type of socialism a country should have. "No one has the right to claim special status in the socialist world," he declared in Prague on April 10, 1987. "We consider the independence of every party, its responsibility to the people of its own country, and its right to decide the questions of its country's development, to be unconditional principles."

The Kremlin leader explained further: "History so willed it that the Soviet Union would be the only country with experience in socialist development at the initial stage... This experience was naturally perceived as a standard. [But] in our time a number of fraternal countries have garnered rich experience in socialist development and, in this, singular forms and unusual approaches have been employed. No one party can have a monopoly on truth."

Not all the leaders of Eastern Europe's six countries – Poland, East Germany, Czechoslovakia, Hungary, Romania, and Bulgaria – were ready for *glasnost*, *perestroika*, and the other new sounds from Moscow. Some enjoyed their dictatorships the way they were. These were not energetic, new-generation leaders in the Gorbachev mould, but the opposite – an orthodox gerontocracy. By the time of Gorbachev's speech, all of Eastern Europe's bosses except Jaruzelski of Poland had been in power for at least 20 years. Four of them were in their seventies, the other two not far behind.

They were often hidden from public view, but one evening in East Berlin, where they had gathered for a meeting of the Warsaw Pact, I caught a glimpse. They arrived in their black limousines one after another at the base of a flight of steps leading up to a Gothic concert hall. Neither the lilt of the outdoor chamber music nor the scattered applause of about 3,000 East Berliners lining the entrance walkway could dispel the funereal atmosphere. Romania's cadaverous Nicolae Ceausescu, the East Bloc's most recalcitrant Stalinist, was first up the aisle. His face had an occult expression and he acknowledged the smattering of applause with some weird, slow-motion hand movements. The Polish leader, Jaruzelski, alien also in his heavy dark glasses, was followed lugubriously by Hungary's Janos Kadar, 75. Bulgaria's Todor Zhivkov, 75, took forever to make it to the door. Czechoslovakia's Gustav Husak, 74, looked ill. With the appearance of Erich Honecker, the 74-year-old leader of the host country, a buzz ran through the spectators. They knew Gorbachev was on his way.

He arrived with a flourish, bounding from his limousine, emanating power. With Raisa, who can sometimes look the empress part, at his shoulder, he moved quickly to the line to greet the East Germans. He eagerly pumped their hands all the way up the length of the promenade. Then, as if he wanted the onlookers to contrast him with the others, he bounded the steps two or three at a time, turned to face the crowd, clasped his hands together above his head and shook them with enthusiasm. The East Germans' applause had by now turned to cheering. "*Hoch, hoch, hoch*," they yelled.

The people in the crowd may have liked Gorbachev, but among the leaders there was division over his new ideas. On *perestroika* and *glasnost*, the block was dividing up quite evenly. Hungary, Poland, and, to a lesser degree, Bulgaria, were in favour. Romania, East Germany, and Czechoslovakia were balking.

Hungary, already the most liberal of the East Bloc states, offered the most radical possibilities. Testing the limits, it looked to be moving in the direction of quasicapitalism economically and quasipluralism politically. Budapest was where the postwar division of Europe might conceivably end. Gorbachev was watching and in some respects encouraging Hungary. As agriculture secretary he had visited the country, asked hundreds of questions, absorbed everything. Now he was looking to Hungarian methods in agriculture and price setting as potential examples for his own domain. Hungary, once the maverick, was now seen as something of a model – though no one knew how long that status would last if it were to break too boldly with socialist tenets.

Gorbachev didn't want a rupture with socialism and neither, ostensibly, did the Hungarian government. But with Gorbachev, the definition of socialism was blurring. He was breaking with the Soviet-style socialism of Stalin and Brezhnev in favour of a democratized socialism where the market could play an increasing role, where the one party dominated society less. But Gorbachev's brand of pluralism was still to exist within the context of one party. The Soviet boss had so far given no indication that he was prepared to allow Western-style parties to get off the ground in Moscow. Chances of that happening were less than chances of a socialist party getting off the ground in the United States.

In Budapest, the architecturally blessed Hungarian capital, the gray cloak of Sovietism was less obvious than in other East Bloc countries. For two decades, Hungary's economic policies had been more liberal, more market-oriented, than those of its East Bloc neighbours. The result was a city with well-stocked stores, fancy cafés, designer boutiques, and a vitality uncommon to the other East Bloc capitals.

No one followed me in Budapest. Later, in Prague, the Czech capital, a man in a brown suit and chequered shirt shadowed me everywhere. He was less than subtle, and for a long time after I left, I regretted that I hadn't confronted him. My hotel in the chilling police-state capital had more cameras in it than people. In the dining room a lens pointed from each corner. In my room another was aimed at the bed.

Shortly before I arrived in Budapest there had been a meeting of 600 members of the intelligentsia – the National Democratic Forum, as they called themselves. They had tabled a list of demands for parliamentary democracy. It was like something out of the Magna Carta days, said one of them. The forum was out to break the one-party Communist lock on the country. Any other parties in Hungary had been mere tokens.

"What is on the agenda is real pluralism," said the writer Miklos

Haraszti. "I think we are in the beginning of real change." Checking that view with the more official crowd, I found concurrence. "There will be some kind of development toward pluralism," said Pal Bokor, the foreign editor of a major state newspaper. "Nobody can say right now whether it will take the form of two parties or something else." He was confused. "I'm not convinced whether we are going from socialism to capitalism or from an authoritarian state to socialism."

The forum was preparing to sponsor candidates in the next parliamentary elections. In the 1985 election about ten percent of the seats in the 352-member assembly had been won by unofficial candidates. The forum felt it had realistic hopes of winning more than 50 percent, establishing a non-Communist majority. The economy had fallen on bad times. A huge foreign debt had crippled possibilities for growth. Hungarians were beginning to taste the bitter side of capitalist experimentation. Words not part of the socialist lexicon – inflation, unemployment, value-added tax – were suddenly the subject of hot debates. Some said the woes were the result of too much Westernization. Most said the problem was not enough of it. Many intellectuals rightly predicted that Janos Kadar would soon be swept aside and replaced by the prime minister, Karoly Grosz. Hungarian intellectuals like film maker Andras Kovacs were enthusiastic about Grosz for what, not too many years ago, would have sounded like the most absurd of reasons – he was much like the Soviet leader. "There is a certain feeling that he is a practical man," said Kovacs. "He likes to see himself in the image of Mikhail Gorbachev."

In what could be seen as an omen for some Bloc brethren, the Hungarians were increasingly looking West. "Tell them they're not bad off compared to the Poles and the Czechs and they tell you that's irrelevant," said the Canadian ambassador, Robert Elliott. "They look to Austria and West Germany."

"Our old model of socialism was based on an unhappy mixture of czarist traditional and Hapsburg-enlightened absolutism," explained the Budapest party secretary, Janos Barabas. "In the fast-developing world of computers and high tech, this mixture no longer works."

In Czechoslovakia, Gorbachev's plea for change created a

delicious irony: many of his reforms were similar to the ones the Czech leader, Alexander Dubcek, had attempted in 1968 – only to see them crushed by Brezhnev's Kremlin. In effect, Gorbachev was now rehabilitating Dubcek just as he had Sakharov – only in the case of the Czech he would not put it in such terms. Gorbachev was prepared to send signals to his Eastern partners, but lauding Dubcek in public would have been to suggest the type of government Prague should have. He wasn't prepared to go that far.

Dubcek himself, however, was indeed prepared to go that far. In an interview with the Italian Communist newspaper *L'Unita*, the retired Czech leader said of Gorbachev's programs, "*Perestroika* is indispensable and I support it because I find in it a profound connection with what presented itself to us 20 years ago. Had there been a political leadership in the U.S.S.R. at that time similar to the one today, the military intervention . . . in Czechoslovakia would have been unthinkable."

Gorbachev disappointed Dubcek's followers with his April speech in Prague when he failed to mention Dubcek or even push *perestroika* strongly on the Czech leadership. In December 1987, Czechoslovakia's Husak became the first of the old-guard East Bloc leaders to step down. His replacement, however, was a close copy: in a quick, smooth transition that crushed the hopes of reformers, Milos Jakes, an anti-Dubcek conservative, took over. It seemed that Moscow had thrown none of its weight into the decision. Gorbachev sent Jakes a congratulatory telegram with a detectable message. "We are confident that the central committee, under your leadership, will ensure the restructuring of your economic mechanism and democratization of public and political life in the country."

Jakes sent a positive reply to the telegram. But a few days later his state-controlled press issued strong denunciations of Dubcek and his liberal movement – in effect warning Moscow against rehabilitating him. In Czechoslovakia there was some modest economic *perestroika*, but it appeared that there would be no *glasnost*, no loosening of the totalitarian knot, no matter who was in Moscow.

Hungary was going one way, Czechoslovakia the other, and somewhere in between was Bulgaria. Known in the West for its medal-winning weightlifters, Bulgaria also had a well-known figure in its everlasting leader, Zhivkov, the first-secretary of the Bulgarian Communist Party since 1956. Zhivkov once boasted that he would make his country "the Japan of the Balkans." It was an eye-catching line, and one of my first stops when I arrived in the reasonably attractive capital, Sofia, was the city's main department store – the ZUM.

A Communist consumer classic if ever there was one, Sofia's ZUM was cavernous, dimly lit, and empty-shelved. The ties, pants, shoes, and sofas were all made out of fabrics akin to cardboard. Most everything came in block stock. For T-shirts, men had one choice – a blue-and-white, jail-striped polyester. There were about 500 of them. The sporting-goods department offered crimson track-suit pants made of a fabric charged with enough electricity to make your hair stand.

In the music section, Bulgarian high tech extended to long-playing albums. But Zhivkov's Japanese analogy became most ludicrous in the TV department. One could have searched forever without finding a colour TV. While black-and-white models abounded, it seemed the State was incapable of producing even a small percentage of the colour models required. The shortage had become a serious issue in Bulgaria, and the week I visited, Zhivkov made a major pledge: the new five-year plan, he stated, "envisaged solving once and for all the problem of colour TV sets."

Throughout Zhivkov's decades Bulgaria had been the Soviet Union's most reliable client state. It did what Moscow wanted. Now the Kremlin was changing direction, and Gorbachev was effectively saying that the old road as travelled by the likes of Zhivkov was the wrong road. It didn't bother the Bulgarian leader – he simply changed his lyrics to accommodate Gorbachev's new tunes. No one was quite sure if he meant what he was now saying, but Zhivkov announced a blizzard of Gorbachev-style reforms: multicandidate elections, limited terms for office holders, a reduction in the powers of the Communist Party.

With this so-called new program, which didn't appear to include much *glasnost*, came an admission – a rather noteworthy admission. "Life shows," Zhivkov said, "that the former model of socialism in this country has spent its potential. What we need now is personnel of a new type and leaders of a new type. They should feel that they are subordinate to those who have elected them."

Zhivkov was saying that socialism, as practised before, could no longer work. A Hungarian writer named Istvan Csurka put it more bluntly. "The new reality is that socialism has failed. Of course no one is saying this officially. We are all trying to change the system without making a point of the failure."[1]

22/The Yugoslav Road

CSURKA WAS correct. The Kremlin fathers weren't saying it officially, but East-bloc socialism had failed. The challenge now was to find a new socialist way. They were looking for models but had little to go by. The examples from one-party states that had tried to experiment by moving to a more market-oriented brand of socialism were not encouraging. The Kremlin's own past experiments – the Liebermanism of the late 1960s, the New Economic Policy of Lenin's time – had not worked out. Poland's socialist reforms in the early 1970s had come to naught. Hungary was now suffering economically, and the country offering the best example of modified socialism, Yugoslavia, was near economic collapse. Triple-digit inflation, crippling strikes, a 20-billion-dollar debt, and ethnic conflicts in the republics had plunged Yugoslavia into a desperate crisis.

Belgrade's policies – a decentralized administration, economic self-management, the stimulation of the market mechanism – were of the type Moscow was now embarking on. "There are some people in our country who use the Yugoslav experience as a bad example," said Fyodor Burlatsky, one of Gorbachev's advisors. "But nobody can find a maximum effective model now from the socialist countries. And the Yugoslavs did some very good things. If you go to the markets there you can see there is no problem with food, with goods."

When Yugoslavia, under Josip Broz Tito, split with the Soviet brand of Communism in 1948, Stalin branded Yugoslavia's leader a traitor and a fascist and accused him of ideological heresy. Gorbachev was intent on repudiating Stalin whenever possible and on warming relations around the globe. When he came to Belgrade in March 1988 he said what Yugoslavs wanted to hear him say about those times. "Groundless accusations," he declared, "were made against the leadership of the Communist Party of Yugoslavia."

Cut off by Stalin from trade with the East Bloc, Tito embarked on his new socialism, giving enterprises free rein within the confines of an overall state plan. "The good thing is that they took a very big step from bureaucratic socialism to self-management socialism," said Burlatsky. "This means the State plays not so big a role as it does now in our country."

Moscow was intent on moving in a similar direction, Burlatsky noted, but modern times meant there were new elements to consider. "We are dealing with the new technological revolution. We have lost seven maybe 15 years in comparison to Western Europe, Japan, and the United States." The best model for the Soviet Union, he said, would be a "planned market economy."[1]

With its many nationalities and sometimes fractious republics, Yugoslavia offered Moscow another fascinating comparison. Tito's decentralization had yielded some striking inequalities in the Yugoslav republics. In switching over to a more decentralized market system, the Soviet Union might have the same problems, the Gorbachev advisor said. "Some areas like the Baltic republics would take big steps forward . . . but middle Russia and Siberia will not have such good conditions."

Gorbachev was aware of Yugoslavia's experience. In a speech in 1985 he said that the lack of a strong central government in Belgrade, and the allowing of too much *laissez faire*, had created wide inequalities in living standards. There wasn't enough socialist sharing, he felt. Indeed, it was the consensus among many Yugoslav officials that the central government in Belgrade had grown too weak to manage the economy as a unit. A hodgepodge of economic decisions had created chaos. For a way out, Yugoslavia was looking West for a capitalist solution rather than East for a traditional socialist one.

On the streets of Belgrade, where crisis was not evident, where the living looked easier than in any Soviet city, no two opinions sounded alike. Young Sacha Milovich, a university student in philosophy, didn't think it would be wise for Gorbachev to experiment with the market solution too much. On a wet evening, while Yugoslavs walked briskly through fallen leaves, he was serving beer in a café that opened onto the street. It was dark but there were warm little lamps. Sacha, black hair against a red crew neck, paused in his work and drew an imaginary pie to explain what had happened in Yugoslavia.

In the early days of Tito Communism everybody had an equal portion of the pie, he said. No one was rich but no one was destitute. But then the government relaxed its regulations, and money mongers started gobbling up bigger chunks of the pie for themselves; in the end there wasn't enough left for those less skilled at capitalist gamesmanship. "So now we have some who are very rich and many who are poor. Kind of like in your countries."

Someone had obviously sold Sacha on classic Marxist-Leninist theory. He had only been to the West once, to Italy, but he thought he knew it all. To be wealthy in the West, he continued, you have to work all the time. "Everyone chases money like dogs," he said, repeating a line I had heard often in the Soviet Union. I asked Sacha if he wanted to get out of the East Bloc. He replied no, that he'd rather stay and rebuild his own country than go West and have to work all day like a mad dog just to stay afloat.

I went back to the hotel and played a little blackjack at the first East European casino I had seen, while music wafted up from the strip club one floor below. The next morning, inflation being as bad as it was, I had to bring along three pocketfuls of dinar notes to pay for a cab ride. "This is no good," said the driver. "The people at the top only take care of themselves. They know that being a one-party system they are always going to be there." I told him that Gorbachev probably wished it was that simple.

What was needed, he told me, was a system of choice. He had sent his son, a track-and-field athlete, to train in Sweden. Now, with the crisis in Yugoslavia deepening, he had just sent his son some advice – "Stay there," chase dollars, get a bigger slice of the pie.

I returned to the Soviet Union, which at that point had been tinkering with its economy for more than two years without result. The leading economists concluded that stronger medicine was required. "We cannot continue onward as we once we did," said Aganbegyan. "Our people deserve a much better life than they have at the moment." He noted that since the early 1960s – when the economy registered a number of highs – the number of housing starts had fallen, the life-expectancy rates had dropped, and food supplies had hardly improved.

What could really help, said Aganbegyan, was a turn of fortune. Many people didn't realize that the gravity of the problems – of the food-supply problem in particular – was the result of a factor beyond Soviet control: oil prices. While Western economies were benefiting greatly from the 1980s nosedive in world oil prices, the Soviet Union, an oil exporter, was feeling the opposite effect. In the 1960s and 1970s the Soviets were exchanging their oil for grain and meat, Aganbegyan explained. "But the price of oil had fallen by almost three times and today the State does not have real opportunities to acquire the previous quantities of grain and meat."

But the Kremlin could not count on a sudden leap in oil prices. The voices that now took centre stage were those of economists like Nikolai Shmelyov. Writing in the authoritative *Novy Mir* magazine, he created a sensation by recommending a break with the hallowed tradition of zero unemployment. "We should not close our eyes to the economic harm caused by our parasitic confidence in a guaranteed job. . . . The real chance of losing one's job and having to take temporarily unemployment benefits or work where one is sent is a good cure for sloth, drunkenness and irresponsibility."[2]

It was time, Shmelyov argued, "to decide for once and for all what is important to us – to have enough of our own food products or to be forever indulging those who champion equal poverty for all." His outburst was telling. "Over the centuries humankind has found no more effective measure of work than profit. Our suspicious attitude toward profit is a sort of historical misunderstanding – the cost of the economic illiteracy of people who thought that socialism would eliminate profit and loss."

Shmelyov credited Gorbachev with opening up the road to

common sense but also said he was dooming the country to half-measures, largely because of his unwarranted fear of letting the evil genie, Capitalism, out of its bottle.

Shmelyov's raising the spectre of unemployment was followed by a call for the introduction of the other capitalist evil – inflation. It came from none other than Valentin Pavlov, the head of the State Commission for Prices. According to Pavlov, the huge state subsidies that were cushioning the Soviet population from rising prices were also robbing the State of the money needed to modernize the economy. Subsidies for agriculture had more than quadrupled since 1955, but food prices in the stores had changed little. A Soviet citizen could purchase 2.5 kilograms of meat in a state shop for the same price as the State paid for one kilo. The resulting drain in state coffers kept wages down; at the same time it meant that prices for other consumer goods were artificially high to compensate for the subsidies.

Pavlov wanted the market, not the State, to be the major price-setting force. His capitalistic thinking was in tune with Shmelyov's: both were socialists, but neither was sounding too socialist.

In theory Gorbachev wasn't prepared to break with the Soviet Union's guarantee of full employment. In practice, maybe. . . . Concerning food prices, he appeared to share the Kremlin's traditional fear that increases in the cost of bread and meat would touch off riots in the streets. But he had concluded, like many of his economists, that it was time for radical action, and was preparing public opinion for the change.

In June 1987 the Communist Party's Central Committee met in plenum and decided to, in a sense, start down the Yugoslav road. A new draft law was adopted that put 60 percent of Soviet enterprises on self-financing beginning January 1, 1988. It meant that central bureaucracies were about to be stripped of much of their power to set prices, control the work force and investments, and tell factories and farms what to produce and how much. In a step toward what Burlatsky called a planned market economy, those tools would be placed in the hands of the enterprises themselves. The central ministries would occupy themselves only with broad planning tasks.

The big factories would still not be able to refuse a state contract, Aganbegyan explained. But beginning in the 1990s, state contracts would amount to only 25 to 30 percent of the economy.

"If we are to speak of the past," said Gorbachev, "perhaps the main shortcoming was that we had begun at the top – though that would appear to be logical for a planned economy. But this time we have decided to start everything from the main link [individual enterprises]." Previously, "nothing was left to the enterprises [because] the higher echelons grabbed everything."

Earlier that spring the Soviet leader had talked of the Soviet founders: "Lenin used to say that there will be many times when we will have to complete or even remake something all over again in our system. This is the task we have set for ourselves today."[3]

Time and time again Gorbachev would resort to the father of Soviet socialism when appealing for actions that sounded contrary to the ideal. In the case of his new decentralizing schemes, there was in fact a good Leninist precedent – the New Economic Policy. Under NEP, Lenin had permitted private trade to flourish in the economy. This created a whole new class of traders known as "nepmen," who began competing with the state sector. Their role kept expanding until Stalin came to power, reasserted party strength, and crushed them.

By allowing self-financing, by allowing individual labour and co-ops, by allowing disparity in wage earnings, by opening his borders to foreign capital and joint-venture entrepreneurs, Gorbachev was raising more than a few eyebrows among rank-and-file Soviet socialists.

The more conservative economists such as Mikhail Antonov argued that Kremlin radicals were trying to throw the socialist system overboard. "Sometimes it seems as if they want our country to turn into a second America so that in our country as well everyone's thoughts would revolve around the rouble. But by doing this we will only create a system of educated, unrestrained individualists instead of civilized cooperators. We do not need another America. We need an inviolable union of free nations rallying around the great Rus."

As the radical economists gained credibility, the entrenched bureaucracy dug in. The news of the switchover to self-financing prompted ministry managers, fearing for their job security, to take measures to make it difficult for enterprises to operate without state contracts. One way was by stacking them with so many state orders that there was no time for other work. Another was by making it difficult for them to get raw materials to take on private contracts.

The opposition to economic reforms like the individual-labour law was scoring victories. Among the little entrepreneurs who were thwarted was Pyotr Chugunkin, an old-timer who wanted to supplement his slender state income. Chugunkin thought he might be able to pick up a slow buck at the railway station as a luggage porter. Moscow stations have state-employed porters, and Chugunkin knew they were not pulling their weight. Porters who operated under the state plan were required to bring in only four roubles an hour. As I and most other passengers who had searched for a porter knew, many got their four roubles worth in a few minutes and dozed off thereafter. Chugunkin's idea was to take up that slack, but the government workers wouldn't tolerate the competition. The harassment of Chugunkin included physical threats against him and telling passengers he was a swindler trying to take bread from their mouths. Chugunkin had all the proper documents under the new law, but the station management, in collusion with the porters, kept demanding more and sending him away. Chugunkin drifted from station to station, wearing an armband to signify his status as a free-enterprise labourer and getting the same treatment everywhere he went. Though he had the spirit of the Kremlin behind him, he was up against a recalcitrant monopoly.

Job security, which had never been a big concern in the Soviet Union, was suddenly becoming a priority problem. As a result of Gorbachev's campaign to reduce the central bureaucracy by "one-third to one-half," Moscow's employment commission was being overrun by citizens in anguish. Newspapers reported that the majority believed they had been dismissed without justification. Those who got new jobs right away said they were having to take steep pay cuts.

The newspaper *Industrialnaya Gazeta* asked whether the country was ready for such a mass displacement of labour and said Gorbachev's policy could be carried out less arbitrarily. Pressed on the matter, Gorbachev sought to assure the people that chaos was not around the corner. "I do not want to be understood as if I am issuing calls, in the way that was done during the cultural revolution in China, to open fire on the headquarters. . . . But those who continue to tread water must go."

The administrative bureaucracy, he explained, employed 18 million people. That was 15 percent of the country's manpower – one manager for every six or seven employees. So "it is only natural that we should give serious thought to ways of simplifying the bloated administrative apparatus. Earlier when any problem arose in the sphere of the economy or in society in general it was immediately suggested that an organization be set up for attending to it, as though it could help. But it did not help."

Perestroika was deadly serious business, Gorbachev warned. "We are not playing games in this restructuring. Behind *perestroika* stands the fate of the country and the life of the people."

23/Cancelling History

SEPTEMBER 2, the first day of school, 1987, was brisk but remarkably clear and bright. On the rare all-sunshine days in Moscow it seemed brighter than anywhere. Maybe it had something to do with the topography, with the crouched architecture that never got in the way of the sky.

From our fifth-floor apartment, which was wallpapered ruefully in perpendicular furrows of brown and tangerine, I could see class after class of pupils in freshly-pressed blue uniforms spilling out of worn-out yellow busses. Red flowers in hand, the boys and girls filed toward the Lenin monument. They clustered several metres in front, divided into pairs, solemnly moved forward, and placed their bouquets. Ritual over, they rushed excitedly through the cool breeze to board the busses – girls in front, boys in back.

At school the first lesson of the year was the same for everybody: *oorock mira*, or "the lesson of peace." For 45 minutes teachers throughout the country led their pupils in a discussion of the importance of that great notion. In many classes they sang or read out the traditional children's verse of the writer Lev Oshanin. Ina, my secretary, told me the words, becoming a little sentimental as she did:

Let there always be sunshine,
Let there always be blue sky,
Let there always be mommy,
Let there always be me.

The children gave flowers to the teacher. Those in grade one presented flowers to the graduating class, who in turn gave flowers to the little ones.

Everything seemed typical, traditional, in character for the Soviet school system. Only these were not typical times for education in the Soviet Union. With the new policy of openness, with Gorbachev's dictum that there would be no blank pages in Soviet history, a past that Russians had never heard about was being revealed in their media. All the old pedagogic falsehoods were being exposed; the era of cover-ups was over. Soviets were learning for the first time the real facts about the death of Nicholas II, about Stalin's brutal repression, about how his farm-collectivization policy had cost an untold number of lives, about his mistakes in readying the country for the war, about his barbarous police chief Lavrenti Beria, about the fate of Nikita Khrushchev, about the appalling corruption under Brezhnev.

The schools had always taught the bible according to Stalin and Brezhnev. Soviet history since 1917, as told to the youngsters, was a march of glory and triumph, only occasionally interrupted. The students never questioned it because the U.S.S.R.'s command system of education – though it did produce a fully literate population that was well advanced in the basics – didn't allow them that privilege. The teacher was the god; the teaching of Communist Party doctrine was the gospel. Critics called it a system of learning by coercion, in which memory was rewarded and imagination wasn't. No stimulus was given to independent thinking, complained a student in the Moscow press. "They must first give us a chance to think for ourselves instead of memorizing aphorisms of the greats."

But now the newspapers and magazines were rewriting history, and anyone who read them knew that what they were hearing in school was lies. As the 1987-88 education year progressed, the hypocrisy of the process became too much to bear. In early June in *Izvestia* an announcement appeared that rocked the Soviet education system: all history and social-studies exams for students aged six to 16 were being cancelled; the textbooks were to be thrown out and new ones reissued – if possible, for the start of the new school year.

"Huge and unmeasurable is the guilt of those who deluded generation after generation, poisoning their minds and souls with lies," the newspaper cried. "Today we are reaping the bitter fruits of our moral compromising. . . . Cancelling the exams is the only possible sober and honourable decision. Only yesterday it was impossible to imagine that such a measure could be taken. Everyone – parents, students, teachers – can feel only relief and thanks toward those who had the boldness to say that these exams would not take place. . . ."

Most of the students were too young to get indignant about the development. Their immediate reaction was delight that they would not have to study for the exams: the students ran out of the school cheering. A 15-year-old girl said that her teacher didn't explain the reasons for cancelling the tests. No one asked. Some of the information in the history texts had been looked upon with skepticism by many of the students, she added, but nobody worried too much about it.

We sat around in the foreign compound trying to imagine something like this happening in our own school system. The outrage would be uncontainable. But it was relatively quiet in Moscow. Many seemed to have a sense that they had been duped by the books all along, that this was coming.

Even before the history tests were voided, the schoolchildren received some startling news. For generations of Soviet youngsters, Pavlik Morozov had been the student hero of the building of socialism. In the early 1930s Stalin was stripping everyone of their farm holdings and forcing collectivization. Pavlik was 14 years old in 1932. His parents were strongly opposed to the policy, and young Pavlik ran to the secret police one day and told on them. For being traitors to Stalinism, his parents were arrested and, presumably, shot. Morozov was then killed by friends of his parents. For this he became a martyr of the socialist cause. His picture was on the wall of nearly every Young Pioneer club in the country for decades after.

Now, 55 years later, in the literary monthly for youth *Yonost*, the boy wonder was being exposed as the traitor himself. "Pavlik Morozov . . . is not a symbol of revolution and class consciousness but a symbol of legalized and romanticized treachery," wrote Vladimir Amlinsky, a novelist and historian.

This exposé followed numerous attacks on Stalin in newspaper articles debating the real facts of history. The most powerful of these was the publication of a 48-year-old open letter to the dictator by Fyodor Raskolnikov. While Soviet ambassador to Bulgaria in the 1930s, Raskolnikov received the ominous news that he was being recalled to Moscow. Fearing it was tantamount to a death sentence, the ambassador fled to Paris, where he wrote to Stalin. His letter was finally published in *Ogonyok* by Vitaly Korotich.

"You have enticed almost all your Soviet ambassadors back to Moscow and exterminated them," it said in part. "You have completely destroyed the entire foreign-affairs commissariat apparatus. . . . You have beheaded the Red Army and Red fleet and murdered the most talented generals. . . . With the help of dirty forgeries you staged false trials, and made up accusations which are more ridiculous than the witch trials of the Middle Ages.

" . . . You have squeezed art in a vise where it is suffocating and dying. Inept pulp writers glorify you as a semi-deity born from the sun and moon and you, like an eastern despot, enjoy the incense of crude flattery. You mercilessly exterminate writers who are personally displeasing to you."

After he had fled to France, Raskolnikov was branded an enemy of the state and tried in absentia. During the more liberal Khrushchev era he was posthumously reinstated in the party. But after Leonid Brezhnev came to power the charges were invoked again and his status returned to that of traitor.

With all the revelations in the media, Gorbachev decided in the autumn of 1987 that it was time to give his own version of Soviet history. Beyond the plain morality of such an act, he could, by drawing attention to the horrors of the past, heighten the demand for reforms of the present. He could also alienate further a large segment of Soviets who didn't want to know the truth about their glorious history.

The anxiously awaited address ran a middle course. Gorbachev was blunt in pointing his finger at Stalin. "It is sometimes said that Stalin did not know of many instances of lawlessness. [But] documents at our disposal show that this is not so. The guilt of Stalin and his immediate entourage before the party and the people for the wholesale repressive measures and acts of lawlessness is enormous and unforgivable."[1] But Stalin's crimes of the 1930s – the show trials, the purges, the murders, the millions of deaths brought on by his forced collectivization – were alluded to only in general terms, not in detail.

And Gorbachev said that Stalin, while he made "gross political mistakes," also made an "unquestionable contribution to the struggle for socialism." He supported Stalin's collectivization, though he regretted the methods used. "It was essential not just to cover but literally to race across the distance from the sledgehammer and wooden plough to an advanced industry in the shortest possible time – for without this the cause of the revolution would inevitably have been destroyed."

The sensitive subject of Nikolai Bukharin, Stalin's chief political opponent, who was executed in 1938, was raised. But Gorbachev declined to take the side of the man whom Lenin once called the darling of the revolution; instead, he said that the timing of Bukharin's ideas was inappropriate. Gorbachev acknowledged Khrushchev's bravery in exposing Stalin's crimes but was otherwise uncomplimentary. Brezhnev was given only mild reproach.

It was a political speech. The intelligentsia would have preferred more frankness, the conservatives less. Gorbachev had opted for the majority in the middle. It was becoming obvious that as a leader he was acutely sensitive to timing. He sometimes chose not to show all his cards at once but instead to let his game evolve. On the election reforms, on the economic reforms, there was a lot of experimentation going on, a lot of testing the market so as not to sink before swimming. Anyone who tried to make a definitive assessment of Gorbachev or his policies while the testing was taking place was entering into risky business. The process of democratization was a cumulative one.

That Gorbachev was being very political in his speech on Soviet history became evident in the months that followed, when he demonstrated a truer, more progressive side. The images of Stalin and Brezhnev were blackened; those of Khrushchev and Bukharin, brightened. Gorbachev set up a commission to consider the rehabilitation of Stalin's victims. Before long it had rehabilitated Bukharin. His widow, Anna Larina, 73, had campaigned all her life to clear his name. She had written to Gorbachev and told him how, before his execution as an enemy of the people, her husband had stooped to his knees in front of her to pray. Bukhavin asked that his name some day be cleared and that she work toward that goal.

Bukharin had been a staunch defender of Lenin's New Economic Policy. Stephen Cohen had written a book about Bukharin and saw many parallels between his thinking and Gorbachev's *perestroika*. In December 1987, when Gorbachev was in Washington, he met Cohen, who later recalled that the Soviet leader "grabbed my hand and held it for a long time." Gorbachev told him, "I read your book about Bukharin. It's a serious, interesting and useful book. Of course it's possible to have disagreements with it." Cohen was invited to give a lecture in Moscow on Bukharin. Foreigners didn't usually receive offers to talk on such controversial subjects. The lecture was announced in the Soviet capital only the night before, to avoid a mob scene. It turned into a mob scene anyway.[2]

After Bukharin's rehabilitation I was sitting with a Russian sports writer at Luzhniki Stadium. "This is crazy," I remember him saying. "I was taught that Bukharin was a traitor." As for police chief Lavrenti Beria, he had heard the odd rumour about the man's real character. But now he had seen the film *Repentance*. "Did you see it?" he asked me. "Did you see what he was? He was an animal."

An employee at a radio station whom I had met in Voronezh was visiting me in Moscow to solicit advice on a film he was trying to produce. As we spoke he leaned across the desk and his words came faster and faster. "The war." His grandparents, his relatives. . . . He had lost so many in the war. They had all died with the glory of the motherland and Stalin on their lips. Now he was reading how Stalin's botched preparations had cost the country endless millions of lives. "No wonder we lost so many," he said with rising anger. "How can we call Stalin a hero for this?"

His visit came shortly before the Kremlin announced a decision that would not be received warmly in Stalin's home town of Gori. Just after I visited Gori in 1986, citizens, responding to a rumour that Moscow was planning to shut down the Stalin museum, had formed a cordon around his monument. Now, almost two years later, the rumour had become fact – the museum was being shut down indefinitely.

One of the Soviet Union's best writers, Chingiz Aitmatov, had always felt the "monstrous and sometimes total absence of democracy" in his country. Now he was finally beginning to feel real hope. "We have been too long ensnared by the authoritarian regime created by Stalin. And only now, 30 years after his death, have we begun to free ourselves from being slaves of his personality cult."

For 77-year-old Anatoly Rybakov, author of *Children of the Arbat*, the campaign against Stalin was only beginning. "I want to drive a stake through his heart so he can never rise up again. I want to help kill once and for all the system he created. And to do the job properly I have to live a few years more to show fully what he did to this country."[3]

As articulated so pointedly by Rybakov, what Stalin did was put an entire country under his thrall. "He created an impossible moral and psychological atmosphere. It became inhuman because people were falling and no one spoke up to defend them. Millions died and others lived in terror. People stopped thinking for themselves or showing any initiative." Now, Rybakov said, "we have to shake off that inner serf mentality that he bred in us, shake off fear." *Glasnost*, he said, was doing it.

It was as though, during that school year of 1987-88, all the major figures of Soviet history since 1917 were being given new sets of clothes. Among the more conspicuous cases was that of Khrushchev. Nikita Khrushchev all but vanished from official history after he was toppled in 1964 by Brezhnev and his band. Ever since, there had been no newspaper stories of him, and no pictures, and hardly a mention of his name. To be born in the Soviet Union in the 1960s, to be a Soviet citizen under the age of 25, was to know next to nothing about the man who led your country for a recent decade. You probably didn't even know what he looked like.

A TV film made in the 1980s called *My Contemporaries* looked at the world's first astronaut, Yuri Gagarin. At the moment of his triumphant return to earth, Gagarin had been greeted by Khrushchev. But in the film Khrushchev was not at the welcoming ceremony. Gagarin "had to walk off into a distance somewhere," said Professor Yuri Afanasyev, "from space to another empty space. . . . The young Gagarin is walking along the red carpet. We wonder who will meet him – who will shake his hand? The youngsters don't know what happened. But people of an older generation exchange glances knowingly."

In early 1988, when a newspaper picture of Khrushchev finally appeared, it was the one with Gagarin. A smiling Khrushchev was wearing a dapper tan coat and doffing his hat to onlookers. Gagarin wore a look of pride. An analysis accompanying the photo was complimentary to the forgotten leader.

Thereafter, a bit of a Khrushchev revival began. The name of an area of Moscow built by him and subsequently renamed by Brezhnev was subsequently given back its previous name. Calls came for his remains to be exhumed and reburied in the traditional place of honour near the Kremlin wall. Sergei Khrushchev, his son, was permitted to grant interviews. "Until recently today's generation had forgotten my father's name," said Sergei, a computer engineer in his early fifties.

Like Gorbachev, Khrushchev sought summits with presidents, had a mania for nuclear-test bans, fought to reduce the size of the military, wanted limited terms for office holders, made decentralization a buzzword, and oversaw a cultural thaw. But *glasnost* was never really part of his show. Gorbachev complained in the late 1960s that Khrushchev had ordered too many arbitrary changes from the top. "The failure of [Khrushchev's] reforms," said Gorbachev, "was mainly due to the fact that they were not built up by a broad development of the democratic process." In economic terms, at least, Sergei Khrushchev agreed. "In the 1960s we thought that if someone at the top gave the right orders then we would all have more, but it turns out that isn't how economics works."[4]

Sergei was getting ready to publish a book about his father. An entire generation that had never heard of him would be correctly appraised. Meanwhile, Brezhnev would soon be paid back for erasing the memory of Khrushchev: an order went out from Gorbachev's Kremlin to have Brezhnev's name removed from all cities and towns named after him. Soon after, the writings of both Brezhnev and Chernenko were ordered removed from Soviet libraries.

In these times of record-breaking revision there was one leader who did not undergo a reassessment. He was the one to whom the children paid homage on the first day of school. Criticisms of Lenin could be found in a newspaper article or two, but Lenin was the inspiration – so Gorbachev said – for *perestroika*. And his place of honour, in the form of a lifeless monument in the central square of nearly every Soviet city, would remain.

The children would return to visit Lenin on September 1, 1988. But they would be less lucky at the school year's end. This time they would have to write history exams – only very different ones than they had ever seen before.

24/Black Sea Cruise

WE BOARDED the Russian cruise ship *Byelorussia* in the port city they called "the Pearl of the Black Sea." This was Odessa, on the Ukranian Republic's southern tip, across the water from Turkey. It was a romantic city, one of seaside bluffs, soft climate, wind-blown sand, old limestone buildings, and the crisp walk of sailors. It blended, Odessa did, the bearing of a tough New England port, a Boston, with the lazy caress of a southern one, a Charleston.

Our ship, stocked with 400 white-bodied, holidaying Soviets, would sail east along the coast some call the Soviet Riviera. It would dock each day at a different resort town, allowing me, the photographer Zoran Milich, and the rest of us to test the comforts of the Black Sea Edens – Yalta, Sukhumi, Sochi, and the others. Russians were known to crowd the beaches so thickly in these places that you couldn't see the sand.

Before the *Byelorussia* sailed we spent three days in Odessa, lodged in a grand piece of cherry-painted baroque called the Krasney Hotel. The high ceilings, chandeliers, terraces, majestic marble staircase, and other finery gave the Krasney a sumptuous look; but she hadn't been refurbished since the czarist days. The paint was peeling, the water cold, the food exclusively Russian, and the service as indifferent as in Moscow.

In the hotel's colonnaded dining room, seated alone at the next table, was Andrei Chernakov. He was 29 years old and had a sailor's build, short blond hair, a sunny smile that revealed a chipped tooth, and an all-Western wardrobe – jeans, tennis shirt, Wedgwood-blue sneakers. He was watching the Russian girls go by and, catching my attention, playfully flashing hand signals, rating them from one to ten. "Just another one of Odessa's charms," Andrei Chernakov remarked as he joined my table. "You can't beat this city, unless you go west."

He had completed his four-hour workday as a physical-education instructor at the sanatorium and was having a late lunch. He was planning to meet the guys afterwards, go to the beach, meet the girls. It would be a normal day for Andrei – the Soviet good life. Moscow was a long way off. The talk of Gorbachev's revolution didn't please him much, because if it ever happened he might have to work more. "I don't have to work hard," he said, "and that's good because I don't want to work hard."

He had moved away from Odessa once, to get married. He and his wife had a daughter and lived in a small Russian town. But he got bored. Odessa – the beach, the sun, the girls – beckoned. So he separated from his wife and returned. "I loved my wife and child, still do. But I was cramped, I wanted to move. That's the only thing wrong now. I miss my daughter."

The phys-ed instructor still lived with his parents in Odessa, but he and the guys had a communal flat to take care of other needs. Odessa, Andrei said, was better off than other Soviet cities for two reasons – its status as a major port and its high population of Jews. There were 200,000 Jews in the Pearl of the Black Sea, a city of 1,200,000. "They're good businessmen," Andrei explained. "They've helped make the city wealthier. But they have all the good apartments, they live well in comparison to others and this causes some jealousy."

According to Andrei, the Jews were doing so well in school that, though they were only 15 percent of the population, they had 30 percent of the university graduates. "So you know what the authorities did? They blocked a lot of them from going to the college. They set a quota on the number of Jews allowed in." Most of Odessa's Jews wanted to emigrate, and Andrei feared that with Gorbachev's liberalism, it might happen. "If they leave, the city will decline. There's no doubt."

Outside, in the evening warmth, thousands strolled down the

proletarian mall. The streetscape was free of obvious signs of authority. In a park at the mall's edge, senior citizens had gathered to listen to music. One little man, who looked almost 100, played a screeching fiddle while the golden agers danced a slow sidewalk waltz.

A beautiful, flaxen-haired Finnish girl who was also staying at the Krasney said she often visited Odessa and other Russian cities because she couldn't stand the boredom of Helsinki. She looked with scorn on Westerners who thought of the Soviet people in Cold War stereotypes.

Her high regard for Odessa was shared by the city's residents. "Don't compare us to Leningrad," said Marina Yevgenova, a language instructor. "The Black Sea coast is a different Soviet Union." She was one of many Soviet women who, though they lived in apartments that were almost squalid, had the dress, bearing, and classic beauty of duchesses. She was wearing a lime-green evening dress and had wrapped a linen scarf of matching colour tightly around her foot-long braid of blond hair. Her perfectly carved chin sat naturally high. She didn't want to hear about Moscow – her Odessa pride wouldn't allow the association.

An Intourist employee named Lena took us on a tour of the city. Visiting monument after monument made Milich and me impatient, and when we were taken to an obelisk commemorating the defeat of the Nazis, I allowed myself the ungenerous observation that it was the ugliest obelisk I had ever seen. Lena glared. At tour's end, while I was routinely shaking her hand, she gave me a cold stare and told me, "When you shake hands in Odessa, you either look the person in the eye or you don't shake hands at all."

As we pulled out of the city's harbour, accompanied by the rousing Soviet anthem, gulls – maybe 200 of them – circled and weaved in leisurely swoops, following the boat unceasingly. In the soft evening sun I saw seamen in whites bounding up and down the 192 broad steps that rose sharply from the harbour to Odessa's centre. I fixed on the handsomeness of that tableau, then noticed a young Russian couple embracing near me, then heard a passenger complaining that the boat was dry. In the new Soviet Union, even Russians on vacation wouldn't be drinking. But it was only true only in the official sense. Five minutes into the trip's first meal, a champagne cork rocketed into the dining-room ceiling. It was the first of many mini-Sputniks that night. Just as in Magadan, the Russians had come prepared to beat the edict.

That first mild night some passengers remained on deck till sunrise. Dawn disclosed a mountainous coast descending on small stone buildings the colour of a robin's breast. They were part of Yalta, the home of Russian writers, the vacation resort of czars past and Soviet leaders present, the meeting place of Roosevelt, Churchill, and Stalin to set the aftermath arrangements of the Second World War.

On shore, three local teenagers heard me tearing open a can of beer on the sunlit street that fronted the water. Just as I expected (the Western beer being a ploy to start conversations), they came over. Only days earlier, they told me, Mikhail Gorbachev himself had come to town from his nearby *dacha*. He had strolled along the street and dipped into the stores, talking casually with the people, telling them more changes were on the way. Having informed me of that and more, the young guys now asked for a quid pro quo – gifts from the foreigners' specialty store. Two cartons of Kool menthol cigarettes and 24 Western beers would do fine – they would pay the rouble equivalent. I was on my way to the store anyway, so I agreed. They insisted that I deliver the goods with the utmost secrecy – hand signals and all. Once I had, they ran off into the trees.

That afternoon the Black Sea sun was straight from Florida. Everything was clean. The town looked like a Norman Rockwell painting. A pristine paradise, was Yalta – until you headed for the beach, the fenced-in beach.

Soviet beaches seem to attract a high proportion of Slavs who are very ample of midriff. The country abounds in strong, well-proportioned, squarely built people, but they're not the ones who congregate at the sand and water.

In Yalta the fat ones were arriving at the beaches by the thousands. They had to line up to get their piece of sand or, in most areas, gravel. On this day a giant tanker loomed offshore, seemingly only a stone's throw from the water's edge. It creaked and snarled and did those things tankers do.

The sunbathers were about a thousand abreast on the white stones, aligned in rows so tight to each other that toes almost touched heads. While I observed the scene from the concrete terrace, I heard a wooden fold-back chair groaning underneath a woman in a red two-piecer. She barely fit under her large yellow umbrella, which was thrust into the white stones. A companion of comparable size, reposing about three centimetres next to her, was dipping into a mammoth jar of musty water in which bobbed pickles, eggs, sausages, wieners, and other buoyant food.

The soft thrash of the Black Sea water looked inviting enough, tanker or no tanker, but few Soviets were venturing in. Instead they squirmed in the heat while others waited for them to vacate their patches.

While walking back to town I peered over a man's shoulder to see a *Pravda* account of a Canada-Russia game, which had ended in a tie. The reader snarled, "Ahhhhgg, the referees!" The Soviets had been leading the Canada Cup match, he said, when the officials hit them with a cheap penalty.

The man was a war veteran, retired, tanned, very content to sit on a bench and pass the day chattering with his wife, Victoria, who appeared to disagree with everything he said. His name was Vladimir. He had worked hard all his life, he explained, and was now entitled to enjoy his retirement. "That's the good thing that's happening in the country now," he explained. "Gorbachev is bringing back the work incentive. People got lazy. Oh yes, they got lazy. Everything was taken care of for them. If you lost your job you would get another one. That's what led to problems."

Before Victoria could interrupt, he switched gears. "People who make these judgements about Stalin," he said. "Well, they are not making them in the context of the times. They don't know about the difficulties he faced. They say he didn't prepare the country well enough for war. But he couldn't devote everything to the war effort. He had to have the people working on the farms to feed the population."

Back on board the ship, Valya, the dry-bar waitress – she with the ever-ascending Slav cheekbones, champagne smile, and deep, dark, friendly eyes – was serving two youths who had snuck in their own spirits. At their feet on the blue broadloom lay vodka, wine, and a bottle of something else. "That's forbidden, absolutely forbidden," Valya admonished them in her effortlessly strong voice. "You'll have to remove it right away or I'll bring in the manager." The youths looked timidly at each other until they heard Valya break into laughter – she was only joking. Go ahead, she told them, drink on the sly and enjoy it. She got them to sneak a beer up to the bar for her and then tiptoed off to a side chamber, where she drained it quickly.

Tatiana, the boat's restaurant administrator, talked about her experiences with non-Soviet tourists. "Well, the Spanish, they're easy-going and so much fun. But the French! It takes them ten minutes to make up their mind whether they want a cup of coffee." And the Russians? "I know people in the West think we're so serious," she said, "but it isn't so."

With us at the table was a bespectacled, mellow-looking man from the Moldavian Republic who only wished to laugh and to console people and offer them drinks. "The people get by," he said. "Of course we have our problems in this country but the people get by. This new policy of *glasnost*, it makes things a little easier." But Gorbachev's policies were not putting any more material goods in the stores, he said. "Not yet, anyway."

The Moldavian had a Russian friend, Volodya, about 35, who knew a few words of English and wanted to learn some swear words from us. He memorized some revolting phrases, which he saved for the downstairs disco. There, during a break between songs, Volodya unleashed a four-letter-word gale that seemed to astonish even the Russian patrons. The Russians are well known for their love of dance; they danced that disco floor without inhibition every night until four in the morning and beyond.

Contrasting with Yalta is Novorossisk, a nondescript industrial town where the tourist boat stops anyway. It became better known in August 1986 when the *Admiral Nakhimov*, a passenger ship like the *Byelorussia*, collided with a tanker outside the port. The tanker almost sliced the *Nakhimov* in half. Many passengers were dancing on the outer deck under the moonlight when the horror struck. When the people below decks tried to escape from their cabins, they found that the crash had buckled the doors so that they were impossible to open. They were among the 400 who died.

Our guide in Novorossisk made no mention of the tragedy but did take everyone on a tour of the war monuments, where he droned on for hours. One striking memorial was the size of a football field. Stepping inside, I was greeted by house-of-horrors chamber music and a staircase leading to a pulsating plastic heart.

On the Novorossisk streets, more patriotism surfaced. A big woman in a kitchen dress spotted Milich taking pictures, whereupon she volunteered a 15-minute monologue on the joys of Soviet living. "Not even the Jews have a right to complain," she insisted. "There are no problems for those who work hard." In her gusty wake, a woman from the cruise ship stormed out of the town's main department store, declaring to no one in particular, "Zero – there's nothing in there." By this time, September 1987, I was capable of carrying out reasonable conversations in Russian and was very much enjoying the language.

Alexei and Georgi, two 20-year-olds walking the main drag, discovered we were Canadians. Though this was the iceless south, hockey immediately came to their minds – they wanted to know about Phil Esposito and Bobby Hull. Milich's state-of-the-art photo equipment captivated them. They were also eager to know about Western cars and apartments. "It will take seven years on the waiting list for me to get a car," Alexei said, "and about the same for an apartment." But the comparison session didn't distress them. They said they still liked the Soviet Union better.

In the city's main square I talked with an urbane gentleman named Konstantin. Soon many others were joining in, all having finished their work early in the afternoon of this weekday. Like Sergei in Odessa, they were taking it easy. "There is so much unused energy in the Soviet people, so much potential," said Konstantin. "It's waiting to be tapped." The city fathers of Novorossisk were only paying lip service to Gorbachev's reforms, Konstantin lamented. "We wait and we wait." Then he shrugged, that shrug I saw so many times in the Soviet Union – a "such is life" kind of shrug, neither sad nor happy. The people here felt things were out of their hands, that they were not in control of their own destinies. So they stood around the city centre, doing as little as possible.

At five a.m. the following morning I wandered onto the deck. The ship was thrashing steadily through the Black Sea, its hull churning up a great V of white foam. On the outdoor deck court I picked up a basketball and shot some hoops in the half-dark, blaming the misses on the lack of light and the ship's motion. At dawn I was joined by a short, heavy-set man from the Georgian Republic. He put up some 20-footers of hopelessly low trajectory, all the time cursing the Russians. "They've been screwing up the country for 60 years," he said. "It will take them another 60 years to straighten it around."

Tropical Sukhumi didn't look all that screwed up. I had to keep reminding myself that this was the Soviet Union. The main street was paradise, southern-California-style – a lane of palm trees, magnolias, and sprawling manors that led into a festival of foliage that was the city's centuries-old botanical garden. Around the fringes, however, Sukhumi took on a seedy look. The homes were in disrepair, as were the roads; whores with vacant stares hounded the foreigners, as did youngsters looking for pens or anything Western. This was the Abkhaz Republic, and the Abkhazians, like their neighbours the Georgians, were tanned, more sensuous, more Asian. They liked to drink wine, to feast, to take life lightly.

At a restaurant that had no wall on the side facing the sea, the locals at a nearby table were eating mounds of wonderful Georgian bread and drinking bottles of wine. They joked noisily with the Russian waitresses, one of whom complained kiddingly that her partner received better treatment on account of her bigger top half.

I couldn't tell what kind of dish arrived at their table, but whatever it was, it caused one in their number to break the loud buzz of conversation. He stood up suddenly, plate in hand, cursing it loudly. Looking seaward, he hurled it, Frisbee-like, due west for Sochi. It cleared the heads of his table friends, whistled past my companion's ear out over the railing, where, accompanied by cheers from all diners, it pirouetted into the Black Sea.

The caper brought a rush of laughter to the restaurant. The staff did some perfunctory scolding but soon joined in the fun. When the cook appeared, the patrons at the offending table offered him some wine. Down below we could see floating bottles, corks, other restaurant paraphernalia – testimony to other Soviet good times in Sukhumi.

Milich and I were anxious to get back to Yalta: we had directions to Gorbachev's *dacha* and visions of an exclusive story. We passed quickly through Batumi, which borders on Turkey and, unsurprisingly, has the air of a Turkish bazaar. Amid the heat, the dirt, and the poverty, we saw shoppers throwing loaves of bread into dusty automobile trunks; ancient, fur-hatted men with leathered faces of a thousand lines; thousands of sunbathers lying on a beach of rocks midday of midweek, while rickety trains, tilting dangerously to one side, slowly chugged by.

In Sochi, the most famous Soviet holiday resort along with Yalta, we were not in the mood for another monument tour. So, by taxi, we saw the best of Soviet beaches, the best of Soviet tans, the most of Soviet wealth. For the first time in my stay in the Soviet Union I was seeing people who all seemed to be reasonably well-off. And for this reason, it wasn't long before the well-fed cabbie was gratuitously berating the new economic rules coming out of the Kremlin.

"Who needs them? Life is comfortable here. I have a wife, I have a girlfriend and soon I will have a second car." For the wife? "No. I tried to teach her to drive once but it was useless." For the girlfriend then? "No, it's for me. She already has a car."

He took us up past the sanatorium, where top Kremlin men went to rest their ailing bones. Then he drove off into the woods. "Quietness," he said. "Breathe that air. It's so warm here we can come in January and cook out." On the way back, as he stopped at an intersection, he rested his eyes on a prostitute. "I don't like prostitutes," he declared. "As a matter of fact, I can't stand them." We passed a rather ordinary-looking hotel. "You have beautiful-looking hotels like that in Canada?"

On the ship, Milich and I had made friends with the Moldavian. He had been to Gorbachev's cottage and so knew the directions. He even offered to come with us. The *dacha* – more accurately, it was a villa – was near Livadia, a few kilometres west of Yalta. The taxi driver, whom we had promised a hefty sum, wound his yellow Volga along the steep embankment facing the sea for the longest time. Finally he turned down a dirt road, pointed to the place from which we could see the *dacha*, and told us not to be too long.

Set against a landscape that the Soviet poet Vladimir Mayakovsky described as the "very image of ancient paradise" the Gorbachev compound made the Kennedy one at Hyannisport,

Massachusetts, look subordinate. On a plateau of sunlit serenity, the rectangular, classical main building looked to have at least 50 rooms. Gray-white in colour, it was framed spectacularly by the sea, the forest, wonderfully manicured lawns, paths, and gardens.

We were told it was one of three Black Sea *dachas* at the Soviet leader's disposal. Even in times of *glasnost*, the government tried to hide the locations of these palaces, which had been used by previous Soviet leaders as well. One reason was security; another was that the classless society was supposed to be just that – classless. Most of the people on Yalta's streets knew the locations, however. A Russian who worked in a liquor outlet said he had made home movies of the villa. "You visit me sometime," he said. "I will show you."

The *Byelorussia* sailed back to Odessa. The sun shone brilliantly, as it had all week. A Russian I had met on board, who was constantly cursing Gorbachev because vodka wasn't sold on the ship, would not stop asking me for one of my shirts. Finally, after his wife joined in the pleading, I surrendered. I took them to my room and handed over a blue button-down – 100-percent cotton. He was so grateful he said he would wear it every day.

25/Boris the Basher

THROUGH THE summer and fall of 1987 Gorbachev made vital political steps that lessened the threat from the domestic forces opposing him. He moved against those who were going too slowly on reform as well as those who wanted to surge ahead precipitously.

Gorbachev belonged to the radical camp, but he was also a political realist who knew that to be isolated on the liberal fringe of the Communist Party was to leave too much room for his opponents. Khrushchev had proceeded with intemperate haste; Gorbachev was moving with diplomatic dispatch. He wanted Soviet society rebuilt not solely through orders from the top but with participation from the ground up. The command nature of the Soviet political tradition and infrastructure, as well as Gorbachev's time constraints, made the realization of this hope rather unlikely, but by rushing in *glasnost*'s freedom-of-speech reforms, by allowing dissent a voice, and by meeting one on one with comrades on the streets, he was at least giving the process a participatory veneer.

Timing was a thorny problem. From the far liberal side, from Andrei Sakharov and other reformist voices, Gorbachev was hearing that his domestic reforms were neither deep enough nor fast enough. From the conservative side the lament was the opposite.

Along with the intellectuals' argument that speedy democratic measures were a moral imperative, there were other compelling reasons for Gorbachev to take a sprinter's approach. The country had fallen into such a state of totalitarian lethargy that only a series of jolts could break the chains. Half-measures produced over a long period of time would be ineffective, Gorbachev was warned. Party bosses would pay only lip service to them. Turning a nation of socialist receivers into one of market doers involved such a change in the basic Soviet mentality that it was easy to wonder whether it was possible at all. I remembered the woman who said that only revolution, only a spilling of blood, could change the Soviet state.

Yet another argument for moving quickly and moving radically was the importance of achieving a new détente with the West. Improving the economy was going to require a relaxed relationship with the West, so that present Soviet expenditures on defence could be redirected to the economy. But détente demanded more than a conciliatory approach to foreign policy; another prerequisite was quick action on human rights. Washington would be much more inclined to enter into arms agreements with a Soviet Union that was in pursuit of democratization. More trade for the Soviet Union, more Western technology, and the integration of the economy with that of the rest of the world, would not come without it. He had to move.

Gorbachev was conscious of dooming the country to half-measures, but aware also that reckless abandon would increasingly frighten a nation of conservatives, rally the opposition around a point man, and bring about his downfall. "The thought invariably comes to mind," said Nikolai Shmelyov, "that a silent conspiracy may take shape or has already taken shape in the country against *perestroika* – a conspiracy in which the interests of a certain part of the local leadership and a number of central departments are drawing ever closer."

Even though the state of the economy approached that of many Third World countries, Andrei Chernakov in Odessa, and millions like him, didn't want an upheaval in their lives. The status quo ensured them they would have the basic necessities without having to work hard.

Changes such as giving more vent to market forces could only succeed if introduced methodically, the conservatives argued. With time and luck, with an increase in world oil prices, with some good crop years, and with the introduction of measured reforms, all would be well again. Why risk upsetting the stability of the nation?

The choice fell between trying to improve the old system and trying to change that system. The risks were far greater with the latter. The country was in a period of stagnation and declining economic growth. The transition to radically new methods would require reeducating and redeploying the labour force, which in turn would likely entail a further decline in productivity. "The leadership faces an acute dilemma," wrote Seweryn Bialer. "The shortcomings of the system are creating enormous pressure for radical change, but successful reform requires previous performance to subsidize the transition. The political risks of attempting a radical reform during a period of declining economic growth must seem grave to the leadership, probably graver than the consequences of living with a somewhat improved old system and its shortcomings."[1]

The thought that Gorbachev's political future was imperilled by his reform efforts sometimes worked in his favour. When he disappointed his Western audience with old-fashioned Communist rhetoric, the foreign press often rallied to the line that he really didn't mean it, but that he had to do if for political reasons. Sometimes in Moscow I found myself quietly hoping he would take a reactionary step or two just to allay the opposition. I felt he was the Soviet Union's last chance, that if anything happened to him the East-West schism and the arms race might endure till it reached the desperation point.

To my thinking and that of most observers, Gorbachev's timing appeared to be right. Usually it was three or four steps forward and one step back. Given the sheer sweep of what he was attempting, the coordination of it all was a staggering task. The Politburo's Alexander Yakovlev once remarked to a couple of Canadian diplomats that the government was undertaking so many changes it could hardly keep track. It seemed impossible that one man could manage four revolutions at once, but Gorbachev was revolutionizing (there wasn't a better word for it) the Soviet Union in the areas of human rights, the economy, foreign policy, and, as would soon be evident, political institutions. Many of the ideas, as well as much of the conceptualizing, were his own. Unlike the president of the United States, he was writing the script as well as reading it.

In the second half of 1987 some of the questions about the pace of his *perestroika* came to a head. There was evidence of sustained obstructionism from Brezhnev-era *apparatchiks* on the right, as well as criticism for lagging behind from the leading voices of the radical left. Gorbachev saw these as threats to his efforts at consensus-building and to the unity of the Communist Party; he responded by nudging conservative Yegor Ligachev away from influence and dropping Boris Yeltsin from power altogether.

In terms of the public profile of Gorbachev's reforms, three figures stood out – Gorbachev, Ligachev, and Yeltsin. Ligachev and Yeltsin represented separate camps, if not in reality then in the public's imagination. Gorbachev didn't want the divisions. He wanted cohesion.

In the case of Ligachev, the main strike would come the following year. But before then, in mid-1987, in the course of the plenum that adopted his economic self-financing plans, Gorbachev moved Alexander Yakovlev into the Politburo. Yakovlev, a former ambassador to Canada, was recognized as one of the fathers of *glasnost*. His promotion was regarded as a signal to Ligachev, who was cooler on *glasnost* than on other aspects of *perestroika*, that his ideology portfolio was being encroached upon. It had always been an anomaly that a man like Ligachev was overseeing ideology while *glasnost* was the rage. Now, although ideology was still Ligachev's official portfolio, the intelligentsia could breathe a little easier.

Gorbachev also promoted defence minister Dmitri Yazov to the Politburo. The Soviet leader had found the proverbial silver lining to the cloud that had recently come over Moscow in the form of Mathias Rust. Rust, a young amateur pilot from West Germany, had flown a Cessna into Red Square the spring before in a startling dash from Helsinki, through the supposedly crack Soviet defences. It had captivated the world's imagination but done little for the career of Sergei Sokolov, the defence chief. The incident was Gorbachev's excuse to dismiss him outright, shake up the armed forces, and bring yet another ally to the Politburo team in the form of Yazov.

The most sensational power move of the year, however, involved Moscow's first secretary, Yeltsin. Since his outburst at the 27th Party Congress against privilege, Yeltsin had continued his radical course, along the way establishing a reputation as a bull-headed maverick who took on anybody and anything that crossed his path.

Moscow was in such a mess, declared Boris the Basher, as he came to be called, that to buy a decent pair of shoes he had to go to his home town of Sverdlovsk. Venturing into a Moscow market one day to check out the vegetables, the city leader told a vendor, "what a miserable bunch of parsley." Muscovites, he said, were worse off than people in most other areas of the country; the rate of housing construction in the capital had tumbled in the rankings, from top-ten to 58th, he added. Architecturally, the city was in "a pitiable state." The police were doing a lousy job, according to Yeltsin, and the academic institutes were so useless he was shutting down 15 of them. He followed up his clobber campaign with mass firings, sometimes on a whim, sometimes for no good reason.

On the more positive side, Yeltsin bravely took on the Moscow mafia. Of corruption in the city, he offered the view that "we are digging in and we still don't see the bottom of this pit of dirt." In his first few months 800 Moscow businessmen were arrested on corruption charges.

His attacks on privilege didn't stop. He closed down a specialty store in Moscow catering to the very elite. He curbed limousine privileges for Moscow's city hierarchy and exposed the system's nepotism, revealing that 70 percent of the students in top academic institutes were children of leading officials of various ranks. Drug problems were serious in the schools, Yeltsin said, but owing to an "ostrich-like" attitude, nobody knew about them. He permitted the formation in Moscow of groups that were independent of the Communist Party and the Komsomol. He even allowed them to hold a convention at which radical platforms, such as one proposing a multiparty system, were passed.

Because Gorbachev had promoted him so quickly, and because he was a torrid reformer, Yeltsin became closely identified with the Soviet leader. Some said Gorbachev was his protector, that Yeltsin would be safe as long as Gorbachev was around, as would Korotich, the magazine editor. At a Moscow city party meeting Yeltsin once received an anonymous note: "We know you are Gorbachev's stooge. Why don't you go back where you came from?"[2]

To those of us in the foreign press corps and many in the diplomatic corps, Yeltsin was a star because his values were closer to our own. While his lust for democratic change was appealing, he had plenty of faults. Yeltsin was overemotional, brash, loose-lipped, and given to authoritarian rampages. He was also becoming intoxicated with his growing popularity among the common people.

Though the information system in the capital was more open, it was still difficult to judge what was transpiring behind the Kremlin walls, to judge how those in the Politburo and Central Committee, including Yeltsin, interrelated. It was generally accepted wisdom that the Politburo had three conservatively inclined figures who might be given to oppose the leader. They were Ligachev, the Ukrainian party chief Vladimir Shcherbitsky, and KGB chief Viktor Chebrikov. For all the Western press knew, there may have been spectacular infighting going on. Of the 307-member Central Committee, which met only two or three times a year, even less was known. It was assumed that a good majority supported continued *perestroika*, but none of us knew whether the degree of opposition on the committee was threatening. (The Central Committee was the ultimate authority. If Gorbachev came to be opposed by a majority on the Politburo, he could appeal to the Central Committee for majority support there.)

When reports of a crisis surrounding Yeltsin surfaced in October, many of us were caught by surprise. Yeltsin had apparently become frustrated by what he considered to be the slow pace of reform. As would later be revealed, he offered his resignation to Gorbachev while the general secretary was on holiday in late August and early September. Gorbachev advised Yeltsin to stay on until the 70th anniversary of the 1917 revolution in early November and then the two could discuss the problems.

But Yeltsin ignored the boss's order. On October 21 at a Central Committee meeting, he delivered a pounding denunciation of the pace of *perestroika*, levelling broadsides in his customary gratuitous manner. While Ligachev was apparently his main target of abuse, Yeltsin, short on allies to begin with, seemed determined to alienate the ones he had left. No text of Yeltsin's speech was published at the time but rumours suggested he even weighed in against Raisa Gorbachev with her husband present, saying she had no business meddling in the affairs of state.

Whether Yeltsin actually stated it or not, the negative view of

Raisa was a surprisingly common one: wherever I travelled I found resentment of her. Traditionally, since 1917 anyway, the Soviet leader's wife had been invisible. Much of the population seemed to feel that this kind of role – first *babushka* of the Kremlin – should continue. They wanted Raisa in the background, peeling potatoes. To me and other Western observers she was the perfect partner for Gorbachev – intelligent, educated, attractive, personable. But the image of the thoroughly modern Raisa rankled so much that an underground film reportedly was made in Moscow ridiculing her credit-card shopping and foreign fashions.

After the speech, rumours abounded that Yeltsin was about to be dumped. Yakovlev, a fast-rising star in the reform constellation, appeared for his first full-fledged press conference. A big fuss was being made of little, he said. Yeltsin would not have to resign. "Why is it such a big deal?" Yakovlev asked. "We have arguments in our meetings. Of course we do. There is nothing special in that."

This was rather vintage Yakovlev. This short, heavy man with receding hair, a large head, and glasses had lived in both the United States and Canada and knew how to play the game of putting the shoe on the other foot. Thus, in his view, the Politburo had arguments but so did cabinets in other countries. Thus it was true that the Soviet Union banned Western publications, but the United States banned an even greater number of Soviet publications. Western experts said Stalin killed millions, but why is that opinion, Yakovlev asked, any more valid than that of Gorbachev and Soviet specialists who said thousands? On a question about whether the Soviets were learning much from the Western capitalist experience, he replied, "In contrast to some Western countries which reject the socialist experience point blank, we study the Western experience and don't reject nearly so much."

Details of Yeltsin's speech had not yet surfaced by the time of Yakovlev's press conference. Unfortunately, because he was Alexander Yakovlev, I believed him on Yeltsin. Then I learned how egregiously wrong he had been. Within days of that press conference Gorbachev himself made it clear that Yeltsin was on the ropes. "We must not give in to pressure from those overly headstrong and impatient people who do not want to take into account the objective logic of restructuring," he said in a speech opening the Soviet anniversary festivities. Gorbachev, who also attacked conservatives in his speech, didn't single out Yeltsin by name, but it was clear he had Boris in mind. It should be made clear to "impatient elements," he asserted, "that we cannot skip stages and try to do everything with one wave of the hand."

The following week Yeltsin was dismissed from his Moscow position, and a short time later he lost his position as a non-voting member of the Politburo. The decision was made at a meeting of the Moscow Communist Party Committee, in the presence of Gorbachev and other Kremlin leaders. The official reason was "major shortcomings" in his work. As well, Yeltsin's remarks in his speech of October 21 were "politically mistaken," Tass announced. On being tossed overboard, Yeltsin was not even accorded the customary compassion – the line about having to retire due to poor health. Even so, he had to be taken to hospital immediately after the meeting – he had nearly collapsed after all the attacks on his character.

Pravda published an account of the debate, during which Gorbachev had inscribed Yeltsin's epitaph: "As life showed, pronouncing appeals and slogans sufficed for him, but when the time came to support words with concrete deeds, a helpless, fidgety, panicked mood appeared." Yeltsin's speech of October 21 was "an irresponsible and immoral act," the Soviet leader said, adding that the Moscow boss had erred badly in saying nothing good was happening.

Yeltsin, who had poured out so much abuse on everyone else, got his comeuppance that night. One Moscow party official accused him of stabbing the party in the back. Others said he was guilty of "Bonapartism" and "huge party crimes."

According to the *Pravda* account, Yeltsin then confessed to his sins. "One of my most characteristic personal traits, ambition, manifested itself of late. I tried to check it but regrettably without success. I have lost the face of a political Communist leader. I am very guilty. . . . " This statement had all the appearance of a forced confession written for him – a carry-over, perhaps, from Stalinist days.

At the meeting the new sensitivity to public opinion in the West showed itself. In the midst of all the spilled emotions, one official rose to warn that if Yeltsin was dismissed, the West would seek to make a martyr out of him, "to turn Boris Nikolayevich into Jesus Christ."

The West's reaction was almost that explicit. The foreign press immediately responded with knee-jerk despair and anguish. The simplistic analysis was that the leader of reform had just been ousted and that therefore reform had suffered a crushing blow. Gorbachev wasn't such a progressive after all, reports said.

Given the nature of his outburst, however, Yeltsin more or less had to go. If a cabinet minister in a Western democracy stood up in Cabinet, with the president or prime minister attending, and assailed his government's program and half the cabinet – which is what Yeltsin had done in Moscow – he would most likely be dismissed. As for his firing damaging the prospects for *glasnost* and *perestroika*, the long-range result was perhaps closer to the opposite.

In the short term there was a marked outpouring of sympathy for Yeltsin. Moscow intellectuals expressed doubts about the viability of the reform drive. Vitaly Korotich, who was holding weekly public forums, heard little but pessimism at the forum that followed Yeltsin's dismissal. "Stalinism is returning," said one participant. "Who will now dare to express his opinion?" asked another.[3] Korotich was uncharacteristically noncommittal in his responses. The extent of the ennui may have contributed to Gorbachev's next move: less than a week after all the histrionics, he appointed Yeltsin to a minister's job as coordinator for Soviet construction. But within a couple of months it became obvious that the Soviet leader was plunging ahead with reform, and the Yeltsin crisis, the first of more Yeltsin crises to come, faded in significance.

In the long run the Yeltsin controversy moved Gorbachev away from his position on the more radical fringe and back toward the consensus-building centre. It showed that he was taking a rational approach to reform. His continuing to support Yeltsin in the wake of such reckless conduct would have been politically foolhardy. Instead, by creating some opposition on his left flank, Gorbachev took away some of the ammunition available to the right.

Within weeks the man from Stavropol was demonstrating that his true leanings hadn't changed. "You should have no doubts," he declared. "We will concede nothing in our *perestroika* policy. We are dedicated to take this policy through to the end. The choice is made and we will not turn off course. . . . To stop now would be disastrous."

"In questions of democracy," the leader of the Soviet Union added, "no one will go so far as we will."[4]

26/The View from Stavropol

IN EARLY DECEMBER, Mikhail Gorbachev was preparing to travel to Washington for his third summit with Ronald Reagan, and I was facing the uninteresting prospect of staying behind in Moscow and writing reaction stories from Gorky Street. In the back of my mind for some time, however, had perched the thought of journeying to Gorbachev's home region of Stavropol. The occasion of the summit would be the best time to try it. I was mildly surprised when officials at the foreign ministry gave me permission to make the trip, particularly while the big event was in progress. They would not, however, lift their ban on visits to Privolnoye, the farming village outside Stavropol where Gorbachev was born.

Wrongly, I expected to find some aura of excitement in Stavropol in those early days of December 1987. Instead, the tone and temper of the city was not unlike what I'd felt in most provincial Russian cities on any day. The people were neither friendly nor unfriendly, neither miserable nor content. They were preoccupied with life's daily routines – shuffling into and out of the shops on Karl Marx Street, standing at the bus stops complaining of the damp weather, trying to stay awake at a socialist library, pretending to work at a socialist job.

At my cold-water hotel the rooms were small and remarkably narrow. Though it was a fair-sized city, getting a phone line required three days booking in advance, unless you were prepared to give gifts of dollars. Just because it was Gorbachev's home city didn't mean the food supplies were better. Gorbachev himself had made the point a year earlier. "In 1969 in Stavropol we had a problem – what to do with all the meat and milk. Butter, too – heaps of it. And now there is nothing. We have forgotten how to work."

I kept looking for evidence that Gorbachev had lived here – a sign, a street name, a poster, a plaque – but found nothing. The lack of recognition was what Gorbachev wanted; however, it rankled the rarely shy Raisa when she visited the city in 1986. At the Komsomol offices, where Gorbachev had started his career, she saw pictures of other noteworthy members but none of husband Mikhail, the most famous of them all. She politely suggested they do something about it.

I met a tall, intense 40-year-old named Slava Solodskik. He had brown eyes and dishevelled brown hair, and wore a brown mohair sweater, brown corduroy pants, and brown shoes. He worked as an organizer of youth events at the city's sprawling recreational palace, which had been slated to house government bureaucrats until Gorbachev ordered it to be given over to the young. Solodskik was a transplanted Leningrader. He had moved to Stavropol because the housing shortfall in his home city on the Baltic was so drastic it might take him a lifetime to get his own flat.

He was a passionate, thinking Russian. He greatly admired *Ogonyok*, the marauding magazine – so much, in fact, that he had recently organized a political club called the Friends of *Ogonyok*. It was his attempt to give more impetus to *perestroika* in Stavropol. "The problem is people can't get accustomed to it. My father was always defending Stalin. Since I have the opposite opinion, we always had quarrels. You see, he fought with Stalin's name on his lips."

Solodskik had been a boozer several years earlier, driven that way partly, he said, by the numbing Brezhnev years. "Politics wasn't touching me as a person. Now there's an absolutely different picture." Now he was becoming religious as well, and was especially interested in the religions of the East. "The thing is, five years ago we couldn't talk openly about these things." To Solodskik, Gorbachev's going to Washington and opening a dialogue with the West was a beginning step toward mutual understanding. "That's the problem.

We don't know each other and we have to know each other. Maybe we can't be big friends but we can be little friends. We are civilized peoples. The systems are different but we are civilized peoples."

I found one of his remarks particularly striking. "I want to be an honest man without being forced to be a political dissident," he said. "I want to be a human among humans. I think Gorbachev is the type of leader who understands my desire."

At the city library, which was big, clean, modern, and jammed with row upon row of books about Communist ideology, I figured I might get a good idea of what the citizens of Stavropol thought of their home-town hero's visit to the White House. For a few minutes I browsed the sports shelves in an unsuccessful bid to come up with anything written in the past five years on Soviet hockey. Then I parked myself a few feet inside the main door, where, it being the day after Reagan and Gorbachev had signed the treaty eliminating medium-range weapons from Europe, I expected to find Russians marginally more roused than usual.

Almost everybody was ho-hum. "This is good," they said, or, "It's a start," or, "People want peace," or, "We have to get rid of these weapons of death." No one turned away my request to talk, but no one lingered. In Stavropol, as in most Soviet places I visited, I couldn't find much hatred or deep animosity toward the Americans. A woman named Luboff, which means "love" in Russian, was an exception – she told me they were all mixed up in the head and that Gorbachev would straighten them out. Someone else joined in to say that American presidents needed the support of the military-industrial complex, which meant that no president would ever agree to Gorbachev's call for deep cuts.

Beyond the generalities the people in the Stavropol library, dressed tidily in low-budget fabrics, didn't know much about what was going on. That their man was in the course of reshaping the Soviet Union's relationship with the rest of the world hadn't yet hit home. As for Raisa, the residents of Stavropol were content not to hear anything at all.

The Reagan-Gorbachev summit was being given unexceptional coverage in the Stavropol newspapers. There were usually two basic news reports a day – no analysis, no colour, no reminiscences about the younger Gorbachev. On the first day the *Stavropolskaya Pravda*, unlike all the country's central papers, did not carry the picture of Raisa in Washington standing with her husband and other leading Soviet figures.

A local journalist told me that Raisa was even less popular in Stavropol, her home of 23 years, than in the rest of the country. Olga Trubeetzena, a businesswoman, seconded the notion, saying her fellow Russians seemed to want Soviet women to maintain their image as dumpy provincials. The Soviet's sensitivity to Raisa was clear in how the media played Tom Brokaw's TV interview with her husband. Brokaw asked the Soviet leader if he sought his wife's views on national politics and policy. "We discuss everything," replied Gorbachev. "Including Soviet affairs at the highest level?" asked Brokaw. "I think I have answered your question fully," Gorbachev retorted. In the delayed transmission to the Soviet audience, that exchange was altered: the translator rephrased the first question so that Brokaw was asking whether he and his wife discussed public affairs in general; the second question was dropped entirely.

Solodskik remembered Raisa as a prominent booster of the arts in Stavropol. She and her husband were regulars at the Lermontov Dramatic Theatre, which, with its pink Ionic columns, is one among several architecturally pleasant structures in the city. Raisa would sometimes come by on her own and congratulate the actors. "She wasn't the type to turn up her nose at anyone," said Solodskik.

A friend of Solodskik's went to Moscow for a meeting of the theatrical union. He'd met Raisa briefly in Stavropol. When she entered the hall he called over to her. Raisa went over to him, said hello, and apologized for not remembering his name. The two got chatting and Raisa ended up sitting with him through the entire meeting. The dignitaries at the front waited and waited for Raisa to come forward and join them, but she preferred the man at the back from Stavropol.

The man asked her about the controversy over her high profile. She said it was only natural for her to be this way, that political wives all over the world did the same, that her contacts with other world leaders were helpful to the Soviet image.

While I was in Stavropol, Raisa was in Washington having her usual problems with Nancy Reagan. Their first meeting in Geneva had turned into a duel to see who could upstage the other. Nancy did not attend the Reykjavik summit that followed. The wives' dialogue in Washington opened curtly: "We missed you at Reykjavik," Raisa said. "I was told women weren't invited," Nancy replied. Raisa went on to say no less than three times that 20 million Soviets died during the Second World War. Finally Nancy said, "Yes you mentioned that." During a tour of the White House, someone asked Raisa whether she would like to live there. "This is an official residence," she replied. "I would say, humanly speaking, that a human being would like to live in a regular house."

Fortunately, their husbands got along better. They were meeting to sign the INF agreement – the first superpower treaty aimed at reducing rather than merely limiting nuclear weapons. After the ceremony President Reagan suggested the two men should have the courage to recognize that there are "weighty differences between our governments and systems." In his response Gorbachev asserted, "The wisdom of politics today lies in not using those differences as a pretext for confrontation, enmity and the arms race."

The final details of the INF treaty had been agreed to shortly before the signing, which meant that the Washington summit could open with its success assured. Gorbachev would finally have something concrete to show the people back home; Reagan, with his popularity tumbling in the wake of the Iran-Contra scandal and the stock-market crash, would have something with which to resurrect his image.

The treaty aside, the summit story was in the atmospherics. Reagan and Gorbachev, despite their fundamentally dissimilar personalities, somehow achieved a public harmony and warmth that moved people. These were two masters of the public-relations game. Their rapport transcended underlying hostilities.

The summit wasn't all smooth. In a worrisome development, the two leaders clashed at their first meeting when Reagan dove directly into the subject of human-rights abuses. Before he could go on too far, Gorbachev snapped, "I am not on trial here and you are not a prosecutor." He asked him what kind of human rights America had, that allowed citizens to lie homeless on the streets of its capital and saw the guns of the nation of freedom targeted on the southern border to prevent destitute Mexicans from partaking of that freedom. Reagan said there was a big difference between wanting out and wanting in. On two other occasions at the summit, these while talking to the media, Gorbachev would overreact, becoming chillingly angry over accusations about human rights and, by extension, reminding Americans that hidden beneath the Madison Avenue veneer was a man of steel.

With Reagan the dialogue was soon set right. At the treaty-signing ceremony the president cited the Russian phrase "trust but verify" as a good axiom in dealing with the Soviets. Gorbachev replied light-heartedly, "You repeat that at every meeting." Laughter followed, whereupon Reagan, with actor's timing, rejoindered, "I like it." The audience erupted.

The two leaders were somehow able to move the potentially explosive issue of SDI to a side table – though not without a tense moment. When Reagan vowed not to let the Soviets or anyone else scuttle his intentions to build a nuclear shield, Gorbachev grew deeply serious before rising to reply. "Mr. President, do what you think you have to do. And if in the end you think you have a system you want to deploy, go ahead and deploy it. Who am I to tell you what to do? I think you are wasting your money. I don't think it will work. But if that's what you want to do, go ahead."

It was blunt talk that Reagan could understand. "We are moving in another direction," Gorbachev added, "and we preserve our option to do what we think is necessary and in our own national interests at the time. And we think we can do it less expensively and with greater effectiveness."

Gorbachev was in the American capital to sell his views to more than the president. He held separate sessions with the cream of the media, business, and political worlds. At one point, in a dazzling bit of p.r., he told his limo driver, "Stop the car!" and stepped out into midtown Washington for an impromptu session with pedestrians. It was a carry-over from the curbside chats he conducted when travelling in his own country. Those were tremendously popular with the foreign media, and Gorbachev did seem to derive benefit from direct dialogue with the people. Whenever someone tried to tell him everything was fine, he would bore in on them because he knew it wasn't true.

His final session with the media in Washington was close to a disaster, as he again lost his temper on human rights and began lecturing the hall in dictatorial, Stalinesque fashion. It was a surprising display of bad politics on his part. Usually he had better sense.

Generally, however, the reviews of his summit performance were gushing. At one point Jack Valente, the president of the Motion Picture Association, told Gorbachev he was so popular he was "now running third in the Iowa primary." Gorbachev enjoyed the remark, joking, "But I already have a job." Even Richard Perle, the retiring assistant defence secretary known as the Prince of Darkness for his raging anti-Soviet views, emerged impressed from a talk with the Soviet leader. "He's a very intelligent man, very engaging, forceful. . . ."

The columnist Richard Reeves called the summit "the peace conference of the Cold War." John Steinbruner, an arms specialist at the Brookings Institute, held a similar view. "The Cold War has been over for some time and the United States is now in the final stages of coming to that realization." After a summit with Dwight Eisenhower in 1959, Nikita Khrushchev had been optimistic too: "The ice of the Cold War already is not only showing signs of a crack but has started to crumble." The year 1959 was too early for that type of optimism, and it was too early to leap to such conclusions in the late 1980s. But no one was denying the promise.

By then, evidence of a new Soviet approach to the world had been accumulating for two years. Before the summit the Kremlin rolled its peace ball to the United Nations. In an about-face in its attitude to that body, Moscow paid back 111 million dollars in arrears and pledged a further 197 million for UN peace-keeping missions going back to the 1960s. As well, it put forward several proposals designed to increase the UN's stature and power.

With the United States, Gorbachev had retooled his country's evil-empire image in less than three years. A new détente was in the works, inter-superpower communications were tripling, Gorbachev was riding high in American opinion polls, and the sensational goal of cutting strategic nuclear arsenals in half now rose as a genuine possibility.

Gorbachev had room to manoeuvre. His country had plenty of surplus stock in the munitions factories to use as bargaining chips; he could make concessions without jeopardizing the Soviets' status as a military superpower. While the United States was in a position to do the same, the idea of making unilateral concessions to score points in the court of world opinion was not a realistic option for a Republican White House. Gorbachev also had to concern himself with public opinion and with the hard-line elements in his country – but not to the extent that Reagan did.

Past Soviet leaders had sought influence by threat; Gorbachev was seeking influence by concession. It was expansion of power not by Marxism, guns, and Stalin Street diplomacy, but by good will, gift giving and Madison Avenue.

Gorbachev could afford a 19-month moratorium on nuclear explosions. He could afford to give away more weapons stocks than the Americans in the INF treaty. He could allow full-scale on-site inspection in his country. He could cut back troop contingents in Eastern Europe and along the Chinese border. He could pull out of Afghanistan. He could pledge to get rid of chemical-weapons stocks. He could grant Sweden rights to exploit resources in the Baltic Sea. He could reduce his nation's strength in mainland troops by ten percent. He could do all this and still blow up the world a couple of dozen times over.

All of this worked, as White Knight diplomacy is inclined to do. By the end of 1987, wherever on the globe one chose to look, the Soviets had registered diplomatic gains – some of them major.

With China, Gorbachev was playing the card. Beijing had put three demands on the table for a recommencement of the dialogue between the two Communist giants: withdrawal from Afghanistan, a Soviet prodding of Vietnam to pull out of Cambodia, and concessions on a territorial dispute along their shared border. In due time Gorbachev would accede to all three demands, and China would agree to a summit to begin a new era of friendship.

In Eastern Europe, Moscow had once been the barrier to change; now it was the major proponent of change. That a Soviet leader could be popular in Eastern Europe had once been unthinkable. Not any more; Gorbachev was holding out hope for millions that they would be able to live without bondage to totalitarianism. He was the Great Red Hope. The INF treaty and, later, the withdrawal of some Soviet forces from bloc countries were evidence the hope was not misguided.

In Western Europe, Gorbachev's liberalism was paying dividends in the form of better relations. He met the Iron Lady, Margaret Thatcher, on his way to Washington and turned her into butter. Her praise of him verged on the fulsome. The French, Spanish, and even German leaders were also admiring, and well prepared to do business with the new Kremlin. Polls began to show that the Soviet Union was no longer seen as the number-one menace to world peace.

In the Middle East, the Irangate scandal, during which it was disclosed that the White House had secretly helped Iran, had badly tarnished the Americans' reputation. Meanwhile the Kremlin's dovish comportment – most notably its high-profile proposal for a Middle East peace conference – was building bridges. Moscow relaxed the terms of Egypt's war-loan repayments. Major increases in Jewish emigration were beginning to produce a thaw in relations with Israel. At the same time, the treatment of Arabs in the occupied territories was damaging Israel's credibility when it tried to complain about the human-rights abuses of others.

Not a week was going by without the Kremlin wooing a Third World leader. The Soviets were paying less attention to old clients such as Angola, Syria, and Libya, while cultivating new relationships in South America, Africa, and elsewhere.

Gorbachev as much as acknowledged that his country bore a significant share of responsibility for the collapse of détente in the mid-1970s. The confrontational relationship with Washington that resulted had prepared the ground for Reagan's unprecedented peacetime military build-up. That in turn put further demands on the Soviet's defence budget, and further strain on their stagnating economy.

The INF signing was a potential turning point, a harbinger of a new era. Gorbachev was repudiating Brezhnev's mindless militarism in the form of the SS-20 deployments of the 1970s in Europe; he was also agreeing to accept minute foreign inspection of Soviet SS-20 munitions factories. The latter move startled American arms experts. "If someone had asked me about this ten years ago, I would have said it's wildly improbable," said Harold Brown, who had been defence secretary under Jimmy Carter. "I thought on-site inspection was something they would resist to the last moment," said Richard Pipes, Havard's leading anti-Soviet hard-liner. "I still find it hard to believe."

British and French leaders in particular had frowned on Gorbachev's 1986 proposal to totally eliminate nuclear arms, saying the nuclear deterrent was essential. The idea of abolishing the weapons altogether seemed strange in the first place, coming from the Soviets. Those weapons were almost all that gave them their superpower status: take them away and what was left but a third rate economy? But while total abandonment of nuclear weapons was still not viewed as a possibility, INF brought credence to the notion that the superpowers could remain secure with greatly reduced arsenals.

Gorbachev got the break he needed in late 1987 with the retirement of Caspar Weinberger, the Americans' defence secretary. Weinberger was the hawk of hawks, regarded by the Kremlin as an uncompromising, closed-minded bigot. The Soviets considered him and top advisor Richard Perle to be the main obstacles to superpower peace. As other hard-liners left the White House – bunker strategist Oliver North, chief of staff Donald Regan, national-security advisor John Poindexter – the playing field was left more open to the more moderate George Shultz. American foreign policy had often amounted to a battle between him and Weinberger for the president's ear; Weinberger was said to rule Reagan's heart, which was big, and Shultz was said to rule his mind, which wasn't. Weinberger had often won.

Eduard Shevardnadze reflected some of the Kremlin's frustration with Weinberger during a press conference in Washington in September 1987. For openers, he smiled mischievously at the assembled scribes. Then he said, "I hope you influential people will be able to bring pressure on the Pentagon to be reasonable." With Weinberger's departure it became more reasonable – and the chances of a new era more likely.

27/A Superpower Without Toothpaste

WHILE GORBACHEV was away signing an agreement on nuclear weapons, back home his empire ran out of toothpaste. Shortages were first reported in the countryside. Then there was a run on the larger cities, which ultimately hit Moscow, leaving a scenario of the absurd – a superpower without toothpaste; not a Pepsodent smile across 11 time zones.

For the foreign community it wasn't an inconvenience. We didn't use Soviet toothpaste anyway. We just assumed it would be inferior. We could import as much toothpaste as we wanted from the Stockman's store in Finland. Every week a train roared in from Helsinki with a cornucopia of overpriced Western goods to keep the foreign community happy. We got almost everything from the train – pens, cheese, shoe polish, aspirin, milk – though nothing seemed wrong with Russian cows – and batteries. Batteries were critical, given all the equipment that ran on them. There were Soviet-made batteries but they weren't manufactured by Soyuz rocket engineers. They drained of strength within a couple of hours and began to leak a sticky, unpleasant fluid. The day the goods arrived our car drivers would race down to the train depot and stand in line in the cold and then be shuffled from kiosk to kiosk, filling out forms. Then they would carry the boxes to our apartments, where some among our maids would make off with whatever they felt they could get away with. Sometimes my housekeeper or secretary would summon enough confidence to ask me to order something for them. The most frequent request was for facial cream or hair dye.

Given the circumstances, it was difficult not to feel like the ugly Canadian. To be generous with the imported supplies was to be condescending, yet to be sparing was to be selfish, and to be somewhere in between was to be coy.

We thought we had a Russian maid we could trust. On occasion there seemed to be less sugar in the sugar bag or less liquor in the liquor cabinet but, compared with stories we had heard about other housekeepers, our Tanya was clean. When we departed in 1988, we made an inventory – with Tanya looking on – of what was left in the apartment, and wished her well. She was to stay on and work for the family of the paper's new correspondent, Jeff Sallot. When the Sallots arrived, several weeks after we left, they found an apartment fleeced of half the items on the inventory list. Tanya had made off with them, figuring that the newcomers wouldn't know. She was asked to return everything, which she did, and find another family of foreigners to work for.

One thing neither Tanya nor Valery nor Ina ever asked for was toothpaste. There were some things, I think, they simply weren't going to swallow their Russian pride to do, and that was one of them. The toothpaste shortage was one more needless, inexcusable privation Russians had to endure. The farcical nature of it hit home the night Zoran Milich and I were trying to find the slippery Yasmin Karpon at the Belgrade Hotel. We had been sitting with the cockroaches at the dark main-floor bar for a little while when a woman who had all the trademarks of a prostitute pulled up a chair beside us and made herself at home.

Her name was Natalia. She wore an emerald-green silk jacket that sloped provocatively to her bare knees. She had legs as long as Kareem Abdul-Jabbar's and eyes that could stop a train. Her only defect was her ruby-lipped smile. It revealed teeth the colour of Alberta wheatfields.

Before long into our conversation she mentioned the toothpaste shortage. Her teeth were grungy, she said, in need of a good brush. There was no argument there, but in a flash the ever-resourceful Milich had a solution: he reached into his totebag and pulled out a tube of Colgate. "Here," he said matter-of-factly, "take this."

Natalia accepted readily. But as if this wasn't a heady enough display of the new détente, I spotted a toothbrush in the photographer's sack, whipped it out, and said, "Here's a brush, too, Natalia. Now you're all set." Natalia was even more delighted. To everyone's misfortune, she grinned from ear to ear.

Milich didn't like what I had done. "I can't really afford to lose that. It's the only one I've got while I'm over here." Over cognac – the only drink this bar served – he lobbied Natalia until she reluctantly relinquished it. Then, without even an offer of other services, she happily vanished into the night.

It's not often, I thought, that a prostitute joins a table for a drink and makes off with a tube of Colgate. But in a town without toothpaste, in the Soviet Union of 1987, it was a good night's work.

Though the country was well known for its endless variety of shortages, no one could remember a toothpaste crisis. There were several reasons for it. A bureaucrat had goofed on his market estimates. Toothpaste imports were down anyway because of a jump in the international market price. And the Kremlin's cutback in vodka production had resulted in many would-be drinkers switching to drinks made with toothpaste.

When a sugar shortage hit a few weeks later, the government's sobriety crusade was again cited as a cause. Thousands of people were switching to home brew, and home brew required lots of sugar. Gorbachev was beginning to realize how hard it was going to be to cure his country of its alcohol addiction.

One March morning a squabble over the sugar shortage developed at a little grocery store near my apartment. About 30 customers had gathered at the counter by the time the clerk came over. "No sugar for sale today," she yelled. "We're all out."

"How can you be all out?" a man demanded as anger spread through the line. "You just opened."

"It's scandalous," an older woman said. "Every time I come there is no sugar." One disbelieving shopper demanded to see the supply room. Two clerks tried to stop him, but he was finally able to push his way by. He returned a few minutes later, shaking his head. "No sugar."

Then a woman accused the counter clerk of hoarding all the sugar for herself. The two got in a terrible argument, whereupon the clerk picked up her bag, tore it open, and glared at her accuser: "You see! There's no sugar in there." Slowly the patrons began drifting out, grumbling to the last one.

Muscovites were sending sugar to needy friends and relatives out in the provinces, where there was none. A woman who worked in my building sent weekly packages to her parents in Minsk, the capital of Byelorussia. Her parents were wealthy, but that didn't help them find sugar in Minsk. The city's residents were on a rationing system: the authorities there handed out coupons, which people had to turn in when purchasing sugar. Adding to the indignity, they had to bring along their passports to prove the coupons were their own.

Along with sugar and toothpaste, the times saw a shortage which could not be blamed on the anti-alcohol campaign: it was in ball bearings. Entire sectors of Soviet industry were grinding to a halt because factories had provided 24 million fewer ball bearings than planned. It was an example of how vulnerable a centrally planned economy is to small disruptions. "Sometimes a tiny hitch in one place, worth only a few kopecks," *Pravda* explained, "causes a disbalancing chain reaction."

The Soviets, though proud of their nation's athletes, were incapable of outfitting them with quality equipment. I received a call one day from a prominent member of the Soviet national hockey team whom I had met while writing about the Soviet league. He explained he needed hockey sticks and asked if I could help. I asked what was wrong with the Russian-made sticks. "They break all the time," he said. "They're not strong enough."

The player gave me the name of someone he knew in Finland. If this man were to forward the sticks to me, could I then relay them to the team?

Being a strong supporter of Canadian hockey, I wondered about the idea of helping the Soviet nationals get better sticks. Since there were no upcoming tournaments involving Canada, I agreed. The Finn proved to be of no help; but I found another channel in Scandinavia. Pandemonium ensued at customs in Moscow when the three dozen sticks arrived. The bureaucratic regulations were too unfathomable for my secretary to cope with. Finally the player himself had to escape the strict confines of the Soviet training camp and steal into town. After establishing his fame he was allowed to take away the prizes. Later I watched from the stands as his team destroyed opponents with their new, high-calibre, non-Russian sticks.

Though Soviet hockey sticks were of poor quality, at least there were enough of them made to keep the shelves from going bare. It wasn't the case in many other sectors of Soviet society. In the arts, the shortage of film for making movies was reaching catastrophic proportions. In one month alone, work on seven films had to be stopped. Even production of the patriotic epic *Lenin and Children* ground to a halt: the producer had run out of film. For pictures that did get made, only a handful of copies could be produced for distribution.

At the same time the toothpaste disappeared there was a run on women's pantyhose. The trade minister had underestimated the number of pantyhose required from the light-industry ministry, which in turn had failed to get the necessary raw materials from the chemical-industries ministry. Moreover, explained Flora Zalharova of the trade ministry, it so happened that more Soviet women were wearing nylons these days than socks. But they were going to have to be very careful: new production totals indicated that they would be limited to two pairs per person per year.

In Moscow, women's bodybuilding was becoming popular, but there was an acute shortage of barbells. In a newspaper story a trainer advised that women wanting dumb-bells should travel to the Ukraine or Leningrad, where they were in greater supply. "Of course it is not too pleasant to carry them such a long distance," he noted.

The year 1987 saw disappearances or chronic shortages of beds, and meat and other staples. It was a terrible year for potatoes, porridge oats, wallpaper, ordinary paper, and hearing aids. The Soviets had enough forests to supply half the planet with paper, a writer explained, but not enough to stock bookshops with popular works.

The potato shortage hit because ten percent of the production had rotted in storage, and another 40 percent during transportation. Outdated factories were blamed for the shortage of that other great Soviet staple, porridge oats. Of the Soviet Union's 17 cereal factories, only one was considered up-to-date.

Later, when Gorbachev visited the Siberian city of Krasnoyarsk, people started shouting at him. "Go into our shops, Mikhail Sergeyevich," one woman yelled. "You'll see there's nothing there." "We have lines everywhere," cried another, "for meat, for sausage, for everything." Other voices, all carried on national television, said that no one was doing anything for housing, that there was no hot water, that public transit was a disaster. In his remarks, Gorbachev agreed with the protesters and tried to assure them that with *perestroika* all would get better. He told them that Moscow was as much to blame as the local leaders.

The Siberian protest followed Gorbachev's "How can we tolerate this?" speech. In that address he devoted no less than 11 paragraphs to the subject of line-ups and the embarrassment to the country they constituted. "There are queues everywhere," he cried, "in trade, in the services sector, in transport, in public health institutions and in organizations which have to act on various requests of working people."

He had recently visited a Moscow shoe factory. A woman he met there complained about constantly having to queue. "Mikhail Sergeyevich, every day I have to spend two and sometimes three hours lining up in stores. This is exhausting. I don't get tired as much on my job as in the queues."

"And this comrades," said Gorbachev, "is in Moscow where, after all, everything can be purchased. But even here people have to stand in endless queues, and in one and the same store – first in line to one cashier, then to another, then to the counter. People stand for hours in queues after work in order to buy simple things that are on sale. How can we tolerate this?"

At the Washington summit Gorbachev made a striking admission, one that no other Soviet leader had made: he referred to his country as the world's "second ranking power." His spokesman, Gennady Gerasimov, later told *Time* that it was the first time Gorbachev had been so categorical. "He conceded," Gerasimov laughed, "to Japan."

Once past the problem of shortages, once past the line-ups, came the problem of quality. At times there were no sausages. At other times, when there were sausages, there was a two-hour line-up for them. Once those obstacles were overcome, the problems were often just beginning – because now the people had to eat them.

As a result of *glasnost*, Russians were beginning to find out how some of their food was made. An *Izvestia* journalist, Slava Baskov, went with a government inspection team to Moscow's main sausage-and-wiener factory. The reconnaissance mission was prompted in part by a story that Moscow sausage was so foul that even the cats wouldn't touch it any more. At the factory Baskov became suspicious right away when he was told not to swallow sausage samples but to spit them into a box carried by a trailing *babushka*. He did so, along with the rest of the inspection team, creating a tableau not to be dreamed about.

The tour offered many other sights Baskov would later want to forget. The first was the condition of the factory workers. He reported seeing one flock of drunks making their way in and another flock of drunks making their way out. He noticed a fat woman carrying a huge sack of empty liquor bottles. Several workers teetered as they handled the frankfurters. They were dispatched to a big open-air cage to sober up.

The plant manager got annoyed when a member of the inspection brigade uncovered a slab of meat jammed with sand. The odour in the plant was unbearable, and the gooey and greasy floor made the footing so treacherous that the inspectors had to cling to each other like Keystone Kops to stay on their feet.

A woman of generous girth in the quality-control department crashed thunderously as she tried to come over and see them. She grew indignant when an inspector levelled the "even cats won't eat it" broadside at her. Cats had become spoiled nowadays, she retorted. Right after this piece of slapstick the sausage truth squad found a wiener with a nail in it. The inspectors also complained about it smelling too sweet, whereupon the quality-control woman said it should smell sweet, whereupon an inspector pointed out that no, pigs and horses don't smell sweet.

The inspectors found gray frankfurters and green frankfurters. They ordered so many kilograms confiscated that the director complained he would not be able to fulfill the plan. About 35 percent of each wiener was found to be made of protein stabilizers –

starches, flours, salt, and other assorted hormones. But the main reason the sausages and wieners had lost their glory, Baskov concluded, was that they were too full of dirt and sand. "And probably," he mused, "too much salt is then added to kill the dirt infection."

To get around the problem of shortages, queues, and quality, Soviets were still turning, wherever possible, to the black market. Gorbachev had clamped down on it, and the cooperatives and private labourers had stolen some of its customers, but black marketeering was still a big operation.

For normal items like tennis balls, Russians had little choice but to make under-the-table deals. In the 1970s the supply of balls had been fine; now it was anything but. Players were having to make do with five or six balls a season. Since they were such a problem, it wasn't difficult to imagine the predicament with rackets. What few were available on the open market compared with models used in the West three or four decades ago. The only alternative was to pay 300 roubles – about 600 Canadian dollars – for a Western racket on the black market.

On the Black Sea boat tour I met a Russian who was a great tennis enthusiast: he loved the game even more than drinking. I'd spent many days watching him drink more than anyone without ever looking drunk. "You see how good I drink," he told me. "Well wait till you see how well I play tennis." But he had derelict equipment. With a new racket, he said, he could beat anyone. Just like the hockey player, he wanted help. "Is it possible you can get me a new racket?"

Back at my apartment I watched him gush over a Western tennis magazine. It was in English, of which he didn't know a word, but he looked excitedly at the colour pictures of big Western stars like Jimmy Connors and Pat Cash. It was as if he was seeing some of these stars for the first time in his life.

When I asked him what kind of racket he wanted, he said, "It doesn't matter, as long as it's from the West." I had imported a Wilson from Finland. The racket was a disappointment to me because it seemed too light, like a women's model. I gave it to him without the 300-rouble charge. He wrote after I'd returned to Canada to say that the racket was making him the envy of every tennis player in his city. Even when he used it with balls that were a year old, it worked wonderfully, he reported.

His difficulties getting tennis equipment led me to believe that the black market in sporting goods wasn't too active in his city. Gorbachev's 1986 crackdown, which made all black market income illegal, was rather cold-hearted in that it didn't take into account the yawning gap between what the state could offer and what the people needed in everyday life. Something was needed to fill that gap, and for that reason some previous Soviet leaders had turned a blind eye to the underground economy.

All the 1985 law did was assuage the bitterness of conservatives and purists who didn't want any nefarious influences crossing the border from the West. These types were declining in number, but there were still some around. I'd seen a teenager wearing a Western T-shirt with the inscription, "I am a girl of the 81st series." I didn't know what that meant. Some other Russian saw a T-shirt with the same words and didn't like it. This man, named Rudenko, fired off a letter to *Izvestia* demanding to know just what on earth was a girl of the 81st series. He said the girl herself probably didn't even know. "I would like to ask a question to our girl of the 81st series," Rudenko said, "and to those others who wish to pay hard currency for the loss of our national pride. Don't we have our own Soviet symbols honouring our own fatherland?"

It was difficult to imagine the Soviets mass-producing T-shirts with some catch phrase appealing to the youth. The slogans Rudenko had in mind were probably the ones he saw on billboards: SOVIET MASSES – FORGE AHEAD.

At the beginning of 1988, Gennady Lisichkin's assessment of the economy was meeting with much agreement. "Everywhere that we have a monopoly, we have stagnation," that specialist had said.[1] One of the measures designed to throw off the albatross of state monopoly – the one stipulating that the majority of Soviet enterprises change to self-financing – went into effect on January 1. Other measures – increasing the number of co-ops and individual entrepreneurs, and continuing to make deep cuts in the bureaucracy – were also expected to contribute.

At this time the Kremlin relaxed its semiprohibition on spirits. That policy had curbed alcohol consumption, at least temporarily,

but it had also embittered the population and driven many people
to seek out alternatives, such as drugs and toothpaste. On top of
that, the policy was draining the state treasury. Relaxing the
near-ban would help ameliorate the budgetary deficit, which Soviet
officials put at 60 billion dollars for 1987.

As a result of human-rights advances and the new Soviet
attitude that "we're open for business," more economic help would
soon be on the way from the West. Western governments,
particularly European ones, were now much less hesitant to trade,
to provide technology, to give credits. In one two-week period
European bankers agreed to provide Moscow with six billion dollars
in credits. With Gorbachev flying high in polls all over the world,
West European leaders were lining up. "The Soviet Union is our
most important neighbour in the East and a decisive power," said
West Germany's chancellor, Helmut Kohl, while paying his
respects at the Kremlin. "It is only an act of wisdom and prudence,
after all those years of the Cold War to take a first step toward
cooperation." That first step involved a two-billion-dollar business
deal, along with many other economic and cultural agreements.

Moscow's joint-ventures program, which had the potential to
reduce the risk of future shortages, was starting to show some life. A
few thousand fast-food outlets might be just the thing to quiet the
angry voices in food-store line-ups. In April 1988, McDonald's of
Canada, with visions of franchises throughout the Soviet Union,
signed an agreement to open 20 stores in Moscow over a two-year
period.

"I think McDonald's in Moscow will be the highest-volume
McDonald's in the world," said George Cohon, the company
executive who landed the potential bonanza for the chain.

The ebullient Cohon had travelled to Moscow time and again
for more than a decade in his efforts to convince the Soviets that a
fast-food chain did not require an enormous ideological leap. On
one of those trips, in late 1979, after many days of talks in Moscow,
Cohon and his colleagues thought they had a deal. They were told
to wait in their hotel rooms for the word. A day went by, then
another, then five more. "We waited that period out," Cohon
recalled, "and when we were finally called in to a meeting we
had thought was for the purpose of executing the contract we were

told – after 17 days in Moscow – that unfortunately they couldn't go ahead with the deal . . . I never did find out what went wrong, but I was led to believe it was somebody pretty high up who vetoed it for ideological reasons."[2]

Burger diplomacy made little progress in the early 1980s. Then, with Gorbachev and company, came joint ventures and a new, less suspicious attitude to the West. An agreement with McDonald's was inevitable. Its signing gave the chain 49-percent ownership in the venture. In a glittering chamber in Moscow's city hall, a Russian official flanked by replicas of the golden arches noted that the important aspect was not just the food and the profits, but the opportunity for Soviets to learn the technology of fast-food production.

The Soviets were unabashedly looking to the rest of the world for help. In a meeting with Barney Danson, Canada's former defence minister, Alexander Yakovlev jumped at the mention that a school of international business was being opened at York University in Toronto. He wanted to send Soviet business managers over for training. "Then he raised family farms," said Danson. "He said, 'We're going to have more family farms.' "

The new Soviet leadership was addressing the economic dolor. Vast changes were on the way. But given the extent of the shortages, given the growing impatience, given the high expectations now being generated, it was an open question whether it had time to see the changes through.

28/Religious Revival

WE HAD BEEN talking about religion in the officially atheist U.S.S.R. The dark-haired, sleepy-eyed woman from Siberia believed in the devil more than in any god. Life had made her that way.

She was 32 years old. She had been married a few times and had one child, and I asked her if she was contemplating another.

"No, I don't think so," she replied. "I've had eleven abortions."

She said it in a matter-of-fact way, as if double-digit abortion was the norm. "Eleven abortions," I said, making sure I'd got it right the first time. "Yes, eleven. The last one was twins." The doctors, she noted, did not have to tell her about the twins. "That wasn't necessary, was it?"

Her nonchalance left a lasting impression. But I shouldn't have been astonished – this was the U.S.S.R. Women with five or ten or twelve abortions to their name were commonplace. No social stigma or religious stigma or financial pain greeted the act. Abortion had been legalized in the Soviet Union in the 1950s, so there was freedom in that dimension. There was no God in the atheist society to peer into the woman's conscience. Hospitalization – if it could be called that – was paid for. In Soviet schools there was a complete lack of sex education; on the streets there was a shortage of contraceptives. Men's condoms, like sugar and toothpaste, were hard to find.

252

It was only a matter of getting a day off work, the Siberian woman said, explaining the nuts and bolts of getting an abortion. In the morning the patient checked in at one of Moscow's 33 hospital maternity wards, mindful of the nine that did not meet modern-day sanitary standards. If she was fortunate she got a doctor who didn't smoke. The doctor applied a general anaesthetic, or none at all. Then he performed the operation, often though not always with sterilized gloves. By late afternoon the patient was ready to go home – one less child to worry about.

Dmitri Chazov, the Soviet health minister, put the number of official abortions in the country at seven million per year. On the black market there were many, many more. No one knew what the population of the Soviet Union might be without abortion. "It's not like in the West," the 11-abortion woman added. "We don't have sophisticated birth-control methods." She wondered why I judged everything in the context of my North American value system. "We don't think about it the way you do. It's something that is accepted. There is no shame."

Soviet government policy was puritanical: there was a ban on sex-peddling establishments and on anything approaching nudity in the arts. But beyond officialdom, the Soviet sex culture was lax. The divorce rate was exceptionally high. Adultery was fair game. There wasn't much religion to get in the way. Upon completing a trip through the sunny Soviet south, I met with my Russian journalist friend, who asked me what I thought of the women down there. I gave a relatively flattering report, whereupon he asked, while knowing I had a family, "How many did you sleep with?" When I demurred, he became indignant. "You are a man are you not? This is only human. All men do this [adultery]. It's life."

I had rarely seen him so amazed. He was very proud of the beauty of Russian women, as were all Soviet men I knew. Though Russians often showed a bias in favour of things Western, when it came to women they preferred their own. During an interview I had with hockey star Slava Fetisov about the prospects of his playing in the National Hockey League, he noted that he wasn't married and would probably be going overseas alone. When I suggested he might meet some interesting women in North America, he tersely replied, "*Nashe luchee*." (Ours are better.)

In the late 1980s male chauvinism was still an entrenched Soviet tradition. While it wasn't as true as it used to be, the best way for a woman to get ahead professionally was still to sleep with the boss. The Siberian woman, who was a university graduate, explained that she had gone to job interviews during which it was made clear to her more than once that yes, she could have the position – with the understanding, of course, that she have sex with the boss on demand.

Some Soviet experts said that the moral vacuum in Soviet society was the result of atheism. By the end of Brezhnev's rule disillusionment with the Marxist path toward social justice had become so profound that increasing numbers of Soviets were turning away from atheism and back to the prerevolution opiate of the masses – religion. A teacher on the subject at Moscow State University reported that even atheists were beginning to see religion as beneficial to society.

A growing nostalgia for the czarist days, a growing nationalism in the Russian Republic, was contributing to the religious revival. "It is curious," the teacher wrote, "that in the past few decades there are virtually no known works of fiction where atheists and free-thinkers are portrayed as heroes. On the other hand characters from the Bible and the Koran, church activists and even monks are frequently portrayed as examples of morality."[1]

Any reorientation from revolutionary, Communist ideals to religious ones, was not reflected in Kremlin policy before the arrival of Gorbachev. The State's official policy toward religion had remained relatively constant since the Khrushchev years. The Russian Orthodox church was permitted to function on a large scale, as was Islam in the Central Asian republics. Other denominations endured with great difficulty. Anyone who wanted a career in the Communist Party was advised not to practise any religion. According to human-rights groups in the West, more than 200 Soviets were in jail on charges pertaining to religious expression.

Religious freedom had not been enjoyed since 1917. It was then that the freshly empowered Bolsheviks began nationalizing property belonging to religious organizations and carrying out an aggressive atheist campaign. In the early 1920s, when the revolution was stabilized, the campaign was eased; an unofficial peace between religion and State stayed in place until Stalin began a new assault. A 1929 law on religious associations prohibited virtually all private religious practices and confined worship to a strictly limited number of state-licensed premises. Throughout the 1930s severe persecutions saw thousands of clergy arrested and church properties closed. The war effort required Russian patriotism of the traditional kind, however, and so Stalin oversaw a new period of selective religious tolerance. An estimated 18,000 Orthodox parishes were reborn. The rebirth lasted until 1959, when Nikita Khrushchev began a new repressive campaign, which in the following five years closed half the churches that Stalin had reopened. Residents of Kiev still recall with bitterness the time Khrushchev came to their city. He looked around at all the spectacular church domes and complained of how they spoiled the view. Brezhnev maintained a policy of atheistic propaganda, and did not increase the number of places of worship, but generally took a low-key approach to religion. In 1975 he revised Stalin's law on religious associations, restoring the right of religious organizations to exist as legal entities.

When Gorbachev came to power in 1985, an estimated 20 to 30 million Soviets were practising adherents of one religious faith or another. They had available approximately 7,000 churches, the vast majority of which were Russian Orthodox. Roughly one million babies a year were being baptized. But atheism was still taught in the schools and promoted in the newspapers.

The first time I attended a Soviet church service it was at Moscow's only Catholic church. I noticed a couple of men walking around with briefcases who looked as if they were from the KGB headquarters up the street. On the way out, parishioners held up their hands to shield their faces from the photographer taking pictures for my article. For the most part those who attended religious services were pensioners. The grandmothers of most of my Soviet acquaintances were churchgoers – their ties were still with the pre-1917 days.

My first sight of Soviet beggars was at the doorway of an Orthodox cathedral in Kharkov, in the Ukraine. They were stooped old women who, with thin, quivering hands held out pussy willows and pleaded for kopecks (pennies). I looked for teenagers or for anyone in their twenties in that dark cathedral where the incense was thick and the roar of the organ descended like a dark cloud on the arched backs of the worshippers. But the atheist teachings had succeeded – no one young was praying this Sunday.

While Gorbachev's mother was a devout Christian who attended church, her son did not evince much interest in religion. In his early days in office he faced many more pressing concerns. Initially, believers were not optimistic that he would change the policies—after all, he had launched his career in the Komsomol, and the Komsomol was one of the Kremlin's main disseminators of atheistic propaganda. When he began to articulate his *glasnost* policy, the religious faithful took note. But at first he did not speak of the new openness in any religious context.

Near Moscow, the small industrial town of Zagorsk (pop. 65,000) is a pilgrimage centre for worshippers and the site of a monastery dating back to 1340. In an enclosure there dotted by spectacular cathedrals and palaces, some built by Ivan the Terrible, one finds young men whose unlikely ambition is to become priests in the Soviet Union.

One sandy-haired seminarian, seated in a drafty wooden study, was Sergei Melnikas. He was 26 years old, married, the father of one child. After a rather standard upbringing, he'd joined the Russian army. That's where he found God.[2]

His father was an engineer and wanted Sergei to become an engineer too. Sergei, while he'd never thought much about religion, found that he had developed an inner restlessness. Everything seemed transient. He wanted to find something permanent. During his mandatory stint in the army in 1981 and 1982, he constantly faced the possibility that he might have to go to Afghanistan. He heard the horror stories about young Russians being tortured by the rebels. He was scared into thinking about religion. "I didn't like the army. It is clear – the army means death."

His father practically disowned him, but Melkinas signed up for the seminary. And now he was living the contradiction, a contradiction made more emphatic by the fact that despite his country's atheism, he professed to love the Soviet Union almost as much as he loved God. Like almost every other Russian I met, Sergei claimed to be a great patriot. "I want to say that I love my motherland."

Maybe he did. The Kremlin's atheism didn't seem to shake him – he took a philosophical view. "My point of view is purely religious. Christ created a church that will exist eternally, irrespective of external conditions. So all the relations between church and state, no matter how bad they are, play a special role."

If there is true *glasnost*, explained Melkinas, then there has to be free religion. "And on *glasnost* our leader is committed." Soviet church-state relations were changing, he said; the impersonal, legalistic attitudes were giving way to warmer, more human ones. He believed that the great majority of the intelligentsia were speaking out for religion, and wasn't it true that under Gorbachev the intelligentsia were making a comeback?

By this time, early in 1988, he was correct: Gorbachev was extending *glasnost* to religion. The State was growing increasingly tolerant, though, as was so often the case during the great reformation, the word from on high was suffering an initial phase of ambush and rape as it spread to the regions. The citizens of Kirov, for example, had but one church. They received the support of Moscow's Council of Religious Affairs to build another one in their city. But Yuri Karacharov, secretary of the Kirov region's Communist Party committee, blocked the bid, saying it was "inexpedient." When a spokesman for the petitioners, Alexander Nezhny, cited the constitution of the country, the regional boss exploded, accusing him of having incited the believers.

Anastasia Nesterenko, an old-age pensioner, wrote to the party committee, "We are advanced in age, we have worked in production for 40 years or so. We have war decorations. Think about us. Don't we have the right to go to church?" Nezhny finally threw the Kremlin angle at party boss Karacharov, saying Moscow was in favour. Karacharov didn't budge. Nezhny reported that his attitude was, in effect, "You and Moscow can do exactly what you please. As for us here in Kirov we'll stick to our guns once we've said no."

The year 1988 marked the 1000th anniversary of the coming of Christianity to Russia. The Russian Orthodox church planned major celebrations. The Kremlin, which seemed intent on showing a fresh face to the world in religion as well as in everything else, was not about to interfere. It made numerous concessions: 35 churches and four monasteries were returned to believers; high-ranking

Vatican officials were invited to Moscow to open a dialogue; for the first time, an American rabbi was allowed to celebrate Passover in Moscow's main synagogue; pro-atheism campaigns were scaled down. Meanwhile, the underground Ukrainian Catholic church, which Stalin had dissolved in 1946, opened talks with the Orthodox hierarchy aimed at official recognition.

Whether all this was just a one-shot Kremlin gift for the anniversary year was a popular subject of debate. But fears that it might be began to diminish as the year progressed and the new attitudes were revealed. "My generation was brought up to believe that religion was backward," said Yuri Asianov, a Moscow inspector who enforced the rules of religion. "But now the state is beginning to appreciate that believers are good patriots and, in their morals, often better than atheists."

The "opiate of the masses" theory had it that people were once made to believe in heaven to distract them from their poverty on earth. Many people were beginning to question this postulate, arguing that Christianity was a positive force in Russian history, and had yet to be negated by modern science, and was therefore viable in the Soviet Union today. "Christianity is not ideology, either bourgeois or socialist," asserted Dmitri Likachev, a leading Soviet academic.

A commentator in *Izvestia*, Konstantin Kedrov, went so far as to suggest that the conversion of the pagan state of Rus to Christianity by Prince Vladimir in 988 was comparable with Gorbachev's attempts to renew Soviet society through *perestroika*.

Easter 1988 saw services attended by Soviet citizens in numbers unprecedented since the revolution. Breaking with tradition, Soviet television broadcast some of the ceremonies from Moscow's Cathedral of the Epiphany. This time there were young people among the tens of thousands who attended the services, though some of the churches were too crowded for them to get in. "You're still young," a militia officer told a group of Moscow teenagers when they tried to gain entry into the Cathedral of Assumption. "You have plenty of time left to go to church." Inside, priests in white brocaded vestments intoned, "Christ is risen." Many Russians were seeing it for the first time. One youth had his arm around his girlfriend. "You're in church, not in the street," a *babushka* snapped. "I'm sorry, but this is our first time," the youth said. "I didn't know the rules."[3]

In its rather sympathetic coverage, Tass quoted Patriarch Pimen, the aging head of the Russian church: "In these days of the resurrection of Jesus Christ, we fix our eyes on the path traversed. We testify that the Christianizing of Russia has exerted a favourable impact on the development of culture, morals, family life and other aspects of the life of the people." Dry prose in the Christian West, but in the Soviet Union, noteworthy.

Then, on April 29, Gorbachev spoke the important words. An "entire depth of differences" in world outlook existed between atheists and believers, he explained. "But at the same time we realistically assess the existing situation. The believers are the Soviet people, workers, patriots, and they have the full right to express their convictions with dignity. *Perestroika*, democratization, concerns them as well – in full measure and without reservations."

In full measure and without reservations. For Russian believers the words were cause for celebration. An older man who drove a taxi told me that he wasn't much of a churchgoer but liked the idea that if he did go it wouldn't be looked down upon. The most important thing, he told me, was that the new attitude might attract more young people to religion. "This is the problem, you understand. The youth – they need something to believe in. In our day when we were young we believed in building the country. There was commitment to our system. But not so many believe in this any more. They are losing their way. Maybe religion can give them something." I told him that not many young people go to church in the Western democracies any more. He asked, "Well, what do they believe in?" I hummed and hawed a bit before he filled in the blank: "Making money," he said.

I said yes, making money and having a good time.

Without mentioning him by name, Gorbachev in his speech on religion referred to what Stalin had done. "Religious organizations were also affected by the tragic developments that occurred in the period of the cult of personality. . . . Mistakes made with regard to the church and believers in the 1930s and the years that followed are being rectified." He promised that in his new law on freedom of conscience, the interests of religious organizations would be reflected.

Wanting to try his words out on some of the flock, I travelled to Lithuania, one of the Baltic republics. Once an independent country, it had been incorporated into the Soviet Union at the beginning of the Second World War. Eighty percent of its 3.6 million people were Lithuanian, and of those, virtually all were Catholic. There were an estimated 700 Catholic churches but only a tiny number of priests. A great many Lithuanians didn't practise their faith openly because, as in the Russian Republic, they feared reprisals.

Without permission, I went to Kaunas, which like many Lithuanian cities felt as if its spirit had been sucked away by some atheist, totalitarian vampire. Next to a Soviet army barracks hid one of the Soviet Union's two Catholic seminaries. Having tried unsuccessfully to contact its administrator, I had decided to present myself at the gates anyway. On this bright and breezy day in May, I was ushered into the courtyard in time to hear the ringing of the bell signalling the close of the final day of a semester of study. With a college roar, the students stormed from their classes to the playing fields for a volleyball game.

Four or five of them came over to me. They seemed keen to meet their first Western correspondent and readily granted me an interview in one of their spartan chambers. These young Lithuanians were far different from their Russian counterparts. They had eagerness written all over them. They were bright-eyed, alert, and almost intoxicated with the possibilities of life. If the strain of their circumstances manifested itself while we spoke, I didn't notice. For them, adversity meant challenge.

A couple of weeks earlier they had been parading through the town as part of the May Day celebrations in honour of Soviet workers and the god of Lenin. By not attending, they explained, they would have risked being thrown out of the academy for being unpatriotic. The authorities knew what was going on inside the seminary because there was likely a KGB mole among them, an imposter who was pretending to worship Jesus Christ while reporting their activities to the secret police.

Kestutis Rugevichus, 30, told me that he had tried for five years to be admitted to the seminary. If he had agreed to cooperate with the KGB, who came to him often back then, he would have been admitted in his first year, he said. "They want us to work for them once inside."

Their fight to build Catholicism in Lithuania included an underground seminary, which they chose not to talk about. "This society is very scared," said Rugevichus. "The people in the professions – teachers, professors, scientists – realize that if you practise as an open Catholic your career is closed."

They were also heavily committed to Lithuanian nationalism. Jonas Valionis, 28, told me that political independence is the right of every people. Faith allowed the seminarians optimism. "The only way to fight is by our example," said Valionis. "We must try to love every man. It is hard but we must try."

So far all *glasnost* meant was that 30 students were being admitted to the seminary every year instead of the usual 10 or 15, and that the army building would be turned over to the seminary for added space. The young Catholics told me that Gorbachev was enterprising and courageous, and applauded his speech on religious rights. But once again they cited the same problem: he was only one man.

The previous summer Lithuania had celebrated its 600th anniversary of Catholicism. Moscow had not allowed John Paul II to visit to commemorate it – it would have caused too much commotion. Now, from the Vatican, the Pontiff was saying that winds of change seemed to be blowing from Moscow, but they must blow stronger to Lithuania. "The freedom they ask for is written in the heart of every man," he declared to a delegation of Lithuanian Catholics. "To be able to honour God without discrimination."

When the official Orthodox millenium celebrations began in June, Gorbachev opened a tentative dialogue with the Vatican by meeting with its second most powerful figure – Cardinal Agostino Casaroli, the Vatican's secretary of state. It was the first time in Soviet history that such a meeting had taken place.

"When will you invite the Pope to Moscow?" a journalist asked Gorbachev as he entered the meeting. "Many things have yet to happen," said the general secretary. The foreign minister, Eduard

Shevardnadze, was more optimistic: "We have big plans. The time will come. Now we will talk about this with Casaroli."

There could be no proper relations between Moscow and the Vatican until the latter respected the former's belief in socialism, Gorbachev told Casaroli. He said he would consider carefully the Vatican's wish to have regular contacts with the Kremlin. And "as far as freedom of religion is concerned," Gorbachev added, "it is sealed in the constitution and we abide by this principle."

Casaroli reported being impressed that Gorbachev, like the Pope, placed an emphasis on "the centrality of man," and added that he liked Gorbachev's view that "the State should serve man and not the reverse." Casaroli had given the Soviet leader a letter from John Paul, and Gorbachev had read it aloud. Casaroli left Moscow smiling.

In early June, when the millenium services were held, thousands of worshippers pressed against churches in Moscow and Kiev. Many Soviet citizens had travelled long distances to see the ceremonies. They had never witnessed a religious atmosphere in their country quite as free as this, and credited the change to *glasnost*.

In Kiev, crowds gathered around an elderly preacher. "At last God has sent us Gorbachev," he cried, while women wept and kissed his crucifix. "But Satan wants to kill him."

Before Satan could get to him, Gorbachev scheduled a trip to Italy for the fall of 1989, where he was to meet the Pope. By then the Government had voided antireligious edicts going back to the Stalin days. Hundreds of new churches and mosques were opening across the country. The Soviet Council on Religious Affairs registered 1,610 new religious congregations in 1988. In 1987 there had been only 104.

With remarkable swiftness, Mikhail Gorbachev was once again breaking with history. The era of religious repression in the Soviet Union was closing.

29/This Sporting Life

THE NEW TOLERANCE that allowed Soviets to worship a real god extended, as well, to another Soviet religion – that of sport.

When I arrived in 1985 the word *professional* was still anathema, training systems were Stalinesque, and sports reporting was public relations. Soviet athletes were not allowed to play for teams in other countries. Western sports such as golf were considered too bourgeois to mention.

When I left in 1988 this sporting life was beginning to change. There was Russian golf, there was Russian baseball. A more critical sports press was developing, Soviet athletes were going abroad to play pro, and players were speaking out against severe training regimens. Teams were moving away from government handouts toward self-financing, and the word *professional* was slowly becoming part of the Soviet sports vocabulary. Soviet society's overall trend toward more honesty, more openness, was being reflected in the sports world. The general Soviet policy thrust with sport was the same as it was with the economy, with international security, with human rights – to further integrate the Soviet Union with the world community.

For some sports *perestroika* came quickly. For others, such as ice hockey, the traditionalists dug in and the forces of the old era waged a searing public battle with those of the new. It was Ligachev versus Yeltsin all over again.

In sports the disciplinarian managers from the war generation always had at their disposal a powerful argument against change. It was called winning. Why change when you're operating a winning system? they asked. And they *were* winning. At the sports on which they chose to concentrate, the Soviets were masters. Since they began competing in the Winter and Summer Olympics in the 1950s, Soviet medals totals in both far outdistanced any other country's. In some big sports the Soviets had the advantage of being able to use all their athletes, while Western countries couldn't, until 1988, use their professionals. This made a difference, but in most Olympics the Soviet margin over the top Western nation was wide enough to negate it.

When the Soviets set their minds on doing something – whether it was space travel, sports, writing novels, dancing the ballet, building a police state, providing empty grocery stores – they usually did it better than anybody else.

The driving imperative of the Soviet sports industry was to win Olympic medals. National championships and international tournaments were important, but all effort was geared to the prestige of winning the Olympics. The games were not merely a test to determine the better athletes; they were viewed also a test of systems, of ideology.

Thus, when it was announced in 1986 that baseball would be an Olympic sport beginning in 1992, the Soviets not only had *glasnost* arguing for them to import the American game, they also had visions of more Olympic gold.

They got a few bats from the Nicaraguan embassy, and some gloves from the Cubans. They sent a hockey goalie to Managua for 40 days of baseball schooling. They imported some video instruction cassettes. And there they were in suburban Moscow in September 1987 – nine Russians on a diamond.

When I arrived, the coach, Alexander Ardatov, the one they sent to Managua, was shaking his head. When I left, he was still shaking his head. Sometime in between I asked him what he considered the team's main weakness. "Hitting and fielding," he declared. Then he paused. "And throwing." Having run the gamut without meaning to, he remarked, "The game of baseball is not really in our blood." Actually, the Russians had played the game of *lapta*, in which a ball and club were used, until early in the 20th century. This led some to claim that they were the fathers of baseball. But it was not a fact they wished to shout about when they saw themselves playing it. Their most recent test had been a 22-0 setback at the hands of the Nicaraguan juniors.

In the batter's box at practice the players were swinging so hard they were almost falling over. Some cuts missed by a foot. One batter pot-lucked on a vicious swing, sending a nose-high line drive torching toward shortstop. The Russian standing upright there, face white, eyes bulged, raised his glove as if saluting a colonel. The ball shot between his ear and his mitt like a train through a tunnel. Two more errors were committed on the same play.

Coach Ardatov explained that his players could throw hard and far. "But we have this problem with aiming," he went on. "In baseball you have to throw very accurately, otherwise it can really cost you. In hockey if you make a bad pass, it's not so bad. Someone can recover for you quickly."

The coach had a lot of learning to do. While it was part of the Russian sports ethic to train hard, he didn't at first realize that pitchers weren't supposed to practise by throwing 300 fastballs a day. He had his best hurler, Yura Trifonyenko, do just that. The results – Yura's arm almost fell off. "I've learned," Ardatov said.

Yuri Chugayev, a 21-year-old who was sampling a number of positions, described baseball as a dynamic, artful game. "I heard about it from the West when I was little but never thought I'd be playing it." Could he hit a baseball? "Well it depends who is throwing. If it's one of our guys, I can."

In the Far Eastern city of Khabarovsk, near Japan, a Soviet team had been developed with Japanese help. It even had real baseball uniforms – made in Japan. The Soviets were starting their own national baseball league, and expected to be competitive in the 1992 Olympics and to challenge for a medal in 1996. To see those routine grounders bounding off kneecaps was to doubt the forecast. But the Soviets didn't take up ice hockey until 1946. They won the world championships in 1954 – the first time they entered.

Golf had not been selected as an Olympic sport, and in the past Soviet officials had rebuffed suggestions that they should develop it. Mikhail Gorbachev was like virtually every other Russian – he had no exposure to the game. Though he had some interest in soccer, he was not known as a sports enthusiast. But all it took was for someone to put the suggestion directly to him – and they were soon building fairways on Russian soil.

During the Washington summit in December 1987, Georgia senator Sam Nunn told the Soviet leader about the game over lunch. Nunn was a six-handicap golfer. He was also a good friend of the golf-course architect Robert Trent Jones, Jr., who had been trying for 15 years to bring golf to the Soviets. When I met Jones at the Masters golf tournament in 1985, he talked at length of all the problems he was having convincing Russians it was a sport of merit. He had almost given up. But as was the case with George Cohon and his hamburgers, Jones kept the idea alive and was there when *glasnost* arrived. It was useful that he was a friend of Nunn's; he also solicited the help of Armand Hammer, an American industrialist who was a favourite with the Soviets. After the lobbying in Washington, it took one more summit – Moscow in June 1988 – for the deal to be sealed and announced. Before the end of the year a championship club was under construction 30 kilometres from Moscow's city centre. At the same time, Sven Johannsen, a Swedish hockey star from decades earlier, received permission to build a club near his country's embassy. It would be used mainly for diplomats. He also got approval to open a golf school to teach the game to Soviet youngsters.

Introducing Western sports to the Soviet Union proved to be easier than introducing Western sports systems or a Western atmosphere. Hockey furnished the best example. When I arrived in Moscow I found a closed hockey world, morose and moribund. The leftovers from the Brezhnev era who were giving the orders paid little heed to those who thought the system needed about a half-century's updating. Within three years, however, a couple of players, emboldened by the words of Gorbachev, had grown fearless enough to stand up and call for changes.

In Canada I had heard some of the stories about the rigid training regimens and the policy of keeping the Soviet players in seclusion. But I had also heard about the privileged lifestyle – the fancy apartments, the cars, the *dachas* – enjoyed by Soviet athletes.

The reality of Soviet hockey, however, was that there was no time for the privileges, only for the regimen. I thought I was being lied to when people told me that for the 11-month hockey year, the players were allowed to go home to their wives and children only one day a week – sometimes only one day a month. But it was no lie.

The coach of both the Central Army team and the Soviet national team was Viktor Tikhonov. While he didn't have all the control, on a day-to-day basis he was the biggest force in Soviet hockey. A believer in military discipline, he ran hockey with a cold, Stalinesque edge. He was emotional, authoritarian, hated by many of his players. His demeanour was fidgety, spiteful. When I saw him, I was always reminded of a hamster.

The Central Army team's training camp, about 45 minutes from Moscow, was like a low-budget American chain hotel. It sat near a big pond, a shaded restaurant, and a picturesque stand of tall pines. Unbelievably, there was no hockey arena at the training centre – for workouts the players had to be bussed in and out of Moscow, sometimes several times a day. The rooms at the camp did not have telephones, this to make sure the players would not divert their attention from hockey by talking with family or friends.

The tournaments on foreign soil, especially in the West, were a highlight for the team. But Tikhonov, doing his utmost to keep the players away from capitalist poison, compelled them to remain in their hotels most of the time. During its entire stay at the 1980 Olympics in Lake Placid, New York, the Soviet club was allowed a single, hour-long walkabout through the town.

The misery of the conditions led the top Soviet goalie, Vladislav Tretiak, to retire early. After his playing days were over he was lucky to be able to maintain his high standard of living as an officer in the army promoting hockey around the world. Many Soviet athletes, after winning their golds, were forgotten, their privileges reduced. "I know a former champion who now works as a gravedigger," said Valery Brumel, the Soviets' classic high jumper of the 1960s. "And an Olympic medal winner who now works for his living by keeping a grocery store clean. That is really sad."

Brumel became an author and composer. He was a little more courageous in speaking out than Tretiak, who played the loyalty game well into the *glasnost* period. I shuddered one day when, after a

Central Army win at Luzhniki Arena, Tretiak came down from the stands, embraced Tikhonov, and kissed him on both cheeks. It was common for Russians to do that, but it seemed to me that Tretiak was kissing plaster, that he was insincere, that his skin should have been crawling.

Luzhniki Arena was so gloomy. It had that gray, frozen-in-time countenance of so many things Soviet. But I used to relish going there for the Soviet-league games. I would hurry out of my office and down seven flights of stairs, then jump into the Volga and bounce her out past the waving militia guard onto Kutuzovsky Prospekt. The arena was a mere five minutes away along the boulevard bordering the Moscow River. In the full-employment society many militiamen would be lining the route, ostensibly for traffic control, though the road was nearly empty. At the stadium only 30 or 40 other cars would be sitting in the parking lot. Almost everyone else got there by the ultracheap (ten cents) and ultra-efficient metro.

Having driven along a lonely, military-patrolled road in a car that felt vintage 1950s, I would enter downcast 1940s Luzhniki to sit among the other spectators in their dark 1950s coats and watch a game being played in a style that in some respects befit those decades. It was one of the most time-warping experiences imaginable.

The excitement level was not a reason for going to the Soviet games. There had been incidents in the early 1980s of crowds getting out of control, particularly at Soviet soccer games. A clampdown ensued on fan behavior in all sports. At hockey matches in 1986 in which the fans did get noisy, a voice would come over the public-address system ordering everyone to calm down and observe the socialist order. Once I sat near two teenagers who occasionally showed their zeal by jumping up from their seats. A man sitting three rows below turned around and berated them with such frozen rancour that I thought the game would stop. Nobody tried to defend the youths. They were silent after that.

Smoking wasn't allowed inside Luzhniki, but between periods I poked my head out the arena doors to observe the smokers' corral — a small zone squared off by a makeshift metal fence and encircled by the constabulary. Hundreds were huddled darkly in the little square, heads bowed, cold fingers and cold lips against their cigarettes. . . .

The lighting in the arena matched the players' sallow complexions. Even victories did little to pick up the spirits of Tikhonov's players. They would win and be driven back to their boot camp, and then they would win again and be driven back to their boot camp. They won all the time, the Central Army team. They were just what their incomparable defenceman Slava Fetisov called them: they were "ice robots."

Tikhonov had designed the system that way. Because it was the army team, and because all young Soviet men had to spend two years in the army, Tikhonov had access to all the best players. Junior stars wanted to play for Central Army anyway, because it was the best club, which meant more championships, which meant higher salaries. Its players also made up about two-thirds of the prestigious national team. In addition, Central Army's players could continue in the army after their hockey days were over. Because of these advantages and others, the Central Army team had become invincible on Soviet soil. By the time I arrived in Moscow it had won every championship since 1977. One season it lost only one game. Some years the club had the championship locked up just past the halfway point. The effect on the league and in turn on the popularity of Soviet hockey was devastating. The fans had little reason to maintain interest, and turned off the game.

At the same time, the quality of the national team was becoming suspect. In the 1980s the national team lost the 1980 Olympics, two world championships, and two Izvestia tournaments. And twice, in 1984 and 1987, it had lost to Canada the prize that counted the most in the more sophisticated eyes of the hockey world – the Canada Cup. No longer were the Soviet nationals invincible.

Yet despite this, and despite the game's collapsing appeal, Tikhonov was hanging on. The Soviet journalists didn't have the guts to challenge him, at least not until *glasnost* was several years underway. They worried that if they did their careers would be finished. Many of us thought that Slava Koloskov, the new director of Soviet hockey, would dump Tikhonov, but he cowered as well. Ultimately it was left to the players to cry out, but a dangerous precedent awaited any who did. In the NHL dissatisfied players often brought their grievances to the press. In the Soviet Union that simply wasn't done. Those who wanted to do it knew better – they knew it would likely mean the end of their career.

With Gorbachev came the sense that the authoritarian mindset was changing. Igor Larionov felt it was changing enough for him to begin speaking out. Larionov, who was in his late twenties, played centre for the most accomplished starting five in the hockey world. The others were Vladimir Krutov and Sergei Makarov (forwards), and Slava Fetisov and Alexei Kasatonov (defence). Larionov was the smallish, artistic play maker who set up Krutov and Makarov, the powerful wingers who careened across the ice surface with the abandon of pinballs.

You could sense that Larionov was more of a thinker than most players. Like Ken Dryden, the Canadian goaltender, he was able to see the game in a wider perspective than the game itself. He often pondered the significance of what he was doing. One time, when a friend told him his life as a hockey player was meaningless, he agreed and said he would some day prove his intellectual worth as a writer. He need not have been so hard on himself: there was a special art in what he and his linemates did – a fleet, physical, beautiful art which required the mind as much as the body.

In December 1987, in the course of an interview with a Russian newspaper, Larionov fired the first of many salvoes to come. "I'm tired," he said. "I'm tired of the training regime, the endless separation from home and family when necessary and when not necessary. I have a seven-month-old daughter Elena whom my wife is alone to take care of. I can do nothing worthwhile to help. For five years winning the national championship has brought no joy or interest to me."

The other teams in the Soviet league, he said, were useless against Central Army's power. They were only going through the motions, he added. Hockey was fading fast. When the interviewer tried to defend the system, saying the training camps outside Moscow offered fresh air to rejuvenate the body, Larionov interrupted. "But why do you talk about that? What about the player's mood? What about the emotion he is supposed to bring to the game?"

In a later interview Larionov was more emphatic. "It's time to speak more pointedly about the style of our leadership in our hockey associations. What has been created is a personality cult where military discipline and unquestioning subordination are substituted for democracy."

The protest of Vladimir Krutov, Larionov's linemate, took place further from the public eye. Since I wasn't allowed into the Soviet training camp, I wrote out some questions one night and sent my Russian secretary in with them. She came back with some taped interviews. The next time I sent her in to do the same, she returned with a drunken Krutov. She had started out talking to Larionov, who had somehow escaped for a few hours, at the restaurant across the road from the training camp. Not long after, Krutov staggered in from the cold night, joined the two of them, and began talking indecipherable blather into the tape recorder.

Earlier in the day Krutov had been in a confrontation with Tikhonov. He had presented a list of grievances about the conditions, about the running of the team, and told the coach he was quitting. Then he had left for the bar to get smashed. Since he was unfit to drive home to his family in Moscow, my secretary and driver piled him into the back of the Volga. In alternate bursts of anger and tears, he told them, "I want to live a normal life. I can't do this any more."

Krutov sobered up and bitterly returned to the team two days later. The incident never made the Soviet newspapers, but writing about it for *The Globe and Mail*, I included a paragraph saying that the team's peerless starting five was headed for a crack-up and that so, perhaps, was the Soviet hockey system itself.

As captain, Slava Fetisov had taken the teams' complaints about the camp regimen to Tikhonov and been rebuffed. After the Larionov article appeared I talked to the new hockey boss, Koloskov. "Larionov is right," he said, in reference to the misery of the players' lives. But he added that though Larionov was right, it didn't mean there would be changes. "From the point of view of the personality, it is not interesting," Koloskov said of the camp life. "But from the point of view of getting the job done, it is the only variant possible." The statement more or less summed up the attitude of the old guard.

Fetisov was one of the two or three best defencemen in the world. With his massive legs, his cold power on the blue line, and his army patriotism, he was the prototype of the great, proud Soviet athlete.

In 1988, while he was preparing for the Calgary Olympics, there was talk that after the Games he would be on his way to the National Hockey League. In keeping with *glasnost*, Soviet sports authorities were allowing players who were past their prime – Fetisov was almost 30 – to play in professional leagues in the West. The reality that Soviet athletes themselves were professional was starting to receive recognition at home. Former athletes like Brumel were campaigning for rights that professionals enjoyed in the West.

"We did not spare ourselves or our health," Brumel said, speaking both for himself and for other past athletes. "We were told, 'For our people's sake, for the fatherland's prestige,' and we went out of our way to win . . . We were not amateurs. But it was not the thing to speak of – that we had professionals in our sports – even though the athletes do get remunerated. I think it is time to recognize our big-time sports as a professional affair, and to think about pensions for athletes."

Fetisov played brilliantly in Calgary. The Soviets glided to gold. The only sad part about it was that the victory meant Tikhonov would probably stay on as coach. Some of the players had discussed losing the gold as a way to ensure that he would be replaced. But that would also have meant losing a lot of bonus money – a gold medal meant 12,000 roubles to each Soviet athlete.

After the Games, Fetisov thought he would soon be leaving to join the New Jersey Devils. Larionov was planning to depart for the NHL the following year. The many bureaucratic hurdles in the Fetisov case appeared to be falling one by one. Tikhonov, reports said, had even given his permission.

But one day, late in the summer, Fetisov was told that it was all off. He also heard that it was Tikhonov who had vetoed it. The coach, it seemed, wanted to make sure that Fetisov was around for the world championships in Stockholm in 1989. Sweden was defending world champion and Tikhonov desperately wanted that medal back.

When the Central Army team went to play a round of

exhibitions with the NHL clubs at the close of 1988 and the beginning of 1989, Fetisov blasted the coach in interviews. Essentially, he said that Tikhonov had double-crossed him and that he wanted out. Like Larionov, he said that hockey was dying in his country.

The statements against Tikhonov were astonishing enough, given Fetisov's status as team captain. But he wasn't finished. In Moscow, a few days after the series with the NHL, Fetisov announced that he was quitting the Central Army team. Then Larionov announced that he was joining him. The other players were with them in spirit, though not in body.

Fetisov said he couldn't take being treated like an ice robot any longer. "I'm tired of Tikhonov's dictatorial regime, which has brought about a constant atmosphere of bad feeling in the team," he said. "And I don't want to play any more for a coach I don't trust."

Fetisov had seen the NHL players and was aware of their lifestyles. He knew that they had four months of holidays every summer, that they didn't have to live in training camps sequestered from their families, that they had rights and pensions and great salaries. He knew that they had all this and that they still won frequently against the Soviets and that they still filled their arenas with spectators.

He knew, therefore, that the Soviet hockey system was living the big Stalinist lie; and because of *glasnost*, he was speaking out. Never in its 42-year history had Soviet hockey witnessed such a display of public dissent. The break with authority had finally been made.

Within a few weeks of the action, Soviet hockey authorities finally caved in and allowed a player to leave to play for an NHL team. Sergei Priakin, a 26-year-old forward who had played for the Soviet nationals, joined the Calgary Flames. Larionov and Fetisov now felt that it was only a matter of time before they too were gone. They knew also that it would enhance their chances if they helped the Soviet nationals to win a gold medal in the world championships in Stockholm. They played, the Soviets won, and Tikhonov, gloating on the fact that his old system had produced another championship, allowed as to how the victory would count positively in regard to the cases of those who wished to leave.

Tikhonov's joy was short-lived, however. On the plane home, a player was missing. Alexander Mogilny, the best junior hockey player in the world, had chosen to defect, to go to the Buffalo Sabres of the NHL. A year earlier, when I had lunch with Mogilny – who had the fastest hands and shot release I had ever seen – he had talked of wanting to play in the NHL some day. He had also talked, off the record, of his strong dislike for Tikhonov and his methods.

It took only one more year of his living in the Tikhonov prison camp to convince him the break had to be made. He didn't want to go through what Larionov and Fetisov had gone through. For him, *glasnost* was taking too long.

30/Freedom and Chaos

IN SOME RESPECTS the story could have been called the Great Red Retreat. As the Soviets opened themselves to the world, as they made friends, as they wiped away the evil image, they were paradoxically retreating from the world. The one was necessary for the other. The turn from the politics of military expansionism to the politics of contractionism earned them a welcome mat to the world and, with planned savings on defence, gave the deathbed economy at least hope of recovery.

In 1988 the Soviets retreated from Afghanistan, they retreated in part from Eastern Europe, they retreated on their defence budget, and they began what in essence would be a retreat from the authority they wielded in some of their own republics. The latter came with the realization that *glasnost* and *perestroika* were, by definition, tantamount to devolution. The power Moscow exerted in the 14 non-Russian republics had to be reduced.

There was no signal that the Soviets were prepared to undertake the process that had inevitably befallen all the world's empires – that of dismemberment. If the laws of political survival would allow him to do so, it was possible that Gorbachev might permit a status of sovereignty-association for, say, the Baltic republics. His expressed ideas on self-determination appeared to support the notion. But while the Soviets were moving more swiftly toward democratic values than anyone would have dreamed a few years earlier, that radical a political possibility was not yet in the cards.

Pulling out of Afghanistan was enough of a swipe at tradition for now. The so-called Brezhnev doctrine had it that once a territory became part of the Soviet socialist camp, it must forever remain in that camp. With Afghanistan, Gorbachev was repudiating the doctrine. Whether Afghanistan had in fact ever been in the Soviet camp was debatable, but it was close enough. There had been other options available to Gorbachev; for example, he could have sent in another 100,000 troops to try to crush the rebels. But integral to Gorbachev's "new thinking" was a novel thought -- that military force wasn't everything.

In the bipolar world, impoverished Afghanistan was a strategic chip of some importance. It was a step closer to the Indian Ocean; it also bordered on Soviet Central Asia, where most of the population was Moslem, and vulnerable, therefore, to cross-border influence from the neighbouring Islamic states. The latter consideration was one reason for the invasion of Afghanistan. It was a reason not fully understood in the West. "We in the West and certainly in North America tend to be insensitive to genuine Soviet security concerns," said Robert Ford, the Canadian ambassador to the Soviet Union at the time of the invasion. The problem of Iran and Afghanistan to the Soviets, he suggested, "would be somewhat similar if Texas and Louisiana were largely populated by Mexicans and Mexico was in a constant state of turmoil." Taking it further, if Mexico were facing the prospect of a leftist overthrow, Washington would likely send in the troops, as it had done so frequently in Latin America. "From the Soviet point of view," said Ford, "American preoccupation with El Salvador, Nicaragua, and Cuba seems like child's play compared with the problems they [the Soviets] face on their own southern frontiers."

By 1988, with the rise of Japan, with the increasing trend toward global interdependence, with the realization that the superpowers' ability to police the globe was diminishing, the bipolar, two-camp way of looking at the world was fading. Moscow and Washington were proceeding toward the sunniest détente ever, and an end to the Cold War was foreseeable. With all these factors at play, and with Moscow beginning to abandon its self-styled mission to dominate the world, chips such as Afghanistan were no longer as vital.

In April, after successful peace negotiations in Geneva,

Gorbachev announced that all 115,000 Soviet troops would be out of Afghanistan by the beginning of 1989. His expressed hope was that a neutral Afghanistan, one not hostile to Soviet interests, would emerge.

There were so many positive effects to the withdrawal – on the Soviet economy, on the morale of Soviet youth, on the image of the Soviets in the world – that the only question was why Gorbachev didn't do it sooner. One reason was that he had to prepare Soviet public opinion for what was to be a tacit admission of military defeat. The Soviet military hadn't been defeated many times in recent decades, and when Gorbachev came to power the Soviet press was telling so many lies about Afghanistan that the Soviet people weren't thinking of defeat this time either. But by introducing some realistic reporting and by allowing the distribution of films like *Is It Easy to Be Young?* the new Kremlin changed the public's perception of the war.

The Soviets' withdrawal made a statement by Gorbachev about foreign affairs seem less ridiculous than it first seemed. "We recognize that every country has the right to choose independently and to decide its destiny, political system and state structure. This should be the point of departure and we reject any attempt at intervention in the affairs of countries and their internal processes." In the same speech, in reference to the gigantic land mass of his own country, the Soviet leader made another, less reassuring remark. "We are happy with our territory. We have enough, though none to spare."

The retreat from Afghanistan was followed by the retreat from Eastern Europe, in the form of cutbacks in troop strength and the Soviet defence budget itself. Gorbachev announced this in his December 1988 speech to the United Nations. He pledged to reduce his military by 500,000 men (ten percent) and 10,000 tanks within two years, with major portions of the reductions coming from his satellites to the east. The Kremlin boss also promised to rearrange his forces on the eastern front so as to be clearly defensive.

"The use of threat or force no longer can or must be an instrument of foreign policy," stated Gorbachev in his UN address. The Soviet leader asserted that, with the INF treaty and with his new cuts, "we are witnessing the emergence of a new historic reality – a turning away from the principle of superarmament to the principle of reasonable defence sufficiency."

The intent of the speech was clear: it was a further invitation – the most explicit invitation yet – for the superpowers to abandon their adversarial roles and become cordial competitors in what Gorbachev called "a fair rivalry of ideologies."

It may have been this speech that put Gorbachev over the top in his efforts to convince Americans that he wasn't talking propaganda. "It is the end of the postwar world," said Jerry Hough. "We're not going to invade them and they're not going to invade us." The *Wall Street Journal*, the hawkish voice of the business right, was all praise. The *Washington Post*'s Robert Kaiser said it was as remarkable as any speech ever given at the United Nations. On the streets of Manhattan, the Soviet leader was cheered by thousands wherever he went. On Broadway he raised his arms in a victory clench like Rocky Balboa. He dodged security guards so he could approach the crowds and shake hands.

Gennady Gerasimov, the Soviets' spokesman, smiled on the sidelines. "We are finally doing away with that endlessly repeated myth of the Soviet threat, the Warsaw Pact threat, of an attack on Europe."

The timing of the grand announcement was curious, coming as it did while the Americans were changing presidents. It also had an ominous ring to it, in that Nikita Khrushchev had been bounced from office shortly after proposing big cuts in the military. "Soldiers will be soldiers," said Khrushchev in his memoirs. "They always want a bigger and stronger army. They always insist on having the very latest weapons and on attaining quantitative as well as qualitative superiority over the enemy."

Senior Soviet army officers were on record in 1988 as opposing unilateral cuts. General Ivan Tretyak, commander of the air-defence forces, was among them, describing, for example, Khrushchev's move as "a terrible blow to our defence capacity."

On the same day Gorbachev made his announcement, the chief of the general staff of the Soviet armed forces, Sergei Akhromeyev, resigned. Soviet officials insisted that it was for health reasons, but that didn't explain why the timing coincided with Gorbachev's address. Asked if he was facing resistance in the military, Gorbachev smiled and said, "*Nyet, nyet, nyet.*"

Gorbachev's plans were to tour Manhattan some more, make a sidetrip to Cuba, and then continue on to Britain. But on the day of his UN appearance, news of overwhelming tragedy arrived from home. Tens of thousands were dead or dying under the rubble of a monstrous earthquake in the Armenian Republic. Gorbachev couldn't be seen toasting the neon of Manhattan in such circumstances. He had no option but to fly home.

The immense tragedy in Armenia stole the thunder of Gorbachev's UN gambit and plunged the tiny republic into overwhelming grief. It came at a time when the Armenian countryside was seething with nationalist ferment over a small parcel of land, Nagorno-Karabakh. Though the vast majority who lived in the enclave were ethnic Armenians, the enclave itself was controlled by the neighbouring Azerbaijan Republic. Galvanized by the liberties of *glasnost*, Armenians had taken to the streets by the hundreds of thousands and entered into a state of virtual civil war with Azerbaijan.

The earthquake had the effect of cooling the conflict by diverting passions to the care of the injured and the rebuilding of the stricken area. It also gave Gorbachev some time to ponder a solution to the outbreak of nationalism that was springing up around him in Armenia and other republics.

Glasnost was paying handsome dividends abroad, but at home it had stirred ethnic passions to the point where the stability of the empire was threatened. Ethnic turmoil was suddenly Gorbachev's greatest danger, a bigger threat to his job security than the still-faltering economy. The emergence of long-suppressed nationalist movements had been easy to foresee. These movements only awaited a Kremlin leader who would loosen the police-state lid. *Glasnost* did exactly that.

What was happening was all written in the clichés about letting the lion out of the cage, about giving people an inch and they'll take a mile, about a little freedom being a dangerous thing, and so on. What had kept the non-Russians in the Soviet Union gagged for so long was police-state intimidation – that and, in particular with respect to the southern and Central Asian republics, Brezhnev's politics of leaving them in the control of corrupt native oligarchies. This form of "devolution by default"[1] demanded absolute loyalty to Brezhnev, the mafia don, in return for his turning a blind eye to their depravity.

Gorbachev lessened the police controls, and broke the mafia chain by replacing the corrupt ethnic leaders with Russian outsiders, who were hand-picked for their willingness to run a clean shop. In Alma-Ata, the capital of the Kazakh Republic, he replaced the native leader, Dinmukhamed Kunayev, with a Russian, Gennady Kolbin. An immediate consequence was two days of street riots. According to the Kremlin version, these riots were incited by Kunayev cronies about to lose their unearned entitlements. That Moscow didn't simply replace Kunayev with another native Kazakh was an indication that Gorbachev couldn't trust anyone in the republic's hierarchy to run a clean and stable ship.

In the Soviet Union half the population of 285 million is non-Russian. Besides the Russians there are no less than 103 other nationalities, each with its own language and culture. Furthermore, 22 of these national groups have more than one million people. There are 15 republics in the Soviet Union, and within these are a host of other subdivisions based on nationalities: 20 autonomous republics, eight autonomous regions, and ten autonomous areas. By early 1989, Gorbachev's Kremlin had witnessed ethnic flare-ups involving eight nationalities – Armenians, Azerbaijanis, Tatars, Kazakhs, Georgians, Estonians, Latvians, and Lithuanians.

Gorbachev wanted democratization, mass participation in decision making, more power at the local and regional levels. He did not presume – though he must have anticipated problems – that his green light on self-expression would so quickly produce nationalist surges all over the empire. Now that they were appearing, he could hardly resort to brute force from the centre. It would have been a repudiation of the policy that was at the heart of his governance. The challenge he faced was to find a middle-ground solution, one that would satisfy or at least mollify the republics by offering them greater economic, cultural, and political power. This was the search Gorbachev undertook.

He was willing to give a lot of rope but was not willing to countenance the type of violence that was occurring over Nagorno-Karabakh. In February 1988 in the Azerbaijani town of Sumgait, 32 people, including 26 Armenians, were slaughtered as the violence reached vicious levels; 46 more would die by the end of the year in the dispute over the enclave, and 300,000 more would flee to safer ground.

The conflict dated back to the early 1920s, when a controversial Kremlin decree awarded the territory to the Azerbaijanis, the majority of whom are Moslems. For more than six decades the Kremlin had ignored Armenian claims on the territory. Most Armenians are Christians, and still remember the holocaust they suffered at the hands of the Turks beginning in 1915. Any ill-treatment they received now at the hands of Moslems was a potential flashpoint.

Gorbachev's Kremlin, which had already instructed Armenian authorities to be more responsive to public opinion, debated many solutions to the crisis. One would have involved returning the enclave to Armenia; another would have made the enclave yet another autonomous region, one of many in the country. Few expected a redrawing of the boundaries, because of the precedent that would have set: a compromise in Armenia might well fan dozens of long-simmering territorial-rights disputes across the country. Making Nagorno-Karabakh an autonomous region would satisfy neither the Armenians nor the Azerbaijanis.

The solution, which the Kremlin announced in January 1989, was the imposition of direct rule on Nagorno-Karabakh from Moscow. There would be no representation for either of the republics involved in the dispute. The Kremlin's decision, though it bore no vestiges of the principles of *glasnost*, met with little indignation abroad, partly because the conflict was taking place in a largely unknown area of the world, and therefore hard for Westerners to identify with. In addition, while the Soviets were sending in troops, the Kremlin was not actually blocking an independence bid. Armenia and Azerbaijan were not trying to secede from the Soviet Union; they were two republics at war over Karabakh. In asserting control from the Kremlin, Gorbachev was doing what central governments in the West might consider doing in similar circumstances. If the peoples of Quebec and New Brunswick, or New York and Pennsylvania, were to start killing each other in a bloody and endless territorial wrangle, Ottawa or Washington would hardly stand idly by.

The Baltics presented Gorbachev with a more classic example of crisis of empire. There the unthinkable was suddenly on the table.

There had long been nationalist murmurings in the Baltic states, but nothing consequential enough to invite the prospect of substantial change. In May, when I visited Vilnius, the capital of Lithuania, I got the feeling that despite the vigour of the thousands of university students, despite the colours of the flowers of spring, despite the promise of *glasnost*, the republic of 3.6 million people was in a state of eternal slumber.

Pranas, a writer I met there, was one of the most forlorn activists I had ever encountered. "We could have been another Denmark," he said gloomily. "The base was here. The potential wealth was here." He threw up his hands. "Now look at us."

Lithuania and the other two Baltic states – Latvia and Estonia – were forcefully incorporated into the Soviet Union in 1940, after 22 years of independence. During those two decades Lithuania, which borders on Poland, didn't have what anyone would call an ideal democracy. Still, it had been a far sight better off than it was now under the Soviets, Pranas noted. He lamented how Soviet control was destroying the ecology, the culture, the economy. He didn't want to listen to Moscow's argument that the Soviet victory in the Second World War had saved the Baltics from the Nazis. He wanted independence.

A 25-year-old actress talked about her grandmother, who lived in Lithuania before the Soviet takeover. "She told me that at Easter she could go to the store and buy any kind of chocolate she wanted. There were dozens of choices. The country was rich. There was food, lots of imports." She paused and pondered. "Why are the Russians on our soil? People who live on others' soil have a destructive attitude toward that soil because it is not their own."

I had met her on my way from Kaunas to Vilnius. The driver of my taxi, who said relations with the Russians were bad because they didn't speak the language, had stopped when he saw her hitchhiking. She wore a black T-shirt with some inscription in Lithuanian emblazoned across her chest. We talked about Lithuanian culture, but it was a short conversation because, as she said, Stalin had deported all the great cultural figures in the late 1940s, leaving nothing.

She was telling me these things even though another man, a Russian, was in the back seat with me. Finally he spoke up. He said the woman should understand that the Lithuanians were not the only ones who had suffered through the years. What about the Russian people themselves? he asked, reminding her of the war, the repressions, the miserable living conditions.

The Baltic region was among the most modern in the Soviet Union. Compared with the Russian Republic, Lithuania had more food, better living accommodations, and more wealth generally. Ethnic Russians often grew bitter when they heard the people in the Baltics and other republics complain. As badly as they were doing, they were still generally better off than the people in the Russian Republic.

Any traveller in the Soviet Union discovered this. When it came to comforts – better hotels, better food, better roads, more colour – the republic to be avoided was the Russian one. "The condition of the social infrastructure in all major Russian republic cities is considerably worse than it is in the other republics' capitals and large cities," said a Soviet specialist, O.I. Shkaraton. "Sadly, even Moscow, our capital and Russia's foremost city, ranks only somewhere between 70th and 80th among the country's cities in terms of development of its social and cultural infrastructure."

What rankled the Russians even more was that the wealthier republics were heavily subsidized from the centre – and with Russian tax money. Several republics held the right to divert to their budgets 100 percent of their consumption tax, the main source of Soviet revenue.

Thus the Russians felt cheated by the provinces, while many of the provinces, because they were not in control of their own destinies, felt cheated by the Russians. Exacerbating the split was the lack of regional representation on the ruling body that meant the most – the Politburo. Under proportional representation, half the Politburo would have been made up of non-Russians.

The reality was that in 1988, only three non-Russians sat on the 13-member Politburo – Shcherbitsky from the Ukraine, Slyunkov from Byelorussia, and Shevardnadze from the Georgian Republic. As part of his anticorruption campaign, Gorbachev had gone after the leaders of the southern and Central Asian republics – the ones who would normally have been members of the Politburo.

In the back of the taxi, on the way through the Lithuanian countryside, the Russian man levelled a gratuitous blast at the woman from Kaunas. He said he didn't have much respect for the Lithuanians because when it came to fighting for their independence they didn't fight very hard; they took everything Moscow handed out. The woman fell into a slow burn that lasted all the way to Vilnius. When she got out of the car she stared icily at the Russian without saying a word.

At the University of Vilnius an old professor was taking me around, showing me lithographs. "The Russians study our language but they don't learn it," he said. "But the professors give them excellent marks anyway to pretend there is no problem." In Lithuania, 80 percent of the people were Lithuanian and Roman Catholic, and only nine percent were Russian. (Most of the rest were Poles.) The professor grew conspicuously annoyed when I brought up the subject of relations with the Russians – it was as if I had ruined his day. Finally he waved his hand through the air in despair. Living under the Soviets was like living under a stone, he said. "We're always dependent on someone else. How would you like to be always dependent on someone else?"

Romauldas Lankauskas, a well-known Vilnius artist and writer, had an apartment bigger than most of the ones I'd seen in the Russian republic. His abstract paintings filled it with a special life and charm. I had trouble understanding their significance. One, I said, appeared to represent an ecological disaster. He explained that no, it was a depiction of the beauty of Vilnius in winter. He was relaxed while he talked about the paintings, but when I got on to politics, he gestured at the ceiling, at where he thought the microphones were buried. Lankauskas belonged to a group of intellectuals who had recently met with Lithuanian government officials to demand a rewriting of the republic's history schoolbooks so that the real story could be taught. They had also demanded that Lithuanian youngsters not have to learn the Russian language beginning in grade one. The authorities, though Communist Party members, were native Lithuanians and not always lackeys of the Moscow party line. They had listened attentively, and Lankauskas had gone away heartened.

"I can feel something," he said, "some hope. But we must wait for a while yet. We must see if Gorbachev survives the party conference in June. Then we can plan our next steps." Gorbachev was their hope. "I fear Ligachev," said Lankauskas. "If he got control, nothing would change. It would be back to the old style."

That weekend in May 1988, about 4,000 Lithuanians showed up at a rally to denounce the 1948 deportation, to northern Siberia, of some 200,000 Lithuanian nationalists. Emboldened by *glasnost*, Lithuanian intellectuals had organized the meeting and, rather than step in, the government of the republic had given it reluctant approval. Some people said it was the first officially sanctioned demonstration against Stalin in Soviet history.

Many demonstrators wept as speaker after speaker detailed how the blameless had been subjected to torture and elimination. A poet, Nikolas Karchiauskas, said the proletarian poets were the first to feel the merciless bloodshed. "There are no words to justify the actions," he told the gathering. "We must not forgive them because they knew what they were doing. Stalin knew and the supporters of Stalinism knew."

A Russian, Alexander Markel, began to speak – in Russian. Soon he was drowned out by shouts that he speak in Lithuanian. He moved away from the microphone while an organizer beseeched the protesters to let him continue. When Markel returned to the microphone, less rumbling greeted him. "I have as much right to denounce Stalin as anyone!" he cried. His father was arrested and shot in 1937 for revolutionary behaviour, he said. His mother was convicted as the wife of an enemy of the people and spent 11 years in prison and exile. Many of his relatives were victims of the bloody repressions. By the end of his address perhaps half the protesters were with him. The other half couldn't sympathize. He was Russian.

Wandering through the gathering, where the young woman in

the black T-shirt could be found, I tried to sense whether the Lithu-anians were really prepared to start pushing for independence. Few wanted to be specific at this point. "Independence is not a word we use," was the frequent reply. Many expressed the view that it was a dream, a Utopia. "I'm Lithuanian," said a student. "That says it all."

The gathering dispersed quietly. I returned to Moscow thinking that any gains would be incremental, that real action was probably years away. Within a month, however, the fires began to burn. This was a republic which had bent to the Soviet will for almost half a century. Now, overnight, it was wakening from the long, forced slumber.

First, the intellectuals organized themselves into a group called the Movement for Support of Perestroika – in Lithuanian, Sajudis. At the end of June came Gorbachev's special all-union party conference. The signals were right. Not only did Gorbachev survive, he rammed through proposals for more watershed political reforms, including one that called for real elections for a real Parliament. Lithuanians were excited. Ten thousand of them turned out to welcome delegates back from the conference. Weeks earlier it had been 4,000 out to protest Stalin. Now it was 10,000 to welcome delegates.

By mid-July the old yellow, green, and red flag of Lithuania was being brandished. On August 23 an estimated 200,000 Lithuanians assembled to commemorate one of the black days in their history – the signing, on the same day in 1939, of the Molotov-Ribbentrop Pact, which divided the Baltic states into areas of Soviet and German influence. The demonstration was broken up by antiriot police. In late September, Sajudis began issuing a private newspaper called *Rebirth*. It was not subject to censorship.

Sajudis was not a blue-collar movement, but a mass of intellectuals and accomplished Lithuanian citizens, some of whom were members of the Communist Party. It was comparable, in some respects at least, to Quebec's early Parti Québécois.

Its activism soon led to political gains. They persuaded the local Communist authorities to formally recognize Lithuanian as the republic's official language, to legalize the national anthem, to grant more religious rights, to adopt the flag of prewar Lithuania as the official flag of the republic.

Unrest broiled to the point where Ringaudas Songaila was compelled to resign as first secretary of the Lithuanian Communist Party. A reformer, the more moderate Algirdas Brazauskas, who was more compatible with Sajudis, was brought in. In by-elections to the Lithuanian Congress, Sajudis-backed candidates won three of four seats. It was becoming apparent that the parliamentary elections scheduled for the fall of 1989 were going to result in a Sajudis majority, one that would support a declaration of sovereignty from Moscow.

The Lithuanian Communist Party did not try to stand firm against these political winds. Only a year earlier any active supporters of Sajudis's platform would have been thrown in jail. But Gorbachev's freedom-of-speech reforms had now taken hold; though not officially on the statute books, they were the new law. The spirit of Stalin was giving ground to the spirit of Sakharov.

In February 1989, Sajudis announced that its ultimate aim was to restore "an independent and neutral Lithuanian state in a demilitarized zone." It was the first Baltic republic to go that far. That provocative declaration brought an invitation for Brazauskas to come to Moscow.[2]

The Kremlin ordered the cancellation of Sajudis's weekly television program. One episode in particular had riled authorities: it had praised the Lithuanian nationalists of the early postwar years for gunning down Soviet troops in guerilla actions. The Kremlin also placed limits on Sajudis's independent press and warned the group not to issue any more separatist declarations. Still, it wasn't the severe type of clampdown many Lithuanians had feared.

"We have told Sajudis that together we can approach that red line, but we, the official leadership, cannot cross it," Brazauskas told the *New York Times*. "On the other side of the line we can no longer remain friends or support their ideas. You can criticize us. You can mistrust us – whatever – but we won't cross that line."

In the March elections for the Soviet Union's new Congress of People's Deputies, Sajudis candidates won a majority of the republic's 42 seats. Supporters of independence now dominated that body's Lithuanian contingent; in all likelihood they would soon dominate the republic's own congress as well. Sajudis wasn't planning on trying to cross the red line in the short term. For the time being it was striving for significantly increased autonomy. And it was succeeding.

In Latvia, where almost half the population was non-Latvian, nationalist fever was cooler; in tiny Estonia, where the population of 1.5 million was 65 percent Estonian, the populist outbursts caused a sensation. Following the escalation of nationalist passions along similar lines as in Lithuania, Estonians issued a stunningly direct challenge to Moscow's authority.

In October 1988 the Kremlin published drafts of proposals that would amend the constitution to allow for real elections, a new parliamentary system, and other liberal reforms. But what most people saw as a major democratic step forward was viewed by Baltic nationalists as an erosion of regional power. They particularly objected to a clause that took away their theoretical right to secede from the Soviet Union. Petitions were circulated demanding the withdrawal of the clauses.

Then, in November, the Estonian legislature dropped a bombshell: it passed laws in direct defiance of the Kremlin. One gave Estonia the right to veto any national law that ran counter to Estonian interests. Another transferred ownership of land, resources, housing, and enterprises to Estonia and legitimized private property. The measures were tantamount to a declaration of independence.

For Gorbachev, this was too much. He summoned the Estonian leaders to Moscow, told them their actions were in contravention of the constitution, and added that they were making a grave error. The resolution on private property, he said, contradicted the achievement of socialism, which was "to stop the exploitation of man by man."

Kostel Gerndorf, an economist and one of Estonia's leading rebels, responded, "I don't think we are dependent on Gorbachev's opinion. This is *perestroika*. It is happening in Estonia. Conflict is the only way now and we will go on."

But with the political skill that was typical of him, Gorbachev moved to ease the crisis. He had his special constitutional committee adjust the draft proposals to allay Baltic fears. The clause affecting the right to secede was removed. In addition, Gorbachev promised the immediate establishment of a constitutional committee to revise the federal relationship between the Soviet state and its 15 republics. The final result was that the Estonians went home somewhat mollified. They had forced a compromise.

Just as in Lithuania, too much long-suppressed passion had been let out of the bottle for anyone to stuff back in. Gorbachev had options on the nationality question, but a return to the pre-*glasnost* status quo was not one of them. He was prepared, it seemed, to move to a much looser federalism, provided the republics did not try to force his hand by violence.

Comparing the situation in the Baltics with the separatist movement in Quebec, and that province's push for recognition as a distinct society, Gorbachev advisor Georgi Arbatov said, "We have no objection to some sort of sovereignty-association among the republics. . . . We want to give them much more authority in economic decisions, in environmental decisions. . . ."[3]

The Politburo had a range of options available for dealing with the Baltic republics. A Finlandization arrangement wasn't to be ruled out. The three states were small and weren't strategically located. Rather than be a thorn in the side of the bear, they could evolve into Finlands – independent, neutral states that traded with the Soviets and never sought to aggravate the relationship. The counter-arguments focussed on what would be done with the large Russian population in the Baltics and, more significantly, on the precedent that would be set by allowing the three republics their freedom. If the Baltics could do it, would the rallying cry of the other republics be, "Why not us?"

In April 1989, after the explosion over Karabakh, after the challenge from the Baltics, nationalist unrest flared in Georgia. Nineteen people were killed and hundreds wounded in bloody clashes between Soviet troops and tens of thousands of demonstrators clamouring for independence. At least two of the deaths were caused by nerve gas. The Georgian party leaders were dumped.

Gorbachev responded by denying any possibility that the

republic could secede. "Restructuring of inter-ethnic relations is not the redrawing of borders, is not the breaking of the national-state structure of the country."

Sixty-eight years under Soviet control had seen Georgia evolve into a republic with the culture and conscience of a nation, but without means of political expression. *Glasnost* had finally given it those means – to the tune of 100,000 filling the streets of central Tbilisi. And the Soviets responded in the old style – with tanks. The aspirations of non-Russians were again threatening the politics of *perestroika* – the very politics that had given vent to the aspirations.

The fear in the Kremlin was that nationalist fever would now spread to the Ukraine. A nationalist eruption there was the most worrisome of all the possibilities. The Ukraine produced one-quarter of the nation's meat and potatoes and one-fifth of its grain. It served as the buffer between the Russian Republic and Eastern Europe. Its population of 52 million was almost five times that of the three Baltic states combined. If nationalism kindled among the Ukrainians, who had endured 70 years of Soviet power, the lid would be off and absolute chaos would loom.

Many of us in Moscow wondered why Gorbachev maintained Vladimir Shcherbitsky as the first secretary of the Ukrainian Communist Party. Shcherbitsky was a Brezhnev-generation conservative and out of step with the new regime. But therein perhaps lay the key. Gorbachev needed a conservative leader in the Ukraine to keep it stable. Shcherbitsky opposed *glasnost*, the spoon that was stirring nationalist passions. His opposition was the type Gorbachev could well afford to have.

Thaws were dangerous politics in the Soviet Union and Eastern Europe. The thaw that followed Stalin's death led to the Hungarian Revolution. Moscow's answer was tanks. Khrushchev's thaw, which continued in some respects into the early Brezhnev years, helped bring on the Prague Spring. Again, Moscow's answer was tanks.

Gorbachev was far more sensitive to world public opinion than his predecessors and less inclined to use force. But he was not about to tolerate internal revolution. The conundrum he faced was that the further down the road to freedom he marched, the closer to chaos he came.

31/See No Evil, Hear No Evil

SCANDINAVIA and the Soviet Union offered visitors the best and the worst respectively that socialism has to offer. Helsinki or Copenhagen or Stockholm were frequent destinations for me, and for other foreigners in Moscow who wanted to escape the worst. For me, however, socialism's best was still a somewhat dismaying experience: Scandinavian socialism, like the Soviet version, featured a population of too many deadened spirits.

The cities had a pretty face and pretty faces. Everything was scrubbed clean and brightly coloured. The affluence was such that even the cabbies drove BMWs. Everyone looked the same – healthy, wealthy, stern. But the surface impression was that life was too easy for them, that the government did too much, ensured too much. Complacency bred boredom and a lack of challenge. Whereas the Soviet Union offered no wealth and no incentive, Scandinavia offered plenty of wealth and no incentive. The pressure was to conform, to be a matching particle in the socialist consensus. Those who dared to stray were looked down upon. "Maybe it's wrong to remove all the stones from [life's] path," said the Danish novelist Tage Skou-Hanson, commenting on the missing dynamism in his country. "We have undervalued the importance of challenge."[1]

In the Soviet Union, where the State guaranteed only the bare essentials, attempts to promote individual initiative were difficult enough: the people were inured to a low standard of living. But in Scandinavia, where the welfare state guaranteed a high living standard, it was even harder: the people were inured to guaranteed wealth.

With little to stimulate them, many Scandinavians drank – most notably the Finns. Most nationalities like to drink, but the Finns – and this was something they shared with the Russians – didn't drink like others, that is, to have a good time. They drank to become unconscious, to erase time from their lives. In Helsinki the Finns poured them back very nicely. But it was when they came over to Leningrad or Moscow in hordes on the weekends that they really put on power-drinking exhibitions.

I was never sure why the Finns came across the Soviet border in such numbers. Supposedly tourists, they seemed to confine themselves to the drinking lounges all weekend. I trampled over Finns flat out in hotel corridors, hissing like steamboats. I saw them outside the hotels, facedown, whoozing at curbside. Why couldn't they do this at home?

Finns and Russians never seemed to say much to each other. So I was a bit surprised one mid-April day in the Hotel Leningrad when I saw a feisty Russian woman and a swillpot Finn squaring off in a corridor. I only caught the end of the conversation, wherein the Russian, who spoke splendid English, was goading the Finn by calling him a "woodcutter."

She poured forth the great Russian names – Tchaikovsky, Rachmaninoff, Tolstoy, Dostoyevsky, Pushkin, Pasternak. "And what have you and Finland given the world, woodcutter? You represent nothing."

The sotted Finn didn't know where to leer. He stumbled away muttering western expletives.

Beyond the Finns, Leningrad, the damp museum on the Baltic, exhibited a sad and dying grandeur. Hailed worldwide for its classic beauty, its despair was becoming harder to hide. Age, wear, the sorrow of war, and corrupt management had left only a veneer. Massive restoration of the palaces, manors, and museums was going to require millions of roubles the city did not have. The housing crisis that had driven away the likes of Solodskik was such that 1.3 million of the city's four million people lived in communal apartments. In these apartments two or three families shared two or three rooms and a toilet.

For this large percentage of the population that was so impossibly cramped and that had to scrounge for basics in half-empty stores, the compensation offered by the princely architectural glamour was insufficient. "The city is a museum, but museums aren't supposed to be lived in," said a local photographer who was fortunate enough to have his own tiny apartment. "Sure they say the situation is getting better, that everyone will have their own flat in a few years. But they always say that."

Nevsky Prospekt, a famous shopping boulevard of four-storeyed baroque splendour, offered nothing in the shops within two decades of vogue.

In untypical Soviet style, Gorbachev blamed the city fathers, not the workers, for the rotten state of affairs. "Yesterday representatives of the city told me that workers in the food industry do not know what they need. What kind of argument is that? I do not think this is true. They know what they need. I would put it this way – the present leadership of the city and of the region to this day does not know what the food industry needs."

At the Maley drama theatre a new Soviet play entitled *Stars in the Morning Sky* was making the headlines. It was a story about how prostitutes had been shipped out of Moscow before the 1980 Olympic Games in an effort to preserve the false image of the Soviet Union as whore-free. Soviet citizens were finally being appraised.

In a wonderfully ancient and ornate Orthodox church, the minister was having a very busy day. Under one of the onion domes, 14 Soviet couples were standing in a semicircle holding crying babies. The sacrament of baptism was about to be administered. No KGB men were clicking cameras.

At the Kirov Theatre, Faruk Ruzimatov, the ballet star who some said was destined to take the place of the defector Mikhail Baryshnikov, was in rehearsal. His trainer and choreographer, Gennady Selyutski, was dissatisfied. "Your head is falling down. Your head is falling down."

Ruzimatov had grown tired of Selyutski over the years. Now his long black curls poured limply over his sallow face, half-hiding a look of dark reproach. In his one-piece maroon leotard he looked unfed, scrawny, exhausted – as if he was on a Leningrad diet. But then Selyutski signalled to the young Russian woman at the piano in the corner. As she hit the keys, a sensation of opening skies and quiet thunder shook the room. Faruk was in the heavens, eyes burning, teeth flashing angrily, muscles tearing through the leotard.[2]

The scene repeated itself – Selyutski's lament, Faruk's frown, the detonation of the air – again and again. Afterwards the skinny, wild-haired dancer could be found, alone and exhausted, in a side chamber. "The tragedy of our profession," he said softly, "is that all the time, every day, from one performance to another, you have to prove yourself and prove yourself again." When he described his training regimen he sounded like Fetisov and Larionov, the hockey players. He was tired of doing the classics, of dancing *Swan Lake* a thousand times. He wanted to expand, explore, create, get Western. Before, Faruk had kept his emotions locked inside, his observers said. Now he was able to get them out and onto the dance floor. But he was still unsatisfied – he wanted to be like other Soviet artists, like the writers, the film makers, the theatre directors beginning to benefit from *glasnost*. He wanted room to move.

Along the road back to Leningrad's airport, big red-lettered signs were still standing, urging workers to work harder. These relics of an era gone by, an era when Soviets really did believe in something called Communism, were now ignored by everyone. "Ever since I was 14 my friends and I have been laughing at all these slogans," said Sergei Kalugin a Muscovite, commenting on the same signs in the capital. He was middle-aged now, but could still remember counting 16 of them along his trolley-bus route. They had a peculiar pattern, he noted: "The worse an organization works, the more posters and slogans are on its walls. . . . Does anyone really believe that even one person in a thousand will be spiritually stirred after seeing a huge slogan reading, 'Workers Accelerate, Deepen and Achieve'?"

In Moscow the dinosaur art had been slowly coming down as part of *perestroika*. It wasn't the case in Leningrad: the city was not in the forefront of *perestroika*. It didn't challenge Moscow on any fronts any more. It was the capital of a past that was fading further into the past. Foreign dignitaries seldom included Leningrad on their itinerary anymore. Recently, Margaret Thatcher and George Shultz had passed it up in favour of Tbilisi.

But the old capital was not entirely subdued. As the fourth Reagan-Gorbachev summit opened in Moscow in early June, an estimated 2,000 demonstrators in Leningrad battled with police. They were out in the streets to show solidarity with a new opposition party, the Democratic Union, which was attempting to get started in Moscow. Reports reaching Moscow said that the demonstration had turned violent and had taken the police two hours to disperse.

Glasnost had progressed to the point where debate swirled as to whether political groups outside the Communist Party should be allowed to form. Activists made hay with the argument, "How can there be real democratization if you don't allow more than one party?" The authorities were not ready to sanction an official opposition party. In Hungary there was one on the way; in the Soviet Union the Kremlin was busy trying to keep in line the competing wings in its own Communist Party. The Democratic Union was repeatedly harassed. The Kremlin elite argued that there were so many nationalities and competing interests in the Soviet Union that if the door were opened, dozens of parties would spring up and the result would be worse political chaos than in Italy. The argument wasn't convincing: the Democratic Union was only trying to become the second official party in the Soviet Union. Chaos was not yet on the horizon.

The late spring of 1988 was a time of stirring developments. Soviet troops were getting ready to leave Afghanistan; Reagan was on his way to Moscow, where he would be the first American president to step on Soviet soil in 14 years; the celebrations marking the millenium of the coming of Christianity to Russia were about to begin; and most of all, the special all-union communist Party Conference, a colloquy that would do much to determine the fate of *perestroika* and Gorbachev, was set for the end of June.

After the signing of the INF accord at the Washington summit, hope had surfaced, slim hope, that Gorbachev and Reagan would be able to do something more spectacular in Moscow – achieve a 50-percent reduction in long-range strategic arsenals. But such a treaty was going to require far more complex negotiations than the INF treaty. After INF the Kremlin's eagerness to make arms agreements seemed to abate; Gorbachev was concentrating on domestic matters in preparation for the conference. Both he and Reagan could feel satisfied in that they had at least made a start on arms reductions. Reagan was now going to be remembered as the American president who began arms reduction as opposed to arms limitation. The president's right-wingers were already irritated enough over this one agreement; another treaty with the Soviets and they might disown him completely.

It was probably to appease his conservative club that he attacked the Soviets the old-fashioned way in the run-up to the Moscow summit. He called on Gorbachev to tear down the wall of repression, a remark which drew an angry rebuttal from the Soviet leader, who said he was getting tired of sermons from the White House. "We are not going to re-educate the United States and do not accept that it has any right to re-educate us. . . . We should realize once and for all that Soviet and Amerian society have different values, and we should not attempt to foist our customs and our ideas of what is good and what is bad on each other."

It was notable, in this context, that Gorbachev usually practised what his public statements preached. For example, the Soviet leader often criticized the American approach to arms control in his public speeches, but he didn't lecture the Americans on their massive drug problems, or their 19th-century gun laws, or the expanding gap between rich and poor in their country. One exception to this was when he was specifically provoked on human-rights questions. Then he would hammer away at American unemployment, homelessness, crime, discrimination, and so on. One reason Gorbachev could keep the rhetoric cooler, perhaps, was that he didn't have to worry quite so much about catering to political constituencies the way Reagan did. There was the Communist Party hierarchy to keep in mind, but as yet there was no public debate on foreign policy.

The Kremlin preferred to listen to the more judicious and temperate Shultz, who during the run-up to the Moscow summit marvelled at East-West progress. "I think if you compare the situation today with what the situation was like in the middle of 1985 you'll see that it has changed dramatically." At the previous three summits, Reagan had for the most part avoided the type of Red-bashing that prompts Soviet wrath. Curiously, however, he turned the other way for the fourth – just when the relationship was at its warmest. In Moscow, he would dangerously put Soviet human-rights abuses at the top of the agenda, and the summit would be almost crippled as a result.

Human rights was one of the few policy banners that Reagan had accepted from his predecessor, Jimmy Carter. When Richard Nixon and Henry Kissinger were fashioning their détente with Moscow in the early 1970s, they chose to turn a blind eye to the egregious Soviet abuses. Back then Andrei Gromyko could get away with the line that human rights was an internal matter. Jimmy Carter, a democrat, found himself tossed between the moderation of Cyrus Vance and the tomahawk approach of Zbigniew Brzezinski. Initially he favoured the Vance line: in 1977 he said that "being confident of our future we are now free of that inordinate fear of communism which once led us to embrace any dictator who joined us in that fear." It would be a valid statement once Mikhail Gorbachev was in command of the Soviet Union, maybe, but it wasn't while Brezhnev held power. Carter gradually came to the realization that his attitude was premature. While having the integrity to acknowledge his own country's failings in human rights, he legitimately latched onto human rights as his stick to browbeat the Kremlin and drove the Soviets mad in so doing.

By the time of the Moscow summit, Gorbachev had made more advances on human rights than any previous Soviet leader. The release of the political prisoners, the media freedoms, and the promises of free elections were among the many reforms testifying to that. Moreover, Gorbachev had plans for still more dramatic initiatives.

The difference that democratization was making was obvious on the streets. In 1974, the day before Richard Nixon's arrival in Moscow, Soviet authorities arrested four members of a political-discussion group meeting in the Arbat district. A week before Reagan was to arrive for his summit, two Soviet militiamen grinningly looked on as a teenage troubadour entertained a crowd with a song making fun of the KGB.[3]

But the Soviet Union was still a long way from meeting the standards required by the Helsinki accords. For example, while significantly more people were being allowed to emigrate from the Soviet Union, a policy of free emigration, as demanded in the accords, was not in place.

Two days before the summit Reagan made a speech in the hall in Helsinki where the human-rights accords had been signed 13 years earlier. He recognized that there had been good progress on human rights under Gorbachev but went on to demand that the Soviets release all political prisoners, allow free emigration, and introduce full religious tolerance.

It was an astonishing display by the American president. In view of Gorbachev's record, he could have chosen to highlight the positive, thereby guaranteeing a warm summit opening. Not Reagan. To his challenge, the Kremlin predictably launched a counterattack. Tass came out quoting American statistics on homelessness, on inhumane prison conditions, and on the history of discrimination against blacks. Earlier the Soviets had called for an international human-rights conference, to be hosted in Moscow; citing Soviet abuses, Washington had turned down the invitation. After Reagan's outburst in Helsinki one Soviet official had the audacity to suggest that the United States should not be invited to the conference in the first place, unless it cleaned up its human-rights act on the homeless – among them 500,000 children. The Soviets also let it be known that when Gorbachev visited Washington he didn't showcase groups of homeless people or poverty-stricken American blacks. Reagan, they knew, was planning to do the equivalent in Moscow.

On Soviet soil where he was asked how it felt to be in the evil empire and where he replied, "Just fine," Reagan greeted 13 dissidents at the residence of the American ambassador. He told them that the United States applauded Soviet changes, "yet the basic standards that the Soviet Union agreed to almost 13 years ago in the Helsinki accords or a generation ago in the Universal Declaration of Human Rights still need to be met." He put forward an agenda for the Kremlin on freedom of religion, speech, and travel. "I've come to Moscow with this human rights agenda because, as I suggested, it is our belief that this is a moment of hope.

The new Soviet leaders appear to grasp the connection between certain freedoms and economic growth."

In turn, the Kremlin produced evidence that one of the so-called dissidents Reagan had brought to the speech was a Nazi war criminal, and that other invitees were not the heroic freedom fighters Reagan was trying to suggest. The general tendency in the Western press was to greet anyone identified as a dissident as a demigod. Dissidents always got wonderful press. The media's mindset was that if they were dissidents they must be "on our side." When the Soviets revealed that invitee Nikolai Rozhko had joined the Nazis and been sentenced in 1944 for torturing and murdering Soviet citizens, the American embassy didn't refute the information. But the story was quickly forgotten. The Soviets also trotted out a group of American Indians for a press conference where American human-rights standards were deplored.

In sum, however, the Soviet counterprotestations had a limited effect because they had limited validity. Particularly since the passing of McCarthyism and the advent of civil rights in the 1960s, American human-rights abuses simply did not compare with those in the Soviet Union.

Deep down, Gorbachev must have been aware of this. His understanding may have been what saved the summit. For the first 36 hours the progress made at the previous three summits, and the very rapport between the president and the general secretary, hung in the balance. The fear was that Gorbachev, who had dropped his diplomatic demeanour in Washington when faced with human-rights charges, would move to near rage this time and turn the summit into a public polemic. The temptation to go on the attack must have been heightened by what most of the world knew, and what Gorbachev himself knew – that the Soviet leader, who had a brilliant mind, was dealing with an intellectual lightweight in Ronald Reagan.

But Gorbachev demonstrated strong statesmanship: he rode out the human-rights storm, leaving most of the counterattacks to subordinates. He showed his diplomatic cast of mind in a capsule comment he made to the president on a walk through Red Square. "If arguments are at the boiling point, truth evaporates. Therefore, we should have dialogue." It was a magnanimous response to

Reagan's harsh words. The summit in Washington had moved to a comfort level after a stressful opening act; so too would the meeting in Moscow.

Gorbachev addressed Reagan's earlier attacks with the president at his shoulder. "The president has given some criticism. I disagree with some of those criticisms. But Americans are proud of their country. We should understand each other while being different. . . . We are so critical of our own country that even the president's criticisms are weak. We know what our problems are."

The superpower leaders were animated. "We share a view," Reagan told the Russians he met on his walk through Red Square. "We want friendship between our countries." To another group, composed of women, he said, "I have great admiration for the women of Russia. You are courageous and contribute so much to the whole society."

A Russian woman who was holding a small child told him, "We want our children to live in peace." Gorbachev took the child from the mother's arms and said, "Shake hands with Grandfather Reagan."

"I have a dream," said Reagan, "that all young people of the world should get to know each other for peace. . . . It would be a better world."

Back at Gorbachev's office the press asked about the possibilities for a big strategic-arms treaty. Gorbachev said it was possible. The president nodded. "I remember once the president and I had some discussion where we seemed to have an impasse," recalled Gorbachev. "And I remember during one of our discussions in Geneva, the president said, 'Let's stamp our fists on the table,' and I said, 'All right.' And by morning everything was agreed. Maybe now it is again a time to bang our fists on the table."

Reagan said, "I'll do anything that works."

"That's the way," Gorbachev replied.

Raisa Gorbachev and Nancy Reagan were having their usual set-to, but more revealing was Raisa's little talk with journalists at the Tretyakov Gallery. She was waiting for Nancy to arrive. "Maybe we'll have a conversation," she said, "because you are on time and" – getting in a dig here – "the guests are late."

In her talk she emphasized a theme that was central to some of her husband's conversations – the theme of humanism. "I advise you to look at the faces of the saints," she told the journalists, "at the way our icon painters painted them. They are open and friendly. Do you see them as I tell you or do you see them differently from me? We should have a dialogue." When none of the journalists took her up on one, she continued. "Look at the faces, restrained yet open. I would like to quote Dostoyevsky: 'That the heart of Russia, maybe more than the heart of people of any nationality, is prepared for human unity.' "

Mrs. Reagan arrived in a Bill Blass black-and-white suit of geometric print with a black-and-white blouse. After everyone had spent some time looking at icons, a correspondent asked her for her impressions of Communist society. "We have two different ways of living." Was she becoming a convert? "No, and neither are they. I'd call it a Mexican stand-off."[4]

Her husband, however, seemed to soften more to the Soviet people every time he met them. The president told students at Moscow State University, "Your generation is living in one of the most exciting and hopeful times in Soviet history. It is a time when the first breath of freedom stirs the air and the heart beats to the accelerated rhythm of hope, when the accumulated spiritual energies of a long silence yearn to break free."

But the landmark moment of the summit came when he declared that he had changed his mind and no longer saw the Soviets as the evil empire. (He first used that celebrated phrase – at least in public – at a press conference in the Executive Office Building, next door to the White House. I was at that conference, and remember noticing that the other reporters were listening to his harangue with relative nonchalance – it was Reagan, so it was expected. It didn't even make the top of some newscasts. But those two words came to symbolize his attitude toward the Soviets and, indeed, the attitude of his administration in its first term.)

Now, in Moscow, Reagan was asked if it was still the evil empire. "No," he said, "I was talking about another time, another era." His disavowal neatly dovetailed with the Russian proverb Gorbachev had quoted to Reagan on the president's arrival. "Better to see something once than to hear about it a hundred times."

Until that week Reagan had never set foot in the country he had chosen to excoriate for so many decades. But now, being there, he had gained a sense of the place, of its history, of its potential. He now saw the Soviets as humans. Seeing live Communists on their home tundra moved the spirit in the man from Hollywood: he was finding out that they didn't breathe fire, that the sun shone on them, that it wasn't a land of prisons and a dark, cold hell of stereotypes. In the end, he would call the Soviet people friends.

The two leaders held press conferences at the close of their talks. Gorbachev met with the journalists for two hours, and if ever they had needed a lesson in the man's depth they got one this day: he ranged far and wide, providing comprehensive and erudite analyses of every issue put to him. An hour later the Gipper came before the scribes. His home team came out of the conference embarrassed by his responses, which were too shallow for high-school grads. He was clearly out of his depth on every substantive issue. But it didn't matter – the American television networks were going to reduce his answers to six or seven words anyway. Nobody would know.

The summit closed, as had the other summits, without any solid agreements. In Washington they had signed the INF agreement, but that was a formality – all the details had been worked out beforehand. In Moscow a couple of incidental agreements were signed, but no notable headway was made on the proposal to cut long-range strategic arsenals by 50 percent. With a presidential election coming up in the fall, time was running out on those negotiations. In Moscow the two sides were unable to clear the way for a final push.

"Propaganda gambits prevailed," complained Gorbachev in his final summation to the press, "and all sorts of spectacles, all sorts of shows. I'm not filled with admiration for this part of the meeting."

But what mattered most was the symbolism, the big picture, the picture of Ronald Reagan's rethinking his evil-empire thoughts. Those were the gains made in the fourth summit. That's what the Soviets needed. That's also what East-West relations needed.

Gorbachev was businesslike at the departure ceremony. He noted that progress in U.S.-Soviet relations was moving "much more slowly than is required by the real situation," but added that he was holding to his previously expressed view that individual treaties such as INF were not as important for the superpowers as the growth of mutual understanding. In the end, he said, understanding had been advanced some more as a result of Reagan's visit.

The president also wanted to conclude on a personal note. "Earlier this week at Moscow State University I mentioned to young people there that they appeared to me exactly as would any group of students in my own country or anywhere else in the world. So too, Nancy and I find the faces, young and old, here on the streets of Moscow. At first more than anything else, they were curious faces. But as the time went on, the smiles began and then the waves."

32/Temperatures Rising

SOVIET CITIZENS selected 5,000 delegates for the special Communist Party conference called by Gorbachev for the end of June 1988. These conclaves were usually held at five-year intervals, but the Soviet leader was introducing so many changes that he had called this additional one as a way to build a greater sense of participation in the process.

The delegate-selection procedure for party gatherings had traditionally been controlled by local and regional party bosses, who hand-picked the delegates, always choosing comrades who would dutifully embrace the orders from the top. But those days were fading now: for this conference the delegates would be selected democratically. In the Kremlin's thinking, this fit under the rubric of *glasnost* and created the likelihood of more grass-roots representation. This conceivably could work in Gorbachev's favour, since among the entrenched party members who would otherwise have attended, there was more opposition to his revolutionary ways.

Actually, none of us in the media had an accurate handle on where Gorbachev's support lay and didn't lay. The science of opinon polling was only now being introduced in a serious way in the Soviet Union – another offshoot of the *glasnost* campaign. There were not enough surveys available to accurately gauge public sentiment. But journalists had to write something, so we took our own tiny opinion samplings and scanned the Soviet media for clues, and judged from there.

The sampling area I chose prior to the Conference was Lenin's home town of Ulyanovsk, formerly Simbirsk; it had been renamed Ulyanovsk in honour of the Soviet founder. (Lenin's birth name was Vladimir Ilyich Ulyanov – he adopted the name Lenin much later.)

Eight hundred kilometres southeast of Moscow dozed Ulyanovsk, an industrial centre of 500,000 lining the bluffs of Europe's longest river, the Volga. Lenin was born there on April 10, 1870, and moved away when he was 17. While the official texts say he loved Simbirsk, it seems he never cared enough to return. His letters suggested that he missed the river but not the town. In the late 19th century it was a deplorably backward town full of drunks and serfs. Today, despite the glory of its native son, Ulyanovsk is still backward, no better than its dreary provincial neighbours. One would have expected Moscow to be more generous. When I visited Ulyanovsk for a few days that June, 71 years after Lenin's revolution and two years after the beginnings of *perestroika*, meat and butter were being rationed. Two other mainstays of Soviet life – an opera theatre and a covered hockey arena – had not yet come to the city. In the central bookstore the new-releases section offered three hot new arrivals on Lenin, but nothing on *perestroika*. Outside the window of my room in what was supposed to be the best hotel in town, an abandoned and rotting platform for window washers hung precariously.

Before there was a rationing system the townspeople used to stockpile meat and butter, a practice that had helped induce the shortages. Now every citizen, by producing a stamped card, was entitled to a kilogram of meat per month – the equivalent of seven small porkchops. "With the rationing system, at least we are assured of getting something," said my hotel floor lady while she delivered biscuits and hot tea in a samovar to my room. A Muscovite whose visit overlapped with my own lowered his eyes when he heard the details of the rationing system. "They say we're a superpower," he said. "But what good is being a superpower? For the good of the people? Huh, we're living like shit."

Young Lenin, the son of an educator, lived well here. The two-floor, ten-room home of his parents still stands. A verandah at the back overlooks a family courtyard that extends for a city block. His czarist-period home is leagues better than the housing that has been built in Ulyanovsk in the seven decades since the revolution. "Were Lenin to visit here now," the Muscovite said, "he would be appalled at what his system has done."

Ulyanovsk was sending 27 delegates to the party conference. In Moscow they would debate and vote on the next, far-reaching phase of *perestroika*. Gorbachev had just released the new "theses" of his revolution. They called for no less than an entirely new, presidential form of government, a stripping of the power of the Communist Party, and a limit to the number of terms elected office holders – including Gorbachev himself – could serve.

Gorbachev was now moving quickly. In order to broaden *glasnost* and democracy, it was vital that he break the Communist Party's monopoly on power. Lenin's revolution had been carried out under the slogan, "All power to the *soviets*." Gorbachev was reinvoking that slogan: his new plans envisaged the elected *soviets*, or local councils, having real legislative authority, replacing a system that saw them in the total grip of party bosses.

The slide away from the Leninist ideal with respect to the *soviets* had begun shortly after the Soviet founder's death in 1924. Boris Kurashvili, a doctor of juridical science, provided a perspective: "Our society spent years developing in extraordinary circumstances. In the 1930s it was necessary to forcibly prepare the country for a military invasion. In the 1940s to repulse it and then restore the economy. An emergency system of government was developed, typically characterized by the concentration of power in the hands of the ruling organs. More specifically, in the hands of the highest ruling political leader, and the organs subordinate to him. . . . In this system the *soviets* in effect fulfilled the role of an institute of approval and support of state policy."

In the 1950s, Kurashvili added, the emergency system of management should have been replaced. But inertia and incompetence kept it afloat. "It [the system] was cleansed, for the most part, of gross lawlessness and cruelty, but it was not restructured."

In the months prior to the congress, Gorbachev summoned

leading party officials from all the republics to Moscow to discuss reform. Around that time, *Pravda* published a scathing critique of the Communist Party, describing its rule as dictatorial and destructive. The editorial heaped scorn on the party's practice of dictating to voters what their anonymous choice should be in the ballot box; it castigated the party for not establishing a rotation system for its leaders, adding that the result had been a lack of accountability and a virtual ban on criticism. Clans had taken over the country, *Pravda* asserted – clans whose egotism, incompetence, and corruption had left honest people feeling humiliated and without faith in justice.

The 19-million-member Communist Party had long practised absolutism on the rest of the population. It had control of all the country's economic, military, social, and cultural bodies. It made all the decisions on policy and the appointment of personnel. Party members occupied all key positions in state institutions. Now Gorbachev was planning to move the party out of its command position in Soviet life. By increasing the powers of the *soviets* he would be placing limits on the party's role in Soviet society; it would be more or less restricted to the areas of theory, ideological guidance, and the promotion of ideals. "A revolution is taking place," said the deputy justice minister, Mikhail Vyshinsky. "Not everyone realizes it, but that is what it is."

Leading political scientists in both the East and the West were excited about Gorbachev's move on the party. At the same time, however, they recognized that he was further threatening the security of the entrenched party establishment. He was dependent – at least until democratization was well in swing – on its support.

In Ulyanovsk the 27 delegates to the conference had been chosen from a pool of 80 candidates. Those 80 had been chosen from meetings of farmers, factory workers, teachers, and the like. This process represented a striking departure from the norm and did not come off smoothly: many citizens later complained that they were shut out of the process, or that it was too rushed. Among the delegates was Nadya Mazheikina, a secondary-school teacher. She was going to Moscow first and foremost to grouse about education. "The main flaw with the education system today," she explained, "is that all the pupils are taught the same way, even though they are all different." Also, she estimated that in Ulyanovsk, 200 teachers were in desperate need of basic living accommodation. Yet, she claimed, the city could only supply one new apartment per year to the teachers' community.

Mazheikina was keen about carving up the party's authority. The story the citizens of Ulyanovsk told was a common one. The chairman of the state farm, say, was experienced in the business of farming; he knew the soil, he knew the weather, he knew the capability of his work brigade. He would make his plans and set his harvesting schedule. But then the word would come down like a hammer from the bureau of the Communist Party boss – all crops had to be harvested by a stipulated date. The crops might not be ready by that date, but that didn't matter – the order was the order.

More than three months before the Party Congress, those in favour of this old system of party dominance began to organize. What came to be regarded as their manifesto was printed in the prominent newspaper *Sovyetskaya Rossiya* on March 13. It was a defence of Stalinism authored by a Leningrad schoolteacher named Nina Andreevna. Because of the newspaper's prestige, and because no rebuttal or explanation was carried with her analysis, it appeared to many to be a statement of official policy.

Whispers in Moscow suggested that Yegor Ligachev, whose responsibilities still included the media, had approved the article. Support for its anti-*perestroika* sentiments was noticeable. Public gatherings, mostly in Leningrad, sought to raise the article's profile. For three weeks – three weeks of apprehension for the *glasnost* forces – no public rebuttal was published. The Soviet press was silent. There was talk that Gorbachev had caved in to pressures.

Finally a *Pravda* editorial appeared that decried the article, accusing opponents of *perestroika* of seeking to promote an alternative political platform and asserting that the reform course was the only way. The intellectual community could breathe easily again. Playwright Mikhail Shatrov and others wondered, however, where everyone had disappeared to during the weeks when it appeared the tide was turning in the other direction. "Where were our historians, sociologists, who now express such close solidarity with the *Pravda* article?" Shatrov asked. "Why was it essential to wait for the impulse from the top floor?"

It soon became evident from Gorbachev's words that an internal crisis of some kind had been played out, and might even still be in course. The Soviet leader told visiting American businessmen of a "head-on collision of opposing views. . . . The administration by command system and its worshippers are not surrendering ground without a fight. . . . A veritable struggle in real life, in party and local government organizations, in work collectives, and in all sectors of society has erupted over this central issue."

A month before the conference, Ligachev denied a split in the Politburo leadership. "Adversaries in the West, and some people in our country too, are making allegations about differences among the Soviet leadership, in the Politburo. What can be said about that? In the first place these allegations have been made more than once, which means that they are being made deliberately. Trying to drive a wedge among the leadership is a notorious trick."

At the same time, however, Ligachev railed against a weakening of the party's role and against plans for integrating the Soviet economy more closely with that of the West. "If we consider the advice that our country's economy be placed on the footing of the Western market economy there is little that remains of socialism," he said. "All this is aimed at weakening political stability in the country, upsetting social justice and stimulating a far-reaching social stratification of society." Gorbachev, while not going as far as some Soviet economists, had stated a clear preference for opening the economy to more foreign participation.

On the future of the Communist Party, Ligachev propounded that "the guarantee of the irreversibility of *perestroika* is the Communist Party, its own healthy democratic development. This development will not, certainly, go along the lines of dissolution of the party in society. Proposals of this kind are unacceptable."

It was a puzzlingly undiplomatic performance, coming as it did after the controversy over the Andreevna article. Ligachev surely was aware of the dangers of going to bat for orthodoxy in Gorbachev's Politburo. He surely knew how savvy a political infighter the secretary general could be. Was Ligachev trying to gather enough support to topple Gorbachev at the conference? Was he simply trying to slow down *perestroika*? Or was he simply too bull-headed to reign in his instincts?

In early June none other than Boris Yeltsin resurfaced, from his deputy minister's job in state construction. For the many who thought Yeltsin would go silently after his dismissal from the party hierarchy the previous autumn, the answer came in the form of another blast at Ligachev. Challenging the gods of Communism again, the irrepressible Yeltsin declared that Ligachev had to leave in order for *perestroika* to move ahead more swiftly.

These words were not exactly hurtful to Gorbachev – and Yeltsin probably had that in the back of his mind. The Soviet leader, without getting personal about it, was in rather fair flight against the conservatives himself. He didn't want to board Yeltsin's runaway train, and politically, he couldn't afford to; besides, he thought that the hellishly swift reform pace Yeltsin wanted would be hurtful to the stability of the country. Finally, being a man of discipline and control who demanded things to be done in an orderly way, he could not condone Yeltsin's style, which almost invited pandemonium. Even so, he was with Yeltsin in spirit, just as the Soviet Union's blue-collar masses were with Yeltsin in spirit.

The common man was beginning to see Boris Yeltsin as a David against Goliath. In the past the David figures had been the dissidents – the Scharanskys, the Sakharovs. Those people had had no chance of gaining broad public support because the pre-*glasnost* press had told only one side of the story – that of their accusers. With *glasnost*, Yeltsin had a platform. The people could hear his views and choose sides – just as it is supposed to be when democracy knocks.

At Gorbachev's press conference during the Moscow summit, Martin Walker, the astute correspondent for the British newspaper *The Guardian*, went face to face with the Soviet leader, asking him what would come of the Ligachev-Yeltsin imbroglio. It was not an on-topic question, in that it had little to do with the summit, but it was a good one. Gorbachev's answer was that moving Ligachev out was completely out of the question, that the Siberian would stay in his present position. But he didn't say for how long.

While the pre-conference infighting continued in Moscow, out in the hinterlands there were signs of Russian political activism that had not been witnessed in decades. The political-selection process may have been calm in Ulyanovsk, but in other Soviet cities tensions spilled over. Far off in Siberia, in Omsk, thousands came down from the stands at a football stadium to protest the announcing of a hand-picked list of conference delegates. The meeting had been organized by the citizens themselves, and marked the first time they had come together in Omsk without orders to do so from above. As well as denouncing the delegate-selection process, they spoke out against their living conditions and ecological ruin. None of them were carted off to jail.

In Yaroslavl, some 5,000 protested against the closed-door selection of delegates and against the shortage of apartments and food. Demonstrators booed the party delegates, one of whom confessed that he had been selected "according to the rules of the old stagnation period."

At Moscow State University, students erupted when the names of two pre-selected delegates were announced. Shouts of "We want Gavril Popov" filled the air. Popov, an economist, was a leading proponent of reform.

The demonstrations suggested that the spirit of *perestroika* and *glasnost* was entering the bloodstream of the people. Gorbachev had gambled in calling the party conference. To get what he wanted, he could have acted as Soviet leaders had acted in the past: he could have passed his grandiose plans quietly through the Politburo and the Central Committee and then announced them as law. But he didn't want the old style – he wanted a consensus revolution, and there were signs that he might get his wish.

The old modus vivendi was taking a beating. One of the more egregious of Soviet customs had been for the Kremlin to lie whenever someone was dismissed from high office. The Tass announcement would unfailingly reveal that the high official was stepping down due to failing health. The nature of the failing health was never specified. But now *Pravda* was printing letters from readers pointing out the absurdity of the practice. When the leaders of the Azerbaijan and Armenian Republics were sacked as a result of the crisis in Nagorno-Karabakh, this issue came to a head. Tass reported that on the day they were dismissed "for health reasons," the editors' telephones did not stop ringing: readers were asking that they not be treated so stupidly. Tass agreed that the lies must cease.

Robert Redford came to town in cowboy boots, blue shirt, and a gray tweed sports coat. He signed an agreement with the Soviet Academy of Sciences to produce a film with that body on the subject of global warming. He signed another agreement to begin an exchange program for film makers and artists. He wowed the Russian women at a seminar he gave on his films. They wondered why his hair was so messy in *Jeremiah Johnson*. Redford was one of hundreds of big names now coming to Moscow to give talks or to arrange joint projects or to explore the new environment. When I first arrived in Moscow, such traffic had been a trickle.

Still, the Cold War games went on. In June, shortly after the advances in détente at the Moscow summit, the Canadian government decided to expel eight Soviet diplomats on spying charges, and to declare persona non grata an additional nine who had already left the country. The Kremlin didn't respond with expulsions of equal magnitude, as it sometimes had; instead it expelled only two Canadians on spying charges and declared three others PNG. Rather than let the minicrisis die, Canada hit back with matching measures. At that point the Kremlin, in an irate mood now, played its winning card: it withdrew 26 important Soviet staffers from the Canadian embassy, hampering in many respects the ability of Ambassador Turner, Canada's voice of reason in the Soviet capital, to function.

"The Soviet Union is a great power which cannot allow itself to be insulted in this way," said the Soviet deputy foreign minister, Yuli Vorontsov. "People who do insult it will not be allowed to do so without impunity." Since Ottawa did not have Canadian staff it could withdraw from the Soviet embassy in Ottawa, it could not retaliate further. It had lost one to the bear and would have to wait for the next hockey series to try to exact revenge.

I wrote a sarcastic column about the matter, questioning the behaviour of both sides and speculating about the motives and timing of Ottawa's action. The initial expulsion of Soviets may not have been a victory for Canadian politicians, but it was probably one for the Canadian spy agency, or Canadian "spookery," as I called it. The Canadian spies hadn't caught much lately. Tass, which occasionally printed Western correspondents' opinions supporting a Soviet position, quoted me as saying the Canadian government was on a "witch hunt." I angrily called Tass, whose correspondent explained that he thought the word spookery meant witch hunt. He was an aging veteran of the old Soviet school. Tass ran a correction.

33/Unparalleled

ON THE EVE OF the party conference, demonstrators on the streets of Moscow cried, "Down with the KGB, down with the KGB. . . ." At another rally, human-rights campaigner Andrei Sakharov led the cry for a memorial to be built in memory of Stalin's victims. "We must do everything we can so that our history develops in a way that is worthy of our great people," he said. "*Perestroika* is our last chance to be a great country. *Perestroika* must be pure. It must be for all the people."

So now, instead of building monuments to Stalin, the Soviets were calling for monuments to be built to those he killed. Hundreds of visiting Western reporters put in requests for an interview with Sakharov. The Soviet foreign ministry gladly supplied a hall for him to say things for which he would have been imprisoned a few years earlier.

On the conference's first day Gorbachev spoke for three-and-a-half hours. The highlight of his new plans was the proposed presidential system of government, which would begin functioning the following spring. Its president would be elected by a new, 2,250-member national congress, which would be chosen in multicandidate, secret-ballot elections. The president would handle foreign policy and defence and name a prime minister. The newly elected body, to be called the Congress of People's Deputies, would meet in full session only once a year. But it would elect from its members a smaller body that would sit in permanent session and "consider and decide all legislative, administrative and monetary questions." The Congress would be elected every five years: 1,500 of its members would be elected on a territorial basis; the other 750 would be chosen by central bodies of the party – trade, youth, veterans', and women's movements, and the like. The president was to be chosen by a vote of the Congress.

Gorbachev was vague on how power would be divided between the Communist Party and the new assembly. His remarks suggested that the head of the Communist Party – that is, himself – might concurrently hold the position of president. The Soviet leader explained that on the local level, the powers of the *soviets* had long ago been usurped by the local parties' first secretaries and that the full authority of the *soviets* must be restored. But then he added that the local-party first secretaries would still sit as chairmen of the *soviets*, though their appointments and mandates would be controlled by the *soviet*'s members in secret-ballot elections.

"If the political system remains unchanged," Gorbachev asserted before the conference body, "we will not succeed with *perestroika*. We must exclude any possibility of the usurpation of power. . . . We encounter direct attempts to distort the substance of reform. [Reforms] would have been doing much better if it were not for the conservatism of the administrative bodies which are trying to maintain tough centralized control."

The leader declared that "there can be no compromise. The people demand total democracy, full-blooded democracy with no reservations. . . . We are learning democracy and openness, learning to argue and debate and tell each other the truth."

Gorbachev believed that there could be enough pluralism within the one party for the new presidential system to be considered a full-blooded democracy. A Soviet citizen would not have to be a party member in order to be elected. Non-party members, while sitting as independents, would likely team up with either the radicals or the conservatives within the party.

The call for a new presidential system – which, as was clear to all, would inevitably mean a downgrading of the Communist Party's role – was perhaps the most revolutionary of all Gorbachev's reforms. It wouldn't be a two-party democracy, because the independents would not be a party as such, but considering the clashing divisions in Soviet society, it could well function as one. The elections, at least for many of the seats, would be real contests. Many major powers would reside with the elected assembly, not the Politburo. In effect, Gorbachev had announced the beginning of the end of the 71-year-old Soviet dictatorship.

But there weren't many instant believers. The story ran in the Western press, but without the thunderous headlines it merited. It was as if Gorbachev's proposals were too unbelievable to be taken seriously, as if there had to be some trap. Many Moscow correspondents seemed to be more excited about the personality battle between Ligachev and Yeltsin, which, while fascinating to watch, wasn't nearly as important as the announcement of a proposed new system of government. Happily, my editors in Toronto – Norman Webster, Geoffrey Stevens, Gene Allen, and Stan Oziewicz – had the good sense to realize that this *was* the hot news. As was the case with all the other reports I'd filed from Moscow asserting that Gorbachev's pronouncements should be taken seriously, they did not succumb to pressure from conservatives who suggested that anyone who believed the man was being buffaloed by propaganda.

The conference was closed to Western reporters, so we had to rely on Tass reports, interviews with departing delegates, and Soviet television. Still, it was a joy to watch these historic happenings even from a distance. What followed Gorbachev's address was a series of the unprecedented.

Economist Leonid Abalkin stood up and took direct aim at Gorbachev, voicing serious doubts about having the party bosses serve concurrently as the leaders of the *soviet*s. "This innovation hardly fits the concept of delimiting the functions of party and government bodies," he said. From the debate that followed, it soon became clear that Gorbachev had indeed left considerable confusion over the party's new role. Delegates wondered what was meant by the power to set "political and ideological guidelines."

Another part of the debate focussed on Gorbachev's plan for limiting elected officials to two five-year terms. It was not known whether the new rule would be retroactive. Mikhail Ulyanov, a prominent Soviet actor, told the assembly that Gorbachev should be an exception to the new law, because the Soviet people needed him.

A schoolteacher from Perm was not so sure, stating that two terms would be enough for him and that "Mikhail Sergeyevich has enough time yet to do what he has to do." Gorbachev told them not to worry about his case specifically but to get on with more important matters.

The next day's session had to open a few minutes early because of the clamour to get started. The conference was being held in the Kremlin's Palace of Congresses, a glass and white-marble hall totally out of sync with the architecture adjoining it. Outside the Kremlin, Soviet citizens milled about in the warm weather, enthusiastically discussing developments. About 60 black Zil limousines with chauffeurs were lined up to serve the elite. But it was not an all-elite affair: the cast of 5,000 delegates included 1,638 industrial workers, 866 agricultural workers, and 182 farm managers. More than one-quarter of the delegates were women. The police presence was noticeable, but the atmosphere was relaxed.

At the foot of one of the Kremlin towers was a small office with a sign over the door reading, PROPOSALS FROM THE PUBLIC TO THE COMMUNIST PARTY CONFERENCE. Mostly women were inside, writing on window ledges, chairs, wherever there was a flat space. When asked why many men weren't present, one woman declared they were out working. "Out drinking is more like it," said another. Their scribbled suggestions were for real elections, more human rights, more food.

The party's newspaper for young people *Komsomolskaya Pravda* printed telephone numbers so people could call in their suggestions. The Lenin library opened a book for people to record their comments. Newspapers printed letters criticizing Gorbachev's proposals.

On the third day, the conference was barely underway when Vladimir Melnikov, a heavy-set party boss from Siberia, rose. "Those who in earlier times actively carried out the policy of stagnation," he declared, "cannot now, in the period of *perestroika*, remain in the central party and Soviet organs."

Gorbachev broke in, half-seriously. "Perhaps you have some concrete proposals. We're sitting up here and don't know whether you're talking about me or him or someone else."

Wittingly or unwittingly, Gorbachev had committed an

incautious deed: Melnikov was asking for resignations and the Soviet leader was asking for names. Melnikov quickly took up the invitation. "I would aim this first of all at comrade Solomentsev and to comrades Gromyko, Afanasyev and Arbatov."

They were all in attendance: Mikhail Solomentsev, the 75-year-old Politburo veteran appointed by Brezhnev; Andrei Gromyko, the country's president; Viktor Afanasyev, the editor of *Pravda*; and Georgi Arbatov, an advisor to Gorbachev and head of the Canada-U.S. Institute. None of the accused defended themselves before the now-buzzing hall, but a note from a delegate on Gromyko's behalf was passed up to the front and read out.

Gromyko, the note read, was "a man respected by the people and the party. His life has been dedicated to us. . . . Now the principle of 'always blame the driver' seems to be at work again. We have driven him hard. And now Comrade Gromyko is lagging behind life. He has done his bit and the noble deeds remain in the people's memory. He should not have been attacked on the run like this."

After Melnikov's outburst a delegate told the leaders seated across the front that they were "a cast of untouchables." Another, a steelworker from the Urals, blasted the State for leaving the cupboard bare. "The workers are asking outright – where is the *perestroika*? In the shops, everything is the same. There was no meat and there still isn't any. Consumer goods have dropped from sight."

It was becoming more and more obvious that the conference was going to favour radical measures of the type Gorbachev was demanding. Little was said on behalf of the conservatives, though Gorbachev defended their right to be heard. The leader cautioned the rank and file that *glasnost* meant everyone had a right to speak. In the past only the conservatives had the public voice, he told the conference, yet now, he added disapprovingly, "we see that gradually another group of people want to use the press as a national tribune."

The conference had no fixed finishing time. By the fourth day, nowhere near the slotted number of speakers had made their way to the podium. Some officials thought it might drag on several days more. But Gorbachev was not prepared to let it.

On Friday a few of us in the huge press contingent were captivated by the sight of Fyodor Morgun. Two years earlier he had been the party boss in Poltava. We remembered meeting him on our tour of his region, and hearing him talk glowingly about the Kennedys and the American entrepreneurial spirit. His appearance at the Moscow conference reminded us of our own prediction that Gorbachev would spot this maverick and give him a major role to play in the march toward a new country.

We could applaud ourselves now. Our prediction had been realized: Morgun was now the Soviet chairman for environmental protection. The environment was suddenly a high priority in the Soviet Union, as it had long been in other countries. Morgun was a step away from the Politburo.

Under Brezhnev's stewardship – or "brewership," as some called it – dissidents who talked ecology had frequently been jailed for anti-Soviet slander. But under Gorbachev the public was becoming increasingly alarmed about the prospect of environmental ruin – about the severe contamination of the Amur River and Lake Baikal and the Baltic Sea, about chemical plants causing high rates of cancer and birth defects, about automobile emissions killing the air, about the random demolition of historic buildings. At the conference podium Morgun railed away in his pounding manner. He vowed to name those who were guilty of turning regions of the country into ecological disaster areas. "Comrade chemists!" he yelled. "Stop today's expansion for a while. Have a rest and give us a chance to breathe normal air. Clean up the rubbish!"

Morgun's appearance was overshadowed by Boris Yeltsin's. He had been chosen as a conference delegate, but few expected he would be given an opportunity to speak. At best he was unpredictable, at worst he was a walking grenade. He had already called for the resignation of Ligachev, and decried the pace of Gorbachev's *perestroika* program. There was no telling what he would do at the podium. But Gorbachev wanted him to be heard.

"I believe my only error was to speak at the wrong time," Yeltsin said, recalling the events of the previous autumn, when he was dismissed as Moscow's first secretary. "I ask the conference to announce my political rehabilitation. I regard this as a question of principle. . . . If you decide on this, you will rehabilitate me in the eyes of my fellow Communists."

He appeared to have little support in the hall. The murmurs of disapproval grew louder. Yeltsin stepped away from the podium, not sure whether he should continue. Gorbachev signalled for him to go ahead. Yeltsin said that his appeal for rehabilitation was appropriate, given the socialist pluralism of views, the new freedom to criticize, and Gorbachev's own clear declaration, in his opening address to the conference, that opponents must be tolerated. Yeltsin reminded the delegates, as he had earlier reminded a TV inter- viewer, that almost everyone was now making controversial speeches of the type that had led to his dismissal. "So if it were necessary to punish all the people who have made these speeches, that would be too much and there would be too many people who would need to be punished."

Yet even while asking for clemency, the old Yeltsin reemerged. The preparations for the conference, he said, had been made in haste. Gorbachev's new proposals weren't getting enough discus- sion, and comrades weren't striving hard enough for *perestroika*. And in apparent support of Melnikov's position, Yeltsin also raised ques- tions about the personal accountability of the present-day leaders who had been part of Brezhnev's stagnation-era administration.

The drama, all of which could be seen on Soviet television, gathered tension when the burly Ligachev took the floor. In a strong, unyielding voice he alleged that Yeltsin had split the leadership and had no right to be forgiven. He cited examples of Yeltsin's eccentric stewardship of Moscow, of how he had driven great servants of the State to emotional ruin. He defended his own reputation by claiming that "the policy of *perestroika* has become the cause of my life," and reminded the conference that some of his friends and relatives were shot during Stalin's repressions. He added that he had helped ensure the election of Gorbachev in March 1985, and had been instrumental in bringing Yeltsin into the leadership in the first place.

Yeltsin had been surrounded by supporters at the close of his address. It was clear, however, from the hall's reaction to Ligachev's speech, that the Siberian's condemnation of Yeltsin had struck home. This wasn't surprising, since even some radical reformers were questioning Yeltsin's stability. Gorbachev chose to be the referee in the Ligachev-Yeltsin debate. He played it more or less down the middle, making some positive remarks about both. But he stopped short of calling for Yeltsin's rehabilitation, and it was not granted.

The conference debate was cut off, the meeting was adjourned for a break. When the delegates returned they quickly voted, show-of-hands style, on all of Gorbachev's major reform proposals. All of them passed, including one that stipulated that there would be no exceptions to the ten-years rule for any holder of elective office. A Central Committee secretary told a press conference that "this covers all levels of party committees, from the district committees to the Central Committee. It covers the general secretary."

Also adopted was the controversial proposal that party leaders double as chairmen of the *soviets*. In his summary remarks Gorbachev explained that the party would stringently observe Soviet laws and the democratic principles of Soviet life. It would have "no substitution for state bodies, no *diktat* over the trade unions, Komsomol, other public organizations and other associations." Would this mean, he asked, that the party's guiding role might weaken? "Such apprehensions were voiced. To my opinion the conference has given a sufficiently clear and convincing answer to this question – No."

The conference ended in a victory for the reformers. The anti-*perestroika* forces had not amassed, the major programs had been passed, and Gorbachev was safe. But in keeping with the leader's political style, the other side had not been subjected to humiliation. While the party would definitely lose much of its authority, it would still maintain its primacy – Gorbachev had stated as much in his summation. Yeltsin would not be rehabilitated, and Melnikov, at least for the moment, would not get his way. Gorbachev was marching boldly ahead but at the same time trying to hold close enough to the centre to maintain a consensus.

Foreign observers shook their heads again. It was all so unparalleled. Many wished openly that the party meetings in their home countries could be as honest, as open, and as plain-dealing as this one had been. We had to keep reminding ourselves that three years earlier the Soviet Union had been one of the world's most closed societies.

"This Palace of Congresses has not known such discussions, comrades," Mikhail Gorbachev said in closing. "I think we will not err from the truth by saying that nothing of the kind has occurred in this country for nearly six decades."

34/Masterful Moves

GORBACHEV'S triumph at the party conference readied him for yet more arresting measures. In midsummer he left for his customary long vacation in one of the glorious palaces in the Crimea. He was away for about five weeks this time. The year before it had been longer than that.

But Mikhail le Grand got a lot done on these vacations. During his 1987 holiday he had put together his book *Perestroika*. Sitting superpower leaders don't usually write books about their philosophy. This book, which laid out Gorbachev's new thinking, was published all over the world, made many bestseller lists, was reviewed respectably, and played a considerable role in the selling of his ideas. By the spring of 1988 the selling was such that in a major survey, 76 percent of Americans said that they liked the leader of the Soviet Union. In 1985, the figure had been 44 percent. Most Americans now believed that economic competitors like Japan posed more of a threat to America's national security than traditional adversaries such as the U.S.S.R.

On his 1988 vacation by the Black Sea, Gorbachev wrote an addendum to his bestseller, which didn't have much to do with *glasnost* but fit the *perestroika* or "rebuilding" motif. It was a new Politburo roster. The plotted shake-up, or "purge" as some would prefer to call it, would considerably strengthen his hold on power. A bit of a paradox, it was, in that one of the driving imperatives of Gorbachev's governance was for greater power sharing as opposed to power stockpiling. But as someone once said, revolutions are not made with velvet gloves.

The shake-up took effect at the end of September, while Yegor Ligachev was on vacation. Needing approval from the Central Committee, Gorbachev slyly advanced the date of a meeting scheduled for November so that he could score a quick hit, which he did: Andrei Gromyko was suddenly out as Soviet president, Mikhail Gorbachev in. Ligachev lost his ideology portfolio to a reformer of the Soviet school. Mikhail Solomentsev was dropped from the Politburo, and Viktor Chebrikov was out as head of the KGB. A woman, Alexandra Biryukova, became a non-voting member – the only woman since the 1960s to sit at the Politburo table.

The 79-year-old Gromyko once remarked, "You know how it is with the Politburo. It's like the Bermuda Triangle. Every once in a while some of us vanish." Finally, after four decades at or near the centre of Kremlin politics, it was Gromyko's turn. His duties as president had been largely ceremonial; in dropping him, Gorbachev was thinking ahead to the spring, when the radically new system of government would be in place and the president would enjoy greatly advanced authority.

It was good news for anyone who wanted to see Gorbachev at the apex of Soviet power for a long time. From the standpoint of job security, the shake-up was a master stroke. Now the Soviet leader had double-barrelled security: power would soon be divided between the party and the new governmental bodies, and he would be at the head of both – presuming, as was likely, that the newly elected Congress of People's Deputies kept him in the president's post.

In the meantime, the restructuring of the Politburo made any challenge to Gorbachev less likely. At the party conference the delegate Melnikov had called for the dismissal of four holdovers from the Brezhnev era. Within a few months, half his wish – in the form of Solomentsev and Gromyko – had been realized. Gromyko was not an opponent of *perestroika* or a second guesser. He followed the political line of his masters, which was one of the reasons he had survived so long to begin with. But the value in retiring him was that it rid the atmosphere of another embodiment of the old era. As an advocate of new thinking, Gromyko hardly fit the bill.

Kremlinologists had always considered Solomentsev, Ligachev, and Chebrikov to be the three Politburo members most likely to lead any plot to overthrow Gorbachev. That Gorbachev went after all three in his shake-up at least partly substantiated that surmise. Solomentsev's departure, and the shifting of Ligachev away from his ideological responsibilities, opened the door for the promotion of the relatively unheralded Vadim Medvedev. As successor to Ligachev, he would have the delicate task of presiding over the scaling down of Communist Party power. One of Medvedev's first statements gave heart to reformers across the country. "The idea that people should fight to death for one or another ideology should be once and forever forgotten," he stated. "The values of peace, prosperity and humanism are more important than ideology."

This was the new Soviet philosophy in a nutshell – one that the likes of Ligachev could not tolerate. As recently as June, Gorbachev had dismissed the idea of Ligachev being unseated. But now he was being moved down, to the important but precarious agriculture portfolio. The conventional wisdom of Western observers – it was probably simplistic – was that if difficulties in agriculture continued, Gorbachev would be able to use Ligachev as a convenient scapegoat. If harvests improved, Gorbachev would be in line to take the credit himself.

In the case of Chebrikov, whose profile was lower, Gorbachev's moves were more difficult to read. He was no longer KGB chief, but he was still in the Politburo, in charge of the new legal-affairs commission. The country was in the throes of liberalizing its legal system; Gorbachev's putting a conservative in such a position had a look of the bizarre to it, and led some to speculate that the commission would have little real power. At any rate, Chebrikov's hands were now away from direct control of the KGB. His replacement was Vladimir Kryuchkov, a career KGB man whose special area was foreign intelligence. Kryuchkov had developed a personal rapport with Gorbachev and had accompanied the leader to the summit in Washington. He thus had the inside track.

Some people worried about the precedent Gorbachev was setting – that the powers he was accumulating were too broad and sweeping. While today it is Gorbachev, said Andrei Sakharov, tomorrow it could be someone of a more authoritarian nature.

Gorbachev moved to ease that concern in November: while revising the plans for the new government structure, he gave the Congress of People's Deputies the right to veto decisions of the president.

The figure that Sakharov and the intellectual community worried about less now was that of Ligachev. Whatever the scale of his slide from grace in the Politburo shuffle, Ligachev had invited it upon himself. During the spring run-up to the Party Congress he had clearly been siding with the go-slow team in the *perestroika* debate. At the Party Congress he had denounced Yeltsin while claiming that he, Ligachev, was not opposed to *glasnost* and *perestroika*, as the Western press would have it. But only five weeks after the congress he stood at a podium in Gorky with a death-wish text. He delivered a speech there that directly contradicted an address Shevardnadze had made two weeks earlier on foreign policy.

Ligachev declared that Soviet foreign relations must be guided primarily by the model of the class struggle against capitalism. "We proceed from the class character of international relations." Talk of peaceful coexistence, he said, "only confuses the minds of the Soviet people and our friends abroad."

The speech was given shortly after Gorbachev had left for vacation and while Shevardnadze was in Afghanistan. Ligachev had a habit of asserting himself when the boss was away. As second in command he was the de facto leader on such occasions.

Shevardnadze had said the previous month that in order to rid the world of the dangers of nuclear war, ecological disaster, and poverty, peaceful coexistence must take precedence over the ideological tug-of-war: "The struggle between two opposing systems is no longer a determining tendency of the modern epoch. One must not identify coexistence, which is based on such principles as non-aggression, respect for sovereignty and national independence . . . with class struggle."

Gorbachev's position was exactly as stated by Shevardnadze. Wanting to normalize international relations, the Soviet leader was abandoning the policy of spreading socialism by overturning capitalist governments. This approach had long been the foundation block of the Cold War, Washington having decided in the postwar years to pursue a policy of containment against it.

Gorbachev's new line represented a sea change in Soviet thinking; with it he was planting the seeds for East-West convergence. Ligachev could not hope to oppose such a fundamental change of course and remain in the ideology portfolio.

In moving to agriculture, he was not moving to a haven free of controversy: Gorbachev was planning a landmark transformation in this domain as well. In a bid to reverse the 20-year decline in agriculture, which had never done well under Communism, the Soviet leader was moving to a system of leasing. A leasing experiment was now underway in which families or groups of farmers could rent land from the huge collective farms. While Ligachev was on holiday, Gorbachev went on television to announce that "our idea is that all agriculture, the entire agrarian sector, should follow this path. . . . Comrades, the most important thing today is . . . to return the man back to his land as its real master."[1]

Farmers would be entitled to lease land for 50 years or longer, manage the plots independently, and sell crops on the free market or to the State. For those who opted for the new system, there would be no state plan to be filled, no party boss ordering schedules and quotas. The announcement came only two weeks after Ligachev was named to his new post. Just because Ligachev was on holiday, Gennady Gerasimov said, "does not mean we should not deal with agricultural issues."

The new proposal was another repudiation of Stalinism, an admission that the collective-farming system had failed: 70 years after the revolution, the country was importing 19 million tonnes of grain a year and could not produce enough food to adequately feed its population. To judge from Gorbachev's experience – his boyhood years on the collective farm in his home town, his five years of night school at Stavropol's agricultural college, his many years as agriculture secretary – he knew more about farming than about any other subject. But curiously, his record in this area, except for the red stars he earned as a young boy toiling in the Privolnoye fields, was weak. As agriculture boss under Brezhnev, he had produced low yields, which he could blame on the weather, but nothing in the way of successful policy innovations, which he couldn't blame on the weather.

As general secretary one of his early initiatives was to lump the sprawling, octopus-like agricultural bureaucracy into one central superministry called Gosagroprom. Gosagroprom proved to be a disaster, creating even more bureaucracy than the old system. Early in 1989 *Pravda* concluded it was "torturing" farmers. "Experts have calculated," the newspaper said, "that orders from the chairman of Gosagroprom reach collective farms through 32 levels, each of which signs and duplicates them."

Having created a monster, Gorbachev was at least prepared to admit a mistake and move on. As part of the new agricultural reform, Gosagroprom was disbanded. In March 1989 the new leasing system was formally adopted, though not before another skirmish in the Ligachev-versus-Gorbachev story. Shortly before the party meeting to debate the proposals, Ligachev visited Stalinist Czechoslovakia, reported himself well content with the agricultural ways there, and praised the Czechs for having stayed the collectivist course. Again, rumours surged. Ligachev was mounting another anti-Gorbachev campaign they said. Gorbachev could suffer a crucial setback at the meeting.

But again the speculation proved to be wrong. Again Gorbachev emerged unscathed, reforms endorsed. Ligachev appeared at a press conference and found a way to say that there had been no dispute in the leadership over the leasing plan. But to everyone – to foreign observers, to the Russian on the street, to the intelligentsia – it was clear that Ligachev was now a fading force, a dying breed of Communist.

The fate of the new farming system was less clear. Early experiments showed that it led to far greater crop yields than the old system. But there was resistance from the state-farm bosses, who felt their security threatened; from some members of the public, who were disenchanted with the entrepreneurial style; and from farmers, who were reluctant to break with the old methods to which they were accustomed and gamble on the new game. The Kremlin planned a propaganda campaign to engender some enthusiasm. Gorbachev understood there would be opposition. "No fool is going to work on a lease contract," he said, "as long as he can have a salary without earning it."

At a collective farm north of Moscow, the Karpunin family had leased a plot. They had increased milk production by nearly 20 percent over the collective-farm average and doubled the family salary. "No one is hindering us and no one is giving us orders," Tatiana Karpunin said. But the price of the independence and the extra income was high: they worked double the time of the average collective-farm labourer. And there was also the problem any Soviet family that made a lot of money faced – what to do with all the roubles. Once the car was bought and the *dacha* rented and the TV set replaced, there wasn't much left to spend them on.[2]

But the Karpunins felt great about the independence, as did other families who were experimenting with the system, as did other Russians involved in individual labour and cooperatives. For the first time in their lives, every order was not coming down from above. The bureaucracy was still thick, the papers to fill out were still many, but the fate of the project they had started rested with their own decisions rather than the arbitrary commands of some corrupt party boss.

The entrepreneurial spirit was not spreading wildly across the Soviet Union, but some victories were being registered. In far-off Vladivostok, individualism was breeding that rare species – the Soviet millionaire. Sergei Grashkin, a repairman in his thirties, had opened a cooperative only a year before. He had already banked over 450,000 roubles – about 900,000 Canadian dollars. He had a chauffeur-driven Ford Galaxy and an office beside the deputy mayor's. His co-op repair shop, called Guarantee, washed cars, did auto-body work, and repaired flat tires in 30 minutes. In short, it was providing the basic services the State was so hopeless at providing. Guarantee was in the clothing business as well, filling 150 orders a day for made-to-order clothes sewn by Vladivostok women at home.

"I registered my cooperative the first day the law came into effect," said Grashkin. "I borrowed 3,000 roubles and began." Grashkin would pay taxes at a rate of three percent the first year, five percent the second, and ten percent after three. At the close of 1988 his was one of 36 cooperatives in Vladivostok and one of 30,000 in the country. He had started with three partners and now employed 58 people.[3]

He knew he could clobber any competition the State, which was offering services "no one wants," gave him. Sounding very American, he explained that "this is only the beginning. In the next five years I hope to have 1,500 people working." Motivating him was what motivated poeple around the world – "The independence of doing something yourself and seeing the results."

In the Soviet Union a kind of test was being run on the possibility that such a hunger existed there too. In pushing Ligachev aside into agriculture, and in pushing Ligachev's collectivist philosophy aside, Gorbachev was making another little declaration of independence for his country. He was moving one more step down the line in a process tantamount to a declaration of the failure of Communism.

35/Too Romantic?

IT WAS AT THE United Nations in December 1988, with Gorbachev practising the type of politics the West wouldn't match – unilateral force reductions – that a special moment took place. Mikhail Gorbachev, a humanist, a man slowly convincing the world of that fact, was waxing eloquent on his global philosophy. "We need good will not to see the alien as bad and hostile. . . . What we need is unity through variety. If we recognize it in politics and declare our adherence to the principal of freedom of choice, then we shall no longer think that some of us inhabit this world in fulfillment of the Providential will while others are here by mere chance."

It was now time, he said, that "international relations be freed from ideology." He advocated a joint quest for world unity, "for the supremacy of the universal idea over the multitude of centrifugal trends."

Then Gorbachev looked up from his text and paused. "Some of our people at home and some in the West," he continued, "wonder if these views are not a little too romantic, exaggerating the maturity and development of the human mind. But I am convinced we are not floating above reality."

A little too romantic? Given the degree of closed-mindedness on his own political right – and on the American right, where they were still ascribing dark motives to every human gesture he made – probably.

But to hear the idealism, particularly from a leader of the Soviet

Union, was ennobling. And in the months ahead, to see him give further flight to his ideals, to words like *freedom of choice* and *unity*, was yet more uplifting.

The first real Soviet elections in 70 years came in March 1989. Their advent had been played down in the West. While much had been said about Gorbachev's democracy campaign, an event as breathtaking as genuine Soviet elections couldn't quite be grasped until it happened. In these elections more than one name would appear on the ballot, a citizen wouldn't have to be a Communist Party member in order to run, and the elected would serve much more than a rubber-stamping function. The 2,250-member Congress of People's Deputies that was being selected was going to be the main body in the new presidential system of government. It would select from its own numbers a standing legislature of about 500 members and a president. The new system had only been endorsed the previous summer and hadn't been fleshed out until the late fall. The Soviet Union, as Alexander Yakovlev said, wasn't ready for this sudden leap into democracy: the country had never run a real campaign. Its people had never voted in one.

When election day arrived the inexperience showed: in many respects the elections were an embarrassing example of democracy in action. In one-quarter of the electoral districts, lone candidates ran unopposed. The vast majority of those running were Communist Party members. Opposition parties had not been allowed to form. Many of the candidate-nomination meetings had been stacked with supporters of the establishment candidate or rigged in some other way.

At the same time, some of the deficiencies weren't as glaring as they sounded. In the districts where only one name appeared on the ballot, voters could cross out that name; if 50 percent of them did so, as sometimes happened in these elections, the lone candidate was defeated and a new election was called. The single-candidate system had always worked this way, but until now, candidates had never had any trouble getting over 50 percent of the vote. On the question of only one party being represented, the pluralism that existed within the one Communist Party was such that it was tantamount to being two – the reform party and the conservative party.

As for the party establishment controlling much of the electoral process, the Soviets were only experiencing a problem that had plagued Western democracies since day one, and was still plaguing them: in Canadian elections the candidate who was the choice of the party establishment usually got the nod, not the blue-collar worker. Stories of stacked nomination meetings were endless in Canada. On the American side of the border, the establishment so controlled the electoral process that incumbents in the 435-member House of Representatives were guaranteed reelection better than 90 percent of the time.

Despite their lack of democratic traditions, the Soviets did a creditable job. Demonstrations, raucous electioneering, sharp debates, and an impressive degree of citizen participation marked many of the races. The election saw a host of jarringly different platforms represented: one called for the secession of Latvia from the Soviet Union; another, for an end to nuclear-test detonations; still another, for the abolition of the draft.

Ogonyok's editor Vitaly Korotich was running. Some of the election meetings at which he appeared grew so volatile that fights broke out between his supporters and backers of the old guard. The latter carried banners with slogans – KOROTICH IS THE FOREMAN OF THE SCUM OF *PERESTROIKA*. One of the candidates in Yaroslavl, Dmitri Starodubtsev, had served a prison term in the Brezhnev years for "speculation," or using free-market techniques at the collective farm. Now he was running in the election – and winning it – on a platform calling for the introduction of the same free-market techniques for which he had been jailed.[1] He was a member of a grass-roots movement known as the Popular Front for the Support of Perestroika. His opponent Alexander Koryashkin had the support of the party bureaucrats. "Don't be afraid, comrade," a member of the audience member shouted to Starodubtsev at a campaign meeting. "The people are with you. We the supporters of Gorbachev are your supporters."

The results testified that the Soviet people desired an end to the old way. In Leningrad the Communist Party first secretary Yuri Solovyev stood alone on the ballot, but more than 50 percent of the voters crossed out his name to defeat him. Solovyev was an alternate member of the Politburo. The entire leadership of the Communist Party in Leningrad and the surrounding region was defeated. In

Moscow, Valery Saikin, the mayor, was defeated. In the Baltics, nationalist and secessionist candidates carried the day. Across the country, voters, where given the opportunity, opted for independents, reformers, and nationalists – for anyone but the party-establishment figures.

"Although not everybody likes the outcome of the elections," said Gorbachev, "nothing can be done here. The masters of the country have spoken." It was yet another statement to be framed and placed in the Soviet Union's gallery of the unbelievable.

In the most spectacular election fight, the new masters of the country spoke in overwhelming favour of their own would-be Robin Hood – the 57-year-old rogue of a Communist, Boris Yeltsin. In the week of the elections – Easter week – Yeltsin, who had so recently been thrown overboard by the party establishment, rose from the dead on the backs of the people. The populist, the symbol of the little man against the party establishment, was up against a classic establishment opponent – the director of the giant Zil factory, Yevgeny Brakov. It was Brakov who supplied the limousines to the party elite. In his campaigns against privilege, Boris Yeltsin had argued that these were an example of the privileges that the party elite must be stripped of. The little man on the street loved it, but there was some dark irony here, in the form of the big, black, shining Chaika limousine that populist Yeltsin himself drove around in.

In many ways Yeltsin was an establishment man. He sent his granddaughter to a school for the elite.[2] His record showed a fiercely autocratic style of management that drove employees to despair. And having preached to Kremlin leaders the year before about the dangers of developing a cult of personality, he now happily allowed one to be built around himself. An abrasive man given to fits of fantasy, he had in many respects deserved his dismissal from the post of first Moscow secretary.

But in the final analysis, his character flaws matterd little: what counted was his fearlessness and his democratic zeal. His election-day landslide was a triumph for the new Soviet way and the death knell of Brezhnevism.

For Gorbachev it was a victory as well, in that Yeltsin had not run against him but against Ligachev. Yeltsin was the lightning rod of the radicals; the Soviet leader needed him to keep the profile of *perestroika* high, to prod and to scream that the country had to reform itself more quickly. He needed a Ligachev as well, so that the conservatives would have a voice and not feel left entirely in the wilderness. Gorbachev had positioned himself in the consensus centre, playing the broker, flanked by high-profile opponents on either side.

Gorbachev had brought Yeltsin in from the Urals, made him, and then played a role in his fall. But in the end it was Gorbachev's election system that allowed the outcast to take his case to the people and win. A defeat for Yeltsin would have been a setback for Gorbachev in that it would have smashed the credibility of the election experiment – the cries of foul would have been unceasing. Moreover, a defeat of Yeltsin would have been interpreted by the party establishment as a defeat of *glasnost* and *perestroika*; the pressures would have mounted for Gorbachev to turn back. Yeltsin's massive victory – he earned 90 percent of the vote – was a stick the Soviet leader could use to batter the holdovers from the era of stagnation.

A calmer and more reasonable voice elected to the new chamber was that of Andrei Sakharov. While Sakharov didn't have as high a domestic profile as Yeltsin, the election of this spiritual force boded well. Sakharov would be the voice of the intelligentsia, Yeltsin would be the voice of the common man.

In a clear reference to Yeltsin before the vote, Gorbachev noted that he was not prepared to support any reckless leaps forward. Instead, he would use his election-day mandate to plunge ahead with radical measures of his own kind – measures which, while not as radical as Yeltsin would wish, were radical indeed by any past Soviet standards. At the same time he would occasionally compromise with the conservatives in order to hold together the revolution-without-guns.

It wouldn't be easy. In establishing a new election system in the Soviet Union, Gorbachev had torn open another carton of unfathomables. The more the people felt the heat of democratic fever, the more would be their demands. A contest was now on to see who would have the real power – the party hierarchy in the form of the Politburo and the Central Committee, or the new Congress of People's Deputies and its president. The party elite was not going to back down easily, as was evidenced in round one of many skirmishes to come. When the Congress met to elect its smaller standing legislature, the conservative majority defeated the bids of Yeltsin and all the leading Moscow radicals. Such a public outcry on the streets of the capital ensued that Yeltsin was quickly given a seat. One of the chosen resigned to make way for him.

The pressures were now building for the Kremlin to abide the formation of another political party. It was distinctly possible that the elected independents might join forces with the very radical Communist Party members in the assembly. Defeats on important votes might speed that merger, out of which could well come an attempt to form a new party. Yeltsin and Sakharov were both on the record as favouring a multiparty system. Gorbachev had spoken out against it, but his basic values, many in the intellectual community believed, were such that over time he could be persuaded to accept such a system – particularly if he sensed that the will of the people supported the proposition.

But that raised another question: to what extent was he prepared to let the will of the people dictate? If he looked at the voting results coming in from the Baltic republics, he would see that the will of the people there demanded not only a diminution of Communist Party control but a separation, a breaking up of the country. Yet another burning confrontation awaited Gorbachev on that issue. It was one of the conundrums of his time in power: the more monsters he slew, the more he created.

36/The Chance

"TO ESTIMATE the depth of the hole you're in is only possible when you start climbing out of it."[1] – Aban Aganbegyan.

Economic problems deepened. Inflation grew, the deficit grew, supplies in the stores shrank, and a growing sense of desperation surrounded Gorbachev's economic reforms.

In the republics, destabilization threatened. In the armed forces, morale problems mounted. The Afghan pullout was tantamount to an admission of military defeat. Then came the announcement that Soviet troop strength would be cut by half a million men.

The economy was being overhauled. The old political structure was being ripped up. The country's 20th-century history was undergoing a massive rewrite. *Glasnost* was replacing a decades-old system of secrecy. The relationship with the rest of the world was being revamped. How much revolution could the system stand?

No one knew the answer. So many new forces had been unleashed in a country so large that no one dared predict where it would all end. To keep informed of even the major developments required all one's time. Soviet authors, finally free to write without great fear of the censor, didn't have time to write. "You have to read all the time,"[2] said the poet Andrei Voznesensky. "Every night, on television, in the papers, there's something new. It's impossible to keep up with everything that's happening. So artists aren't spending their time writing – they're reading and talking. People want us to help them, to speak for them. . . . But if you spend all your time this way, you don't have time to write a good novel. And if you stop fighting to go off and write a novel, maybe you'll find the freedom has been cut off."

Somehow Gorbachev's reserves of confidence, skill, and courage were keeping the revolutions going. I could hear on the streets a number of arguments for why he wasn't moving quickly enough, and an equal number for why he was moving too quickly. Working greatly in Gorbachev's favour was the lack of alternatives to *perestroika*: his opponents had nothing to offer except a return to the old ways. With *glasnost*, the past was being painted as a living purgatory, and fewer and fewer people wanted that return.

By 1989, confusion and doubt all around him, Mikhail Gorbachev had set in motion four reformations – or, more accurately, "revolutions." There was the moral revolution, the revolution in foreign policy, the revolution in the economy, and the revolution in political structure. In the moral and foreign-policy areas, Gorbachev was succeeding; in overhauling the political system, his start – the elections – was spectacular; in the domain of the economy he had yet to find success.

Of the four, the most successful was the moral revolution won by his *glasnost* policy. When I arrived in Moscow the Soviet Union was a closed society; by the time I left, a hundred different doors had burst open. The list of accomplishments was unimaginable: Soviets could speak their minds in the newspapers, in books, on the picture screens, in the theatres; they could protest in the streets without being thrown in jail; they could vote in real elections. Sakharov and hundreds of other political prisoners were free. It was possible to do private work and keep the profits, to listen to all the foreign radio broadcasts, to practise religion without fear of persecution, to travel outside the country, to emigrate.

In the seven decades that followed the 1917 revolution, dissent had been forbidden in the Soviet Union. The price that society had paid for disallowing it was obvious on every Soviet street, in every Soviet face. Gorbachev's moral revolution broke the silence. By the time I packed my bags to leave Moscow, dissent was "in." It had become part of the Soviet Union's culture – an intriguing juxtaposition to developments in the United States, where the pledge-of-allegiance presidential campaign was underway.

Both superpowers were undergoing changes. The United States was not en route to becoming a closed society, but throughout the Reagan era and through to the dawn of Bush, dissent declined. As if exorcising the demons of the incriminatory 1960s, the country was caught up in an orgy of self-righteousness. Dissent had come to be seen, in the words of novelist E.L. Doctorow, as "a form of betrayal." The attitude, he said, was that "if you speak out or take a critical position, you're somehow giving aid and comfort to the enemy." Thus, Bush's pledge of allegiance and other patriotic blasts worked in the 1988 campaign. Thus, he could score points by accusing his democrat opponent, Michael Dukakis, of being a "liberal."

In January 1989, in the superpower where some light was beginning to shine, John Paul II told Soviet officials that *perestroika* "coincides with the social doctrine of the Roman Catholic church." In February 1989, Edgar Bronfman, president of the World Jewish Congress, pronounced progress on human rights such that "there will be a great revival of Jewish culture in the Soviet Union."[3]

The Soviet people were losing their fear. In my last days in the Soviet Union I saw three faces I will never forget. One was the face of a Moldavian friend whom I met on a bench behind the Lenin monument outside my apartment. The sun was coming from Lenin's far side, its rays shooting across the statue's shoulder and onto those of my friend. He spoke first of how a nationalist movement was sprouting in his own tiny republic and how it excited him. Before this he had never conceded that serious problems existed in Moldavia, but now the apprehensiveness was gone, and he told me everything he knew about them. I wasn't overly interested, because stories about nationalism abounded in the Soviet Union those days. But something more important was on the Moldavian's mind: he wanted to visit Canada, and to do so under the Kremlin's new, relaxed regulations, he needed only an invitation from a Canadian. Could I provide him with one? he asked.

When I told him yes, lights went on all over his face. He was overweight, but seemed to lose all the excess as he rose like a balloon from the bench and kept rising, as if he was about to disappear in the sky. He had only travelled to Eastern Europe, had never been to the democracies. Canada had no special attachment for him, but it was the West, and it was more than that – it was the principle of the thing, the idea that as a Soviet citizen he now had the freedom to go there.

The moment was repeated with the artist I had met in Lithuania. He was older, but no less hesitant to show his joy. Then again with a 30-year-old Soviet journalist whose specialty was hockey. The latter was studiously watching a videotape of the 1972 Canada-Russia hockey series in my apartment. Among his ambitions in life was to visit the birthplace of the game he knew so well. Like the others, he talked excitedly about Gorbachev's new travel regulations. I kidded him about it, because for almost three years running we had argued about Gorbachev, with me taking the positive line and he the pessimist's. Before he could ask me for an invitation to visit, I offered him one, then watched him try unsuccessfully to suppress his exhilaration.

Glasnost had come too far to be reversed without a rebellion against the Kremlin the likes of which the country had never seen. Brezhnev had turned back Khrushchev's inroads to freedom, but those had been short inroads, and had been made at a different time – a time when Russians weren't totally fed up with the way things were. Gorbachev's measures on freedom of expression were taking firm root.

The remarkable progress of the moral revolution was almost matched in the area of foreign policy. The two were connected, in that the fostering of human rights at home was critical to Soviet image gains abroad. At the time of Gorbachev's ascendancy, the face the Kremlin showed the world was glacial: the Brezhnev doctrine remained in place, the view of the world as an eternal struggle between ideologies was unchanged, and the priority given the military budget was unassailable. Intransigence dominated at the summit table, the emigration bars surrounded the country, the occupation of Afghanistan continued.

Four years later, all had changed. Soviet troops had drawn back from Afghanistan, Eastern Europe, and the Chinese border.

Half a million men were being dropped from the military. The military budget was being cut by 14 percent. The quest for military superiority was being abandoned in favour of the concept of "reasonable sufficiency." The master control over Eastern Europe was being relaxed to the extent that the Solidarity movement in Poland was no longer outlawed, but was instead recognized as an official opposition party by the Polish government and competing in an election.

The Soviets made the major concessions to seal the INF treaty, and opened their military facilities to on-site inspection for the first time in their history. They also elevated the role of the United Nations, began much closer observation of the Helsinki accords, and signed a new, sweeping human-rights agreement in Geneva. They were pressuring, more than any other country, for disarmament around the world. They were beginning new, greatly improved relations with the United States, with China, with Western Europe. In all of Cold War history, no one had made more concessions than Gorbachev. He was dismantling the barrier of fear between East and West. In four years he had turned his evil empire into, seemingly, a good-will empire.

George Kennan, the renowned American diplomat who had authored the containment strategy for halting Soviet expansionism, appeared before the U.S. Senate Foreign Relations Committee in April 1989. "What we are witnessing today in Russia," he told that body, "is the break-up of much, if not all, of the system of power by which that country has been held together and governed since 1917."[4]

The political revolution – the creation of a democratized presidential system, the curbing of the powers of the Communist Party, the move to free elections – was only beginning, but there was realistic hope that seven decades of repressive oligarchy was coming to an end. To have suggested in 1985 that within four years Andrei Sakharov and other dissidents would be elected to seats in a legitimate Soviet legislature would have been to invite allegations of madness. But it had happened.

In the sphere of economics the Soviet advances were still largely in the formative stage. Not having adequately grasped the depth of the economic crisis at the time he took power, Gorbachev was long in introducing measures to move the country away from its system of command centralism toward a more market-oriented socialism. By early 1989 most Soviet enterprises had switched over to a system of self-financing, giving them at least some independence from central planners. Bureaucratic fat was still being slashed, farming was still being returned to the farmers, and Soviet business was only beginning to open itself to the world in the form of joint ventures. The cooperative movement was beginning to take root, individual labour was increasing, and other capitalist threats were at hand. At a news conference in January 1989, Soviet official Ivan Korovkin unrolled a calendar pin-up of a naked woman and complained with disgust, "Look at this!" The photos were of such "dubious aesthetic taste," he fumed, and yet they were on sale in the Soviet Union, having been manufactured by a cooperative in Estonia.

Many of the Kremlin's economic ideas sounded good on paper but in practice were being thwarted by the decades-old sloth ethic. The mentality transfer, from collective non-enterprise to individual enterprising spirit, was going to take years. Gorbachev was chained by circumstance: to effect structural change in the economy was going to require moving to a free-market pricing regime; but that was going to require the removal of government subsidies, with big price increases the direct result. The Kremlin feared, for good reason, that this would trigger a rebellion in the streets.

But Gorbachev had at least recognized the failure of command centralism and was giving the economy a chance. What he needed was time. In 1988-89 the reforms were just going into effect. While it was too early to expect results, too early to call economic *perestroika* a failure, the Soviets were becoming impatient. They had become accustomed through the decades to food shortages, but under Gorbachev's leadership their expectations were much higher. Moreover, with *glasnost* they were now able to rant and rave about the shortages. To give public voice to a problem was to give it more urgency.

With this in mind, Gorbachev undertook an important stabilizing initiative in early 1989. Realizing his economy was not capable of quickly providing the consumer goods, he decided to go on a massive overseas shopping spree to fill the most pressing needs of his public. Mass imports of basic items such as sugar, toothpaste, soap, and pantyhose would help make up for the shortages at home. The import policy would run up his trade deficit on a dramatic scale, but would also help buy some peace on the home front till such time as his changing economy began to produce.

The biggest threat to his democratic programs and to his stability in power was not the economy but the explosive ethnic crisis. The genie of freedom of expression was out of the bottle; there could be no stuffing it back in for places like the Baltics. The pressures and claims for independence were likely to mount; the pressures on Gorbachev to send in the tanks in response were likely to mount along with them. To cave in to the former pressures would be to preside over the beginning of the dissolution of the country; to cave in to the latter would be a repudiation of the very principle for which he stood most strongly – democratization.

Though nationalism raged, the possibility that Gorbachev might be overthrown in the near future seemed remote as of mid-1989 – particularly in light of the removal of the so-called "dead souls" of the Communist Party's Central Committee. One hundred and ten of them – more than one-third of that body's members – were dismissed in April in the wake of the election results. The message of the vote, as the Kremlin interpreted it, was that conservatives were no longer wanted. Some of the 110 – labelled dead souls from Nikolai Gogol's novel of the same name – were holdovers from the Stalin era. On important issues of reform, most of them would likely have tilted against Gorbachev. Their removal demonstrated the extent to which the election results had played into Gorbachev's hands, and amounted to a major consolidation of his power.

The debate in the West often centred on whether Gorbachev should be helped or hindered in his grand plans. Those who favoured opposition were pressed to make a good case. The Soviet leader was dismantling the totalitarian elements of his society that were the very reason for the West's opposition to the Soviet Union in the first place.

To argue that Gorbachev should not be helped presumed there was a better alternative to him. But the likely alternative to Gorbachev was a return to the old-style Soviet thinking of a Ligachev, to a closed society, to nuclear-weapons stockpiling.

Gorbachev had almost single-handedly brought the Cold War to its knees. The departing Ronald Reagan naturally tried to take some credit. But almost every East-West initiative of significance in the previous four years had been Gorbachev's. While Reagan was presiding over the biggest peacetime military build-up in American history, Gorbachev cut back militarily, pushed for the summits, made the big compromises for the INF agreement. It was argued that it required a Republican like Reagan to get the INF agreement through Congress. But the Soviet concessions on INF were such that almost every American legislator agreed it was a deal they could not refuse. Public opinion in America had been altered so much by the Gorbachev phenomenon that it would have been hard to imagine any president not getting the agreement through the Democrat-dominated chambers.

As the last decade of the 20th century approached, Gorbachev's revolutions were prompting debate in many foreign capitals on some of the fundamental questions of the times: What is the Soviet threat? Why the Cold War? Why the bipolarized world?

The foundation blocks of the Cold War had been Soviet expansionism, human-rights abuses, emigration restrictions, the Kremlin's arms build-up, the totalitarian nature of the system, and, in the 1980s, Afghanistan. By 1989, Gorbachev had acted to remove or substantially diminish every one of them. He had made the notion of the Soviet threat difficult to define.

Prudence advised that Gorbachev could be toppled and that the next Soviet leader might turn back the clock to raw Communism. But in such a scenario, with the Soviets rearming, Washington and the other NATO countries could also rearm, reestablishing the rough balance of terror with the Kremlin that they had maintained over the previous 40 years. In the meantime NATO could take advantage of the opening and come up with some dramatic initiatives of its own, instead of allowing the Soviets to project themselves around the world as the leading force for peace.

What was clear in 1989 was The Chance. At no time in the previous half-century had there existed such a glorious opportunity of ending the world's most threatening division. It came down to the question of trust – trust in Gorbachev.

The case could be made that in four years he had put in motion one of history's major sea changes. He had taken a bipolar world in the grip of the Cold War and given it a détente that had so much hope of lasting, of becoming an *entente*. He had taken a world surcharged with nuclear weapons and started, with the help of Washington, the process of nuclear reduction. He had taken the world's largest totalitarian empire and begun the process of bringing far-reaching democratic values to it.

The question was whether Western democracies would respond positively or remain forever entrapped by the old thinking, by what Marshall McLuhan called the "rearview mirror phenomenon"[5] – seeing the present in terms of the past, instead of heeding the reality in front of them.

Recalling a meeting with Gorbachev, Margaret Thatcher said she felt that the Soviet leader was trying to point "a giant searchlight into the future. . . . I had a deep instinct that it was the beginning of a quite new relationship." Gorbachev had this great view of the future, she said, one which "really has far more in common with the system we have worked toward and which has given us our prosperity and our freedom."[6]

Some argued that Gorbachev was doing his great deeds out of political expedience, that it was all for the sake of saving the Soviet economy, that he had no option. Indeed, all of that played a part. But as I boarded my last Aeroflot plane, I felt there was something more to it than that, something more to him than political expedience. I felt that the magnificent developments were taking place because Mikhail Gorbachev was that rare breed of leader—a man of moral vision.

Notes

Frozen in Time

1. *Izvestia*, November 3, 1986.

2. Stephen Cohen, *Sovieticus*, New York: W.W. Norton, 1985, p.29.

The Inheritance

1. Robert Ford, *Our Man in Moscow*, Toronto: University of Toronto Press, 1989, pp.80-81.

2. Seweryn Bialer, *The Soviet Paradox*, New York: Alfred A. Knopf, 1986, p.63.

3. Ibid., p.64.

4. Reuter, October 29, 1987.

5. Ibid., November 4, 1987.

An Open-Minded Soviet Man

1. The author interviewed Stavropol residents in December 1987.

2. Easily the best biographical material to date on Gorbachev's boyhood and university years is by the editors of *Time* magazine in *Mikhail S. Gorbachev: An Intimate Biography*, New York: Time Incorporated, 1988, pp.22-106. I am particularly indebted to David Aikman, whose excellent chapter on Gorbachev at Moscow State University I have drawn from substantially.

3. Jerry Hough, *Russia and the West*, New York: Simon and Schuster, 1988, p.24.

4. The material about Gorbachev's tour of Canada with Whelan is from Eugene Whelan with Rick Archbold, *Whelan*, Toronto: Irwin Publishing, 1986, pp.250-251 and 254-261. Also, from author's telephone interview with Whelan, March 1989.

5. Hough, *Russia and the West*, p.29.

6. Minutes of Proceedings and Evidence of the Standing Committee on External Affairs and Defence, Issue no. 95, May 17, 1983, Queen's Printer, Ottawa.

Out of the Blocks

1. A fascinating account of how Gorbachev succeeded Chernenko is in Zhores Medvedev, *Gorbachev*, New York: W.W. Norton, 1986, pp.3-21.

2. Georgi Arbatov, *Toronto Star* Lecture, November 14, 1988.

3. Material on the Gorbachev-Korotich connection is from Ilya Gerol and Geoffrey Molyneux, *The Manipulators*, Toronto: Irwin Publishing, 1988, and from conversations between the author and Gerol in March 1989.

4. *Washington Post* columnist David Broder ran the Eisenhower letter in his column in the first week of September 1983.

Gorky Park

1. Thomas Stevens, *Through Russia on a Mustang*.

2. The author interviewed Morgun and Bubka in February 1986.

The Congress

1. The author interviewed Bordeleau in May 1988.

2. Press conference with Georgi Arbatov, March 3, 1986.

First Crisis

1. Anthony Barnett, *Soviet Freedom*, London: Pan Books, 1988, pp.69-70. Barnett's book on Gorbachev's first two years is first-rate.

2. The author interviewed Chernobyl residents and Kiev officials on May 15-16, 1986.

Georgia on My Mind

1. Robert Kaiser, *Russia, The People and the Power*, New York: Washington Square Press, 1976, pp.121-22.

The Home Team

1. *The Globe and Mail*, November 17, 1988, as reprinted from the *New York Times*.

2. *International Herald Tribune*, October 13, 1986, as reprinted from the *Washington Post*.

Breaking the Chains

1. The account of the Gorbachev phone call to Sakharov was provided by Sakharov in interviews given to reporters when he was in Canada in mid-February 1989. Sakharov provided the most detail in an exclusive interview on February 18 with Ilya Gerol, foreign editor of the *Ottawa Citizen*.

2. The author interviewed Kudriavtsev on February 19, 1987.

The Market Mechanism

1. *International Herald Tribune*, August 4, 1987.

2. The author interviewed Axelson on February 21, 1986.

Telling It Like It Is

1. *Sovyetskaya Kultura*, May 21, 1987.

2. *Washington Post*, August, 1988.

3. Barnett, *Soviet Freedom*, pp.85-95.

Eleven Time Zones

1. A splendid English-language guidebook for tourists is *Motorists' Guide to the Soviet Union*, Moscow: Progress Publishers, 1980.

Internal Resistance

1. *Literaturnaya Gazeta*, December 2, 1987.

2. Bialer, *The Soviet Paradox*, pp.19-40.

The Rockers

1. The author interviewed the motorcycle gang members on November 25, 1987.

2. *New York Times*, February 8, 1988.

The Gospel Goes East

1. *Toronto Star*, August 7, 1988.

The Yugoslav Road

1. Reuter, March 16, 1988.

2. Shmelyov's controversial article appeared in the June 1987 issue of *Novy Mir*. It was excerpted in the *Washington Post*.

2. Gorbachev's speech in Prague was on April 10, 1987.

Cancelling History

1. Gorbachev's speech was on November 2, 1987.

2. *New York Times*, January 28, 1988.

3. Reuter, May 8, 1988.

4. Sergei Khrushchev was interviewed by Stephen Handelman of the *Toronto Star*. The article appeared on January 1, 1989.

Boris the Basher

1. Bialer, *The Soviet Paradox*, p.135.

2. *Los Angeles Times*, October 3, 1986.

3. *New York Times*, November 17, 1988.

4. Tass, January 12, 1988.

A Superpower Without Toothpaste

1. Press conference with Gennady Lisichkin, June 30, 1987.

2. Larry Black, *Report On Business* magazine, August 1988, *The Globe and Mail*.

Religious Revival

1. Z. Tazhurizina, *Komsomolskaya Pravda*, April 10, 1987.

2. Author's interviews in Zagorsk were in mid-February 1988.

3. The material on Soviet Easter, as well as some concerning the millenium celebrations, is from the excellent work of Helen Womack of Reuter.

Freedom and Chaos

1. Patrick Cockburn, "Ethnic Tremors," in *Foreign Policy*, Spring 1989.

2. Bill Keller, *New York Times*, March 14, 1989, and Tom Zizys, *The Globe and Mail*, March 23, 1989.

3. *Toronto Star*, November 19, 1988.

See No Evil, Hear No Evil

1. *Los Angeles Times*, December 1978.

2. The author interviewed Ruzimatov in April 1988.

3. Robert Evans, Reuter, May 24, 1988.

4. The meeting between Nancy Reagan and Raisa Gorbachev from the press-pool report by Nancy Traver, *Time*, June 1, 1988.

Masterful Moves

1. Bill Keller, *New York Times*, October 14, 1988.

2. Knight-Ridder, March 1989.

3. Gerald Nadler, UPI, October 1988.

Too Romantic?

1. Michael Dobbs, the *Washington Post* (series), March 1989.

2. *Wall Street Journal*, March 24, 1989.

The Chance

1. AP, November 8, 1988.

2. *New York Times Book Review*, March 19, 1989.

3. Christopher Young, Southam News, February 1989.

4. Peter Jenkins, INS, April 1989.

5. Philip Marchand, *Marshall McLuhan*, Toronto: Random House, 1989, p.209.

6. AP, April 6, 1989.

INDEX

A

Abalkin, Leonid, 316
abortion, 252-53
Afanasyev, Viktor, 318
Afghanistan, 74-81, 85, 105, 276-77
Aganbeygan, Aban, 28-29, 53, 197, 199
agriculture, 327-30
Aitmatov, Chingiz, 208
Akhromeyev, Sergei, 37, 65, 278
alcohol policy, 50-52, 243, 249-50
Aleed, Said, 79
Aliyev, Geydar, 54-55
Alma-Ata rioting, 152-53, 154, 280
Amin, Hafizullah, 79
Amlinsky, Vladimir, 204
Ammanadin, Said, 80, 81
Andreevna, Nina, 308
Andronov, Iona, 94
Andropov, Yuri, 29, 130
Anikin, Andrei, 167
Antonov, Mikhail, 199
Arbat protest, 109-11
Arbatov, Georgi, 31, 57, 92, 289
Ardatov, Alexander, 264-65, 318
Armenia, 279-81
Asianov, Yuri, 258
Axelson, Carl, 119
Azerbaijan Republic, 279-81

B

Baltic states, 282-90
Barabas, Janos, 190
Barnett, Anthony, 65, 141
Bartchenko, Alexander, 164
baseball, 264-65
Baskov, Slava, 247-48
Beatty, Perrin, 88
Begun, Josef, 110, 112, 125-26
Berkhin, Viktor, 111
Bialer, Seweryn, 15, 223
Bilibino, 163-64
Biryukova, Alexandra, 324
black market, 117, 248, 249

Blinov, Valentin, 164
Bogdanov, Alexander, 158-59
Bokor, Pal, 190
Bonner, Yelena, 105, 106, 128
Bordeleau, Michel, 50
Bradlee, Ben, 4-5, 186
Brakov, Yevgeny, 334
Brazauskas, Algirdas, 287
Brezhnev, Leonid, 14-15, 31, 51, 54, 62, 69, 126, 144, 191, 206, 209, 255, 276, 280, 319
Brokaw, Tom, 91, 234
Bronfman, Edgar, 339
Brown, Harold, 240
Brownyslavovich, Andrei, 51-52
Brumel, Valery, 267-68, 272
Brzezinski, Zbigniew, 297
Bubka, Sergei, 44-46, 49
Bukharin, Nikolai, 206-07
Bulgaria, 188, 191-92
Burlatsky, Fyodor, 136-37, 194, 195, 198

C

Canada: expulsion of diplomats, 312-13; relations with Soviet Union, 87-89; Soviet emigration policy, 124-25
Carter, Jimmy, 297
Casaroli, Cardinal Agostino, 261-62
Casey, William, 96, 97
Ceausescu, Nicolae, 188
Central Asian republics, 152-55, 279-80
Chazov, Dmitri, 13, 253
Chebrikov, Viktor, 30, 226, 324, 325
Chernakov, Andrei, 211-12, 222
Cherenko, Konstantin, 29, 209
Chernobyl nuclear disaster, 59-66
Children of the Arbat, 138, 208
China, 238
Chugayev, Yuri, 265
Chugunkin, Pyotr, 200
Chukchees, 164-65

Památka
mamička 1991.